The Aging American:

AN INTRODUCTION TO
SOCIAL GERONTOLOGY AND GERIATRICS

CROWELL'S NEW SOCIOLOGY SERIES
Alfred McClung Lee, *Editor*

Milton L. Barron   THE AGING AMERICAN: AN INTRODUCTION TO
SOCIAL GERONTOLOGY AND GERIATRICS

George Simpson   PEOPLE IN FAMILIES: SOCIOLOGY, PSYCHO-
ANALYSIS AND THE AMERICAN FAMILY

The Aging American:

AN INTRODUCTION TO
SOCIAL GERONTOLOGY AND GERIATRICS

Milton L. Barron

THE CITY COLLEGE OF NEW YORK

THOMAS Y. CROWELL COMPANY: New York

Established 1834

Library of Congress Catalog Card Number: 61-6171

Manufactured in the United States of America
by the Vail-Ballou Press, Inc., Binghamton, N.Y.

ACKNOWLEDGMENTS

Acknowledgment is gratefully made for permission to reprint the following material:

Chapter 2 first appeared as a series of articles, "The Aging Population's Problems," in *The Delphian Quarterly* (Vol. 39, Winter–Autumn 1956).

Chapter 3 first appeared as "Minority Group Characteristics of the Aged in American Society" in the *Journal of Gerontology* (Vol. 8, Oct. 1953), pp. 477–82.

That part of Chapter 5 beginning with "Retirement Morbidity" on page 82 was written by Milton L. Barron, Gordon Streib, and Edward Suchman and first appeared as "Research on the Social Disorganization of Retirement" in *American Sociological Review* (Vol. 17, Aug. 1952), pp. 479–81.

Chapter 7 first appeared as "A Survey of a Cross-section of the Urban Aged in the United States" in *Old Age in the Modern World,* proceedings of the Third International Gerontological Congress (Edinburgh, E. & S. Livingstone Ltd., 1955), pp. 340–49.

Chapter 8, written by Philip Taietz, Gordon Streib, and Milton L. Barron, first appeared as *Adjustment to Retirement in Rural New York State* (Ithaca, Cornell University Agricultural Experiment Station, Bulletin No. 919, Feb. 1956).

Chapter 10 appeared in 1957 under the same title as a publication of the Community Council of Greater New York.

Chapter 11 first appeared as "The Role of Religion and Religious Institutions in Creating the Milieu of Older People" in Delton L. Scudder, ed., *Organized Religion and the Older Person,* proceedings of a conference at the University of Florida Institute of Gerontology (Gainesville, University of Florida Press, 1958), pp. 12–33.

Chapter 14 first appeared as "The Dynamics of Occupational Roles and Health in Old Age" in John E. Anderson, ed., *Psychological Aspects of Aging* (Washington, D.C., American Psychological Association, 1956), pp. 236–39.

For BENJY

EDITOR'S FOREWORD

Better foods, medicines, physicians, and ways of life are combining both to bless mankind with longer and healthier life and to present new problems and anxieties. Each human baby has a chance to grow up that is usually better than his parents had; in consequence the planet may before long be choked with people striving against each other for resources and living space. Man's dreams of a longer life of activity before possible feebleness and inevitable death are being fulfilled; in consequence we are being overwhelmed with the aging and their problems.

Until recently, a high death rate required a high birth rate for a tribe and for mankind as a whole to survive. Disease, famine, catastrophe, and war made it certain that man would not live long, and for millenniums human procreation just barely replaced and slightly augmented the population from generation to generation. Then, in the three centuries from 1650 to 1950, the world's numbers multiplied by five, and United Nations specialists anticipate a rise of two and a half times again between 1950 and 2000.

No effective population check of a desirable sort appears in sight. In most parts of the world we are practicing death control without balancing it with birth control. Possible H-bomb destructiveness, new diseases induced by fissionable materials or created by germ warfare specialists, and disastrous mutations in human genetic processes arising from bomb fallout may be horrors in our future that will stem the rising tide of humanity or even wipe us all out, but we seldom discuss such matters in sufficient detail and with adequate responsibility.

A great many of the six or seven billions we are told to expect on the globe by A.D. 2000 are going to be sixty-five years of age and more. The older people are increasing more rapidly in proportion to the total population than any other segment, especially in so favored a country as the United States of America. About one tenth of our population is now over sixty-five years of age, and the fraction is likely to continue to get larger.

In this interesting and scholarly volume on *The Aging American,* Professor Milton L. Barron assembles relevant facts and theories on social gerontology and social geriatrics from a wide variety of sources. He brings evidence, plans, and concepts into sensible relationship. With critical judgment, he makes the whole into a challenging and useful work. Professionals in community work and in regional and national planning as well as students in colleges and universities will find helpful guidance in this book. With it, they can learn to cope with the intricate and important problems Barron so thoughtfully discusses.

As we come to understand and to help solve the problems associated with aging in our society, we aid people of all time-levels in life. The prospect of a healthy and self-reliant period of living following sixty-five can remove a source of depression and concern and give a sense of looking forward to new interests rather than to an inevitable ordeal. When an elderly person indicates that his "third life"—his years after formal retirement—is absorbing and rewarding, his cheerfulness can be most infectious. The bitter and confused among the aging blight us all.

Our "first life" of childhood and youth is our most idealized period. Our society and, as Barron points out, our social science as well tend to be overly centered upon youth and to neglect the later years. We even try to solve problems of adjustment to living by attempting to prolong more and more the period of "youth."

During our "second life" of busy and involved adulthood, employment, parenthood, there are both pleasures and pains, excitement and boredom, but a great many find themselves needed, useful, perhaps influential, and loved. In the past, few people went beyond such a second period. Farmers, shopkeepers, and industrial laborers rarely retired; they worked as long as they could, had a brief period of decline, and died, or life was cut short by violence, accident, or disease. Elderly housewives eventually turned their responsibilities over to a daughter or daughter-in-law, but they still had valued things to do in an old-fashioned extended family. The toothless cackle of a gaffer or gammer was rare and no enticement to long life.

The interests, contributions, and even excitements of our new "third life" are opening up to us surprising and invigorating possibilities. At present the costs of supporting the aging may appear vast and dangerously increasing, but we do not yet know how much they themselves might well contribute.

Barron makes it clear that many of our traditional ways of thinking about retirement and planning for it are relics of a period in which life after sixty-five was a much less real possibility. Such ideas are colored with fantasies and are often unworkable. One's "third life" rarely lasts long beyond "retirement shock" if the aging person has nothing to do but take it easy and perhaps play at some hobby. After years of having a sense of contribution, baby-sitting or sewing or answering telephone calls for other people is often more satisfying to a woman than wandering from window to TV to dining room to bed. Making ship models or gardening becomes an exciting later career for a man when he can help young hobbyists to get similar pleasure from work with their hands and imaginations or when he finds that his flowers or vegetables give aid or pleasure.

Barron does much to help correct the "youth bias" of social science. Social scientists need to see how people of all ages function in society. Barron does much to indicate the merits of "whole life" planning in community, region, and nation.

ALFRED McCLUNG LEE

PREFACE

In the decade that has just ended, gerontology "came of age" in the social as well as in the biological sciences. An unprecedented development in theory, research, and action on problems of aging and the aged finally began to close the wide gap between systematic knowledge on the one hand and the unavoidable, often difficult and perplexing reality of prolonged life in the Western world on the other.

A predictable consequence of this emergence of gerontology will be its firm establishment in the curriculum of American colleges and universities during the next generation. Furthermore, we can anticipate that because of the deep-rooted social and cultural aspects of problems of aging, courses in gerontology will appear most often in the offerings of departments of sociology and anthropology, psychology, social work, and to a limited but significant extent also in the other divisions of social science.

In preparing this book as an introduction to social gerontology and its applied counterpart, social geriatrics, I have kept the needs of the aforementioned fields uppermost in mind. Designed to be comprehensive in scope, the book nevertheless has a focus on retirement and the health problems of the aged in American society. We begin by tracing the evolution of gerontology, showing its relationship to geriatrics, and spelling out its organizational scheme both as a multidisciplinary science and as a profession. This is followed by an elementary but extensive coverage of the aging population's problems, thus providing a broad base for the more intensive and critical analyses of problems in the sections that follow.

Section II of the book comprises three chapters in gerontological theory. The thesis is developed that the aged in American society, particularly those who retire from gainful employment reluctantly, may sociologically be viewed as a "quasi-minority" group. Middle-class norms in gerontology and geriatrics, retirement in the light of the meaning of work, and some propositions about retirement morbidity are the other issues of a theoretical nature treated in this section.

In Section III the book turns to three accounts of findings in gerontological research. The first of these describes the results of a pilot survey on attitudes toward retirement. This is followed by a detailed analysis of what researchers learned in a nationwide survey of the urban aged, with special attention given to the relationships between retirement, other occupational roles, and physical and mental health. In contrast, the last chapter in this section presents the patterns of adjustment to retirement found in six rural counties of upstate New York.

There is a growing awareness in gerontology that many of the seeds of trouble in old age are planted in the middle years of life, if not earlier. In Section IV, accordingly, we scrutinize in three chapters the ignored but crucial period of middle age, first with an exploratory overview of the meaning of middle age and of its characteristic problems. Employment difficulties in this period of life and the various practices by public and private agencies to solve them are reviewed in the second chapter. This is followed by a theoretical and empirical analysis of the influence of religion on adjustment to aging in the middle years.

Section V deals with geriatrics and has, first of all, a chapter on the range of treatment and social services that control or seek to prevent the problems of aging in American society. To provide cross-cultural perspective, the second chapter turns to firsthand observation of social geriatrics in western Europe.

The final section, comprising one chapter, briefly examines key ideas and issues raised in the prior sections and sets forth reformulations of the problems of aging that require further clarification and research. For those readers who seek guidance in pursuing special aspects of gerontology and geriatrics in the voluminous writings of both fields, an annotated selection of articles and books appears at the end of each chapter, and a definitive bibliography along with other study aids has been prepared as an appendix to the book.

Contributors in one way or another to my work in gerontology are far too numerous to mention in full. I wish, however, to give special acknowledgments to the Lilly Endowment for making available the substantial grant supporting my first gerontological research. The Social Science Research Center at Cornell University and the Social Research Laboratory of the City College of New York provided the indispensable academic settings.

I am grateful to the various journals, publishers, and associations for granting permission to reprint in this book all or part of eight of my articles, papers, and essays that had been originally published in their own respective media. I also acknowledge my indebtedness to the New York State Joint Legislative Committee on Problems of the Aging for the useful material available in their legislative documents.

Professor Alfred McClung Lee, Mr. John T. Hawes, and especially Mr. Novello Grano of the Thomas Y. Crowell Company helped immeasurably in their constructive and thorough criticisms of the manuscript. Typically, my wife has been a constant source of inspiration and encouragement. And last, but certainly not least, thousands of aging people contributed enormously to whatever value appears in the following effort to comprehend their problems. For whatever deficiencies the book may still have, I assume the usual author's role of full and exclusive responsibility.

M.L.B.

New York, N.Y.
October, 1960

CONTENTS

VI: Retrospect and Prospects

CHARTS AND TABLES

I : Introduction

All would live long, but none would be old.

BENJAMIN FRANKLIN

1 : Introduction

I :

GERONTOLOGY AND GERIATRICS

The field of research on aging is not marked as yet by a high degree of theoretical organization. It is concerned rather with developing methods and personnel, integrating problems, and experimenting with various patterns of individual and group research. Perhaps more than in many areas, it seems necessary in this field to maintain a close relationship between scientific workers and those concerned directly with policy making and with planning and maintaining services for older persons. For this reason, our representatives are not merely from physiology, psychology, and various social sciences, but also from medicine, public health, social welfare, and jurisprudence.*

Pioneers

The first systematic thinking about patterns, processes and meanings of aging (i.e., gerontology) and the earliest efforts to ameliorate, control and prevent the various problems of aging (i.e., geriatrics) were apparently lost somewhere in antiquity. Nevertheless we do know that the rudiments of gerontology and geriatrics go back at least two thousand years. Cicero's classic essay "Old Age and Friendship" (*De Senectute*) was written before the Christian era. Actually, however, it was in a succession of books that were published from the sixteenth through the nineteenth centuries that several European and American authors laid the foundation for contemporary gerontology and geriatrics. As the representative listing at the end of the chapter of a score of their titles suggests, these pioneers were concerned almost exclusively with

* Harold E. Jones, "Introduction," in H. E. Jones, ed., *Research on Aging* (New York, Social Science Research Council, 1950), p. 1.

detecting and describing the ways and means of emulating the rarely achieved longevity of their times.

Shifting Interests in Contemporary Gerontology

In the twentieth century, longevity is no longer an uncommon achievement. The change in life expectancy along with the new emphasis on scientific analysis shifted gerontologic and geriatric attention away from their original search for recipes for longer life toward understanding and control of the processes and problems of aging. An outstanding example of this transition was G. Stanley Hall's *Senescence,* published in 1922. By virtue of this work, the author, a developmental psychologist, became one of the first contemporary gerontologists. Even more widely renowned for a companion work entitled *Adolescence,* Hall thus emerged as the forerunner of many behavioral scientists now specializing in human development and maturation whose studies in the course of their careers inexorably led them from observations and analysis of the early segments of the life cycle, infancy, childhood, and youth, to those at the other extreme, namely, middle and old age. For these scientists, the earlier patterns and problems of life help account for those that appear in the twilight of the mortal span. "The child is father of the [old] man."

Problems of Aging and Youth Reciprocally Linked

In addition to the continuous thread of the life cycle that has brought some scientists and practitioners to acquire an interest in aging after an earlier interest in growing up, there may be still another reason for linked interests in age extremes. Linden, a psychiatrist, proposes that if one probes beneath the surface of everyday life he will note how problems of aging actually provoke problems of youth, the reverse of the aforementioned maturational pattern:

It is probably not a merely fortuitous circumstance that countries having a low juvenile delinquency rate are simultaneously found to be those whose predominant cultural atmosphere is accepting of the aging and the aged. There appears to be an inverse ratio between elder-veneration and youthful misbehavior. Wherever the values of youth are epitomized, aging lacks currency. The elder-discarding tendency of a culture finds its way in the older individual, turning into attitudes of self-rejection, self-degradation and ultimately into personality destruction. Serious as this is for older persons, its implications in the character development of oncoming generations is still more significant.

The authority for modes of discipline as well as the philosophical motivation and power to create and develop systems of social welfare reside in the elders of a culture. The effectiveness of educational systems designed to guide the child's psychological growth into socially desirable ways of thinking and acting depends to a considerable degree upon the inspirational goals that the elders and forebears personify. . . . There is a disquieting possibility of real social danger and potential damage to children in a social setting in which the elders are devalued. The debased elder becomes an object of mixed scorn and pity for the younger generations. The elder's model role as the authority deteriorates. The outcome is diminution of all social authority. This may lead in susceptible and suggestible youth to the illusion of possessing greater personal strength of purpose and judgment than is in accord with reality. The grandiose and unconstrained self-concept thus engendered in the young may lead to the "I-am-the-master" illusion. Unbridled longings and efforts in the young to satisfy their drives, coupled with an exaggerated sense of personal worth, may lead to willful and ultimately socially destructive behavior.[1]

Early Development of Contemporary Gerontology and Geriatrics through Formal Organization and Conference

The interest of individual specialists in aging and its problems was essential but insufficient in itself to give rise to gerontology and geriatrics as new disciplines and professions. Formal organization or structure was necessary, and this began to take shape in 1939 among those specializing in the biological and medical aspects of aging. The Surgeon General of the United States, with the support of the Josiah Macy, Jr. Foundation, appointed a National Advisory Committee on Gerontology and authorized a nationwide canvass of research on aging by the Public Health Service. Supplementing this fact-finding and coordinating census of research was the reorganization of the National Research Council's Committee on Aging into a fund-raising and planning agency to promote further research. The American branch of an International Club for Research on Aging constituted the third structural

---

[1] Maurice E. Linden, "The Relationship between Social Attitudes toward Aging and the Delinquencies of Youth," *Book of Abstracts: First Pan-American Congress of Gerontology* (Mexico City, 1956), pp. 145–47.

basis in the early formal organization of contemporary gerontology. Concerned with the formulation of research and action, it was established by the British gerontologist, Dr. V. Korenchevsky, who came to the United States explicitly for that purpose. The three associations from time to time held meetings that were subsidized by the Macy Foundation, gerontology's earliest source of financial support.

By 1945 interest in aging not only by biologists and physicians but also by sociologists, economists, social workers, nurses, clinical psychologists, and administrators of welfare agencies pointed to the need for a multidisciplinary, professional organization and a journal to publish its ideas and findings. To meet this need, the Gerontological Society was organized that year and the first issue of its *Journal of Gerontology* was published in January, 1946. The Society, its original membership of 80 having grown to 240 persons representing several sciences and professions, held its first meeting in January, 1949. Its present membership exceeds 1,200.

Another professional association, the American Geriatrics Society, was founded by members of the medical profession whose interests were primarily in diseases of elderly people. With a membership initially numbering slightly more than 200 but now counted in the thousands, it publishes the *Journal of the American Geriatrics Society*.

Still another significant organizational step was the appointment by the Federal Security Administrator of a Committee on Gerontology and Geriatrics to integrate activities within the various branches of the federal government and to complement activities of nongovernmental agencies.[2]

An inevitable development was the establishment of committees or divisions on aging by several already established professional associations. In 1946, for instance, the American Psychological Association organized a Division on Maturity and Old Age. At annual meetings of this division with a membership of approximately 250, there have been presentations of scientific papers, symposia on psychological aspects of aging, and discussions of methodological problems in research on aging. In 1956 the American Medical Association established a Committee on Aging to explore the scope and problems of aging so that it could assist medical societies and individual doctors in assuming their professional responsibilities toward older people.

[2] Albert I. Lansing, ed., *Cowdry's Problems of Ageing: Biological and Medical Aspects,* 3d ed. (Baltimore, The Williams & Wilkins Co., 1952), pp. v, ix.

There is also a National Geriatrics Society, an organization of about 200 institutions (old age homes, nursing homes, sanitariums, etc.) that provide care for the aged. Among its purposes are the promulgation of a code of ethics to regulate institutional care and the publication of a registry of institutions caring for the aged that meet the Society's standards.[3]

Beginning in the 1950's, the development of gerontology and geriatrics was further stimulated by local, national, and international conferences and congresses that have attracted attendance by the membership of the formal organizations described above as well as by unaffiliated but interested professionals and laymen. The first National Conference on Aging was held under the auspices of the Federal Security Agency in 1950 in order to facilitate the exchange of ideas among people of diverse backgrounds, to define and explore problems of aging, to promote research, and to inspire action by private and public agencies in all states and communities.[4] By that time, too, most of the European countries and a handful of South American countries had gerontologic and geriatric associations comparable to those in the United States. It was to be expected that all of them would eventually convene at intervals in international congresses. The first International Gerontological Congress, with representatives from fourteen countries, was held in Belgium in 1950, and in 1951 the Second Congress took place in St. Louis with the cooperation of the United States Public Health Service and supported by a grant from the usual source, the Macy Foundation. The Third Congress followed in London in 1954 and the Fourth Congress met in Merano and Venice in 1957.[5] The countries of the Western Hemisphere had their First Pan-American Congress of Gerontology in Mexico City in 1956.

Factors in Gerontologic and Geriatric Development

Eight underlying and related factors account for most of the growth and development of gerontology and geriatrics in recent years. First and probably foremost is the decline of the death rate in Western

---

[3] Nathan W. Shock, *Trends in Gerontology*, 2d ed. (Stanford, Stanford University Press, 1957), pp. 98–100.

[4] See Federal Security Agency, *Man and His Years* (Raleigh, N.C., Health Publications Institute, Inc., 1951), 311 pp.

[5] San Francisco was the site of the Fifth International Congress that met in 1960.

societies, including the United States. In 1860 only 2.7 per cent (860,-000 people) of the American population was over sixty-five years of age. By 1950 the percentage had risen to 7.6 per cent (11,270,000 people) and by 1980, according to census estimates, there will be 12.1 per cent (22,000,000) in that age group. This increase in both the absolute and proportionate numbers of older persons in the population has brought into sharper focus their present and anticipated economic, social, psychological, and medical problems. To bear in mind that the life expectancy of people sixty-five years of age and over is now an average of thirteen more years of life is to appreciate the duration of their problems as older persons as something more than a fleeting matter.

A second underlying factor in gerontologic and geriatric development is the vast panorama of problems the aged confront. For example, the employment of older individuals has diminished markedly alongside their population increase. Accentuating this tense employment situation have been the rising cost of living and the higher standard of living today in contrast with the case a generation and more ago. The difficulties that millions of older Americans accordingly now confront in income maintenance are re-enforced by the facts of social change. The transition from a family-based economy to an industrial economy has come to mean that the retired, indigenous older person cannot rely on children for support as easily as was true for his historical counterpart. Lacking children, or separated from them as the result of family dispersal, the aged man and his wife may also find themselves forced to abandon membership in clubs and other organizations in order to adjust to their reduced income. This can induce social isolation and relegation to the status of a has-been. Neuroses, suspicion, bitterness against the world and its changing ways are frequent consequences. Thus the economic problems of aging merge with a host of social and psychological problems, all of which come under the growing emphasis placed by social scientists on the study of personality and interpersonal relations. Finally, the decline in economic productivity and social integration of the aged in American society is abetted by an increase in the incidence of chronic disease and disability that accompanies advancing age.

A third underlying reason for the more conspicuous role of aging in our society and, consequently, the enhancement of gerontologic and geriatric activity, is that most individuals are not prepared or educated for old age, a situation that accentuates the symptoms of their problems of aging. Retirement, for instance, is frequently unplanned. Too often the gainfully employed worker reaches age sixty-five, the most common age of compulsory retirement, and suddenly realizes that the years ahead of him are an uncharted and frightening vacuum. Preretirement counseling programs in some industries, although still largely operating on an experimental basis, collectively comprise one social geriatric measure that is pointing the way to meeting an important need of the aged in modern society.

A fourth stimulating basis for gerontology and geriatrics is the legislative action in behalf of older people. The Social Security Act and its recent amendments, old age assistance, and the laws passed in a few state legislatures to prohibit discrimination against older workers have been some of the major expressions of such legislative action. Outstanding vehicles have been such state legislative committees as the New York State Joint Legislative Committee on Problems of the Aging and more recently, on the federal level, the Senate Subcommittee on the Problems of the Aged and Aging. Admittedly not a panacea for problems of old age, legislation and legislative efforts nevertheless have made disciplines and professions that touch on these problems more conscious of their roles and have given them the publicity they could not achieve otherwise.

Fifth among the bases of gerontology and geriatrics is the long-festering dissatisfaction with almshouses and homes for the aged as institutional forms of rehabilitation and terminal care, and the rise of newer forms such as the outpatient geriatric clinic. The latter device stems from the growing conviction that the aged need specialized service medically. Whether their medical needs can better be met within the framework of existing medical clinics or by the alternative of special geriatric clinics is a question on which there is still no agreement.

A sixth reason for the new focusing of professional attention on the aged is the impressive increase in the number and variety of clubs and fraternal organizations by and for the aged. Some, such as the Townsend Clubs, have been primarily political pressure groups seeking to promote certain kinds of legislative action. Others, like the Golden Age Clubs, are principally social, seeking to overcome the allegedly detrimental by-products of isolation in old age. All of them, consciously or not, employ group therapy in some measure to help meet some of the needs that the aged no longer can satisfy in the family and employment.

The seventh undergirding factor of gerontology and geriatrics is the evolving awareness of the traditional professions whose interests converge on aging. We have already seen how more and more committees and divisions in the professional organizations of American medicine, psychology, the social sciences, social work, and even architecture and housing have been formed to promote research and action on the problems and needs of the aged.

The eighth and final basis of gerontology and geriatrics is research. Systematic exploration into the aging processes and its problems is now being conducted in every conceivable discipline, including biochemistry and nutrition, physiology and medicine, the behavioral sciences (sociology, psychology, anthropology, economics), housing, law, education, and philosophy. A good deal of research findings on the aged came about as secondary products of studies primarily concerned with other problems. Furthermore, it is not unusual for an old-age research project to have the collaboration of scientists who are only loosely organized because of their regional dispersal. Relatively little research as yet originates in laboratories and institutes where aging is the major concern.

The aspects receiving the most intensive research are the diseases of old age, particularly arteriosclerosis and heart disease, anatomical changes, endocrine factors, nutritional problems, the attitudes of older people, and their adjustment to retirement. Fundamental research on the cellular and biochemical aspects of aging, physiological responses to stress, the nervous system, and specific psychological and social processes in old age are still in a state of relative neglect. A sample of the basic questions still unanswered is as follows:

1. What factors influence the rate of aging?
2. How can morbidity and mortality in old age be reduced?
3. What are the potentialities and capacities of older people?
4. What are the factors that lead to adjustment in old age?
5. How do the personality and emotional traits of individuals change with age?
6. What are the most appropriate methods of care for aged people when senility develops?

The Scope of Gerontology and Geriatrics

Specializing in the aging of human and other organisms but with different purposes and emphases, both gerontology and geriatrics cross disciplinary lines, involving the study, findings, and applications of many diversified sciences, occupations, and professions. However, there is still an unfortunate tendency to define gerontology and geriatrics or to give undue emphasis in each case in terms of its medical and biological aspects, probably because of the early research and organizational foothold by personnel in the fields of medicine and biology. This biased conception of the new fields is apparent, for example, in the definitions that were given at the First Pan-American Congress of Gerontology:

Gerontology (from Greek *geron,* old or ancient) is the biological science which deals with the aging process of life and therefore covers all the vital phenomena from the normal physiological aspect as well as from the pathological, psychological, social, and economic points of view.

Geriatrics (from Greek *geron,* old or ancient, and *iatreia,* to heal) is the medical specialty of gerontology which studies and treats changes and diseases of the aging human system.[6]

When behavioral scientists define the subject matter of gerontology and geriatrics, more than token acknowledgment is given to the importance of the economic, psychological, and sociological aspects of aging. According to Frank, author of the lead article in the first issue of the *Journal of Gerontology:*

It [gerontology] is not just one more highly specialized discipline, the latest addition to the already long and ever lengthening list of "ologies" that make up the academic roster. Nor is it merely an applied science, like much of engineering and technology, which takes over and utilizes the basic research of others. Gerontology reflects the recognition of a new kind of problem that will increasingly command the interest and devotion of a variety of scientists, scholars, and professional workers, all of whom are needed to study such problems as human growth, development and aging. . . . These new problems transcend the knowledge and methods of any one discipline or profession and demand the focussing of the findings of many separate investigators into a synthesized, coherent whole.[7]

[6] Program of the First Pan-American Congress of Gerontology (Mexico City, Sept. 15–22, 1956), p. 2. Similar biased definitions appear in *Birthdays Don't Count,* New York State Joint Legislative Committee on Problems of the Aging (Legislative Document No. 61, 1948), p. 33; Anton J. Carlson and Edward J. Stieglitz, "Physiological Changes in Aging," *The Annals of the American Academy of Political and Social Science* (Vol. 279, Jan. 1952), pp. 18–31; and Shock, *op. cit.,* p. 3.
[7] Lawrence K. Frank, "Gerontology," *Journal of Gerontology* (Vol. 1, No. 1, Jan. 1946), p. 1.

Just as Frank and others have made a legitimate claim for the social sciences in gerontology, so has Fleming,[8] a British sociologist specializing in social and industrial medicine, spoken for those who see geriatrics as something more than a medical specialty. True, he points out, geriatrics is among other things the systematic direction of the art of medicine to treating and preventing problems of health in later years, as pediatrics is for the earlier years. But there is a need to see it in a wider sense. Geriatrics can be thought of not only as the medical care of the old but also as social geriatrics, which seeks to secure the most efficient functioning of the older person in relation to other people by minimizing the individual and social handicaps of old age. "It would seem," he suggests, "that the new development of social medicine . . . could contribute to the required ends, with the partnership of the physician, sociologist, and psychologist directed to this socio-medical-industrial problem, and operating with the collaboration of those responsible for social and industrial administration."

A content analysis of ongoing gerontologic and geriatric research and action helps account for the continuing dominance of biological and medical specialists in these two relatively new fields. Both in quantity and quality of output they supersede the social scientists, although the gap is closing. Pollak explains the situation as follows:

> The greater advance of the medical sciences than of the social sciences in research on problems of aging is understandable. The fight against death has always been the legitimate concern of the former and logically has led their representatives to investigate the medical and biological aspects of aging. But among social scientists the motivation for studying the social impact of aging upon the older individual and upon society is comparatively new, since it has resulted mainly from the relatively recent demographic and cultural developments outlined elsewhere. It was logical, therefore, that they should have been inclined to treat age as a variable in the analysis of social phenomena rather than as a social phenomenon worthy of examination as such. However, where public concern has focused on a special age group, for instance, adolescence, social scientists have responded by revising their approaches and intensifying their efforts, and seem about to do so with respect to old age.[9]

[8] C. E. Fleming, "The Vocational Aspects of Ageing," *The British Journal of Physical Medicine* (July 1957), pp. 1–6.

[9] Otto Pollak, *Social Adjustment in Old Age: A Research Planning Report* (New York, Social Science Research Council, Bulletin No. 59, 1948), pp. 6–7.

Another controversy in gerontology and geriatrics besides the question of the medicobiological versus the social nature of aging concerns the beginning point of aging. One school of thought holds that aging commences at the time of conception; gerontology, therefore, is in effect the study of the whole process of development. According to the other school of thought, aging usually begins in adulthood when the decrements of life, whether biological or social, start to outweigh life's increments.[10] Shock, who represents this more popular position, maintains that

. . . by aging we mean the progressive changes which take place in a cell, a tissue, an organ system, a total organism, or a group of organisms with the passage of time. All living things change with time in both structure and function, and the changes which follow a general trend constitute aging. Although aging begins with conception and ends only with death, gerontology is concerned primarily with the changes which occur between the attainment of maturity and death of the individual, and the factors that influence these progressive changes. These factors may range from the influences of heredity to differences in climatic factors, and include the effects of social customs and usages. Gerontology is concerned not only with changes in structure and function in individuals with the passage of time, but also with their reactions to one another, and to their environment. . . . Because of the diversity of rates of aging among different individuals, as well as between different organ systems within the same individual, no specific answer can be given to the question "When does old age begin?" Aging is a dynamic equilibrium. The individual animal, at any age, is the result of processes of accumulation and degradation that take place simultaneously. In youth, equilibrium is shifted in favor of accumulation. The rate of building up is more rapid than the rate of tearing down.[11]

The reverse obviously is the case in old age.

Subject Categories of Gerontology and Geriatrics

Because the fields of gerontology and geriatrics are still evolving, no one can say yet in precise detail what they cover. Nevertheless the range of subject matter is suggested by the following scheme generally in use in the classification of old age bibliography: [12]

[10] Lansing, *op. cit.*, p. viii.
[11] Shock, *op. cit.*, pp. 1, 3–4.
[12] Nathan W. Shock, *A Classified Bibliography of Gerontology and Geriatrics*

1. BIOLOGY OF AGING. (1) Cellular biology and physiology (includes plants); (2) Longevity (case reports, heredity, marriage, occupation, sex differences, comparative physiology, mortality rates, national groups); (3) Metabolism; (4) Nutrition; (5) Parental age; (6) Theories.

2. ORGAN SYSTEMS. (1) Blood; (2) Cardiovascular System (blood vessels, blood pressure, hypertension, blood volume, veins, and arteriosclerosis); (3) Heart (anatomy and physiology, heart disease, coronary artery disease, myocardial disease); (4) Endocrine System (includes sex glands and climacteric); (5) Gastrointestinal System; (6) Nervous System; (7) Reactions of the Body as a Whole; (8) Reproductive System; (9) Respiratory System; (10) Sense Organs and Perception; (11) Skeletal System (bone, arthritis and rheumatism, gout); (12) Skin and Integument; (13) Urogenital System.

3. PSYCHOLOGICAL PROCESSES.

4. SOCIAL AND ECONOMIC ASPECTS. (1) Accidents; (2) Demography; (3) Education; (4) Economic Problems (employment, retirement, and pensions); (5) Housing and Care; (6) Medical Care; (7) Social Problems (includes social adjustment); (8) Social Groups; (9) Social Security; (10) Social Services and Social Work (recreation and rehabilitation).

5. GERIATRICS. (1) General; (2) Medical Care and Diagnosis; (3) Disease (chronic, infectious, and mental); (4) Surgery.

6. MISCELLANEOUS. Popular articles, etc.

The Literature of Gerontology and Geriatrics

Gerontology and geriatrics owe much of their rapid and marked development in recent decades to the prolific and versatile literature [13] they have inspired. This ranges widely from books for popular consumption [14] that Shock has aptly characterized as "inspirational," and

---

(Stanford, Stanford University Press, 1951). See also the listing of new publications in any issue of the *Journal of Gerontology*.

[13] See the annotated readings at the end of each chapter and the extensive bibliography at the end of the book.

[14] See, for example, C. Crampton, *Live Long and Like It* (New York, Public Affairs Committee, Pamphlet No. 139, 1948); R. Giles, *How to Retire and Enjoy It* (New York, Whittlesey House, 1949); M. Gumpert, *You Are Younger Than You Think* (Cleveland, World Publishing Co., 1947); G. Lawton, *Aging Successfully* (New York, Columbia University Press, 1946); C. W. Lieb, *Outwitting Your Years* (New York, Prentice-Hall, 1949); W. B. Pitkin, *Life Begins at Forty* (New

popular magazines [15] that emphasize adjustment to old age, especially retirement, to newsletters [16] that report succinctly on research developments, action programs, announcements and miscellaneous information on aging, professional journals,[17] monographs, and finally, miscellaneous brochures, pamphlets, conference proceedings, and legislative documents.

Promotion of Research and Action

To facilitate research and action in gerontology and geriatrics in the United States, various devices [18] have been developed. One is the training institute or workshop that meets annually on a number of university campuses (such as the University of Michigan, the University of Connecticut, the State University of Iowa, and the University of Florida) and attracts both professional personnel and the aged themselves. Another is the gerontological research center or institute, now an integral part of Washington University at St. Louis; the State University of Iowa; the University of Florida; the University of Michigan; the University of Kansas Medical School; Moosehaven Laboratory, Orange Park, Florida; National Heart Institute, Baltimore; National Institute of Mental Health, Bethesda, Maryland; University of Miami,

---

York, McGraw-Hill Book Co., 1932); I. Salomon, *Retire and Be Happy* (New York, Greenberg: Publisher, 1951).

[15] The widest circulation of all is probably enjoyed by the monthly *Journal of Lifetime Living*. Others are *Modern Maturity* (published every second month by the American Association of Retired Persons), *Successful Retirement Annual, Senior Citizens* (published monthly by the Senior Citizens of America), *Retirement Life* (published by the National Association of Retired Civil Employees), and *Mature Years* (published by the Methodist Church).

[16] Among the best known are *News Bulletin and Progress Report* of the National Committee on the Aging, the *Newsletter* published by the Gerontological Society, and *Aging*, published by the Committee on Aging of the Department of Health, Education, and Welfare.

[17] Shock, in a world-wide enumeration in 1957, identified the following 16 professional journals: *Acta Gerontologica Japonica, Acta Gerontologica* (Italy), *Archives of Gerontology* (Japan), *De Senectute* (Switzerland), *Geriatria* (Argentine), *Geriatrics* (United States), *Geron* (Finland), *Gerontologia* (Switzerland), *Giornale di Gerontologia* (Italy), *Journal of the American Geriatrics Society* (United States), *Journal of Chronic Diseases* (United States), *Journal of Gerontology* (United States), *Longevita* (Italy), *Revista de Geriatria* (Mexico), *Rivista di Gerontologia e Geriatria* (Italy), and the oldest of all, *Zeitschrift für Altersforschung* (Germany).

[18] Shock, *Trends in Gerontology*, pp. 93–94, 121–22, 139.

Florida; and Duke University. A notable step was the establishment in 1956 of a Center for Research on Aging in the National Institutes of Health, assigned the task of encouraging research programs in gerontology at various universities.

The first private foundation to support gerontology, as we have already noted, was the Josiah Macy, Jr. Foundation. More recently grants for research on aging have also been made by the Kellogg, Schimper, Rockefeller, Ford, Farmer, Dorr, Russell Sage, and Forest Park Foundations, the McGregor Fund, Twentieth Century Fund, and the Lilly Endowment.

Advisory councils, committees, or commissions on aging exist now in the majority of states and, like the pioneering New York State Joint Legislative Committee on Problems of the Aging established in 1947, they provide leadership in the initiation and furtherance of legislative programs to alleviate the problems of aging. On a nationwide basis, gerontology and geriatrics find support in the *Federal Council on Aging* [19] founded in 1956. The Council reviews existing programs in a number of government departments and agencies in terms of emerging needs of the aging, and makes recommendations to the appropriate governmental units concerning priorities and provisions for meeting those needs.

An outstanding private organization fostering gerontology and geriatrics nationally is the *National Committee on the Aging,* established in 1950 as a standing committee of the National Social Welfare Assembly. Composed of 250 members representing the interests and concerns of older people in business, industry, organized labor, health professions, social work, the clergy, education, housing, research, government, and state and local committees on aging, the Committee's support comes primarily from private foundations and the Assembly. In 1956 and again in 1959 the Ford Foundation made large allocations to strengthen and broaden its basic program and to expand its information and consultation services. The Committee's staff includes consultants in health, social welfare, employment and retirement, a librarian, and special project personnel. It was organized at the request of communities, professional and civic groups, agencies of government, and others who face the pressing problems created by the growing number of older people in this country, and who recognized the need for more adequate planning and resources. To help solve these problems, the Committee provides a national information and consultation center, maintains a

[19] *Ibid.,* pp. 105–6.

special library on aging, keeps current on activities in gerontology and geriatrics, holds conferences and workshops, serves as a medium for interchange of information and ideas, encourages experimentation in programs and services for the aged, stimulates studies, conducts special projects and research, presses for the training of professional personnel with competence in the field of aging, prepares books and pamphlets based on the Committee's activities, summarizes and distributes reports on the pertinent work of others, produces films, exhibits, and other visual aids, lends kits of materials on specific problems, works with the mass media of communication to combat the stereotypes about old age and to publicize programs and needs, and gives field consultation within the limits of available resources.

In 1959 another important national spur to research and action in gerontology and geriatrics was organized, the Senate Subcommittee on Problems of the Aged and Aging. It was legally charged as follows:

> The Senate Committee on Labor and Public Welfare or *any duly authorized subcommittee thereof* has the responsibilities of examining, investigating and making a complete study of any and all matters pertaining to the problems of the aging including, but not limited to, (a) a study of the major problems of the aged; (b) a study of the existing programs of agencies, both public and private, dealing with problems of the aged; (c) a study of the present role of the federal government in dealing with the problems of the aged; and (d) a study of any additional federal programs which should be undertaken to help solve the problems of the aged. . . . The committee shall report its findings, together with its recommendations for legislation as it deems advisable, to the Senate at the earliest practicable date, but not later than January 31, 1960.[20]

In pursuit of this mandate,[21] the Subcommittee under the chairmanship of Senator Pat McNamara conducted a series of hearings in seven cities throughout the United States, receiving testimony from the aged themselves as well as from city and state officials and representatives of local agencies. The major subjects covered were housing for the elderly, job discrimination against the worker over forty-five, financing adequate medical care, conditions of nursing homes, measures to prevent physical and mental deterioration, adequate incomes for retired persons, and

---

[20] *Congressional Record* (Vol. 105, No. 160).
[21] *Modern Maturity* (Vol. 2, No. 6, Dec. 1959–Jan. 1960), p. 11.

elements necessary to ensure a productive and meaningful life for those retired from regular employment.

White House Conference on Aging

To open the way for a concerted national movement against the problems of aging, an Act was passed by Congress and signed by President Eisenhower in September, 1958.[22] It authorized immediate action in improving and developing programs to (1) assure middle-aged and older persons equal opportunity in gainful employment; (2) enable retired persons to enjoy incomes sufficient for health and participation in family and community life as self-respecting citizens; (3) provide housing suited to the needs of older persons at prices they can afford to pay; (4) assist middle-aged and older persons to make preparation and develop skills and interests and find social contacts that will make the gift of added years of life a period of reward and satisfaction and avoid unnecessary social costs of premature deterioration and disability; and (5) step up research designed to relieve old age of its burdens of sickness, mental breakdown, and social ostracism.

The Act further authorized and directed the Secretary of Health, Education, and Welfare to establish an Advisory Committee on Aging composed of professional and public personnel, and to plan a White House Conference on Aging to be held in January, 1961. Representatives to the Conference would be delegates from federal, state, and local governments, professionals and laymen working in the field of aging, and the general public including older persons. Lastly, the Act provided for "grants of not less than $5,000 nor more than $15,000 to each state which shall submit an application for funds for the exclusive use in planning and conducting a State Conference on Aging prior to and for the purpose of developing facts and recommendations and preparing a report on the findings for presentation to the White House Conference on Aging and defraying costs incident to the State's delegates attending the White House Conference on Aging."

Summary

In this chapter introducing the book, we have defined gerontology broadly as the systematic, multidisciplinary study of the patterns and

---

[22] *Modern Maturity* (Vol. 2, No. 5, Oct.–Nov. 1959), p. 34; see also *Progress Report,* The National Committee on the Aging (Vol. 1, No. 3, Dec. 1958), pp. 1–2.

meanings of aging, and geriatrics as those techniques that aim to control and reduce its problem aspects. The pioneers of gerontology and geriatrics had as their aim the achievement of recipes leading to longevity. Their contemporary counterparts, however, have turned toward attempts to analyze and comprehend the problems and processes of aging. Many of the newer gerontologists are scientists who extended their interests in the life cycle from youth to old age and who saw that the problems of the two age extremes are linked.

Gerontology and geriatrics achieved rapid development in the decades of the 1940's and 1950's through formal organization, aided by foundation support, that sought to integrate and consolidate the research and action of individual scientists, scholars, and practitioners in medicine and social welfare. Eight underlying and related factors have been the spurs to the development of gerontology and geriatrics: the declining death rate, the numerous economic, psychological, and social problems of the aged, their unpreparedness for their age status, legislative action, dissatisfaction with traditional care and treatment, organizations by and for the aged, the evolving sensitivity of traditional professions to the needs and problems of the aging, and finally, research.

Largely because of their early research and organizational foothold in the new fields, medical and biological specialists have tended to define gerontology and geriatrics in their own image, ignoring or underplaying the importance of the behavioral sciences. But in all disciplines the prevailing position is that the study and treatment of aging properly begins in adulthood, not at conception as a minority of specialists insist. Some order can be given to the vastness of gerontologic and geriatric literature by classification in terms of inspirational books, popular magazines, newsletters, professional journals, monographs, and miscellaneous brochures, pamphlets, proceedings, and documents.

Devices in use to promote research and action are the training institute or workshop, the research center, foundation grants, commissions on aging, and national councils and committees, both public and private. Two of the most recent and important devices are the Senate Subcommittee on Problems of the Aged and Aging and the White House Conference on Aging.

Now that we have explored the history and dimensions of gerontology and geriatrics, we can turn to a survey in some detail of the aging population's problems, with special emphasis on those aspects that are encompassed by *social* gerontology and geriatrics rather than the biological and medical aspects of aging.

Questions and Research Exercises

1. Read Cicero's classic essay "Old Age and Friendship," and show what can be deduced about attitudes toward aging in his place and time in comparison with attitudes toward aging in contemporary American society.
2. In what two ways are the problems of youth and old age allegedly linked?
3. What factors account for the growth of gerontology and geriatrics in recent years?
4. Explain the tendency to give the biological and medical aspects of aging undue emphasis in defining gerontology and geriatrics.
5. Discuss the controversy in gerontology concerning the beginning point of aging.
6. Both gerontology and geriatrics are multidisciplinary, but some disciplines and professions clearly contribute to one and not to the other. Draw up a list of such appropriate disciplines and professions for each of the two fields.

Selected Readings

Drake, Joseph T., *The Aged in American Society* (New York, The Ronald Press Co., 1958). The first textbook on social gerontology and geriatrics. Especially useful for a comprehensive view of the factual material in both fields.

Frank, Lawrence K., "Gerontology," *Journal of Gerontology* (Vol. 1, January 1946), pp. 1–12. The lead article in the first issue of the Journal of Gerontology. Gives unusually well-balanced view of the various disciplines involved in gerontology.

Hall, G. Stanley, *Senescence* (New York, D. Appleton & Co., 1922). A work that represents the transition between pioneering and contemporary gerontology.

Jones, Harold E., ed., *Research on Aging* (New York, Social Science Research Council, 1950). One of the best symposia on problems of theory and methodology in old age research.

Journal of Gerontology, published by the Gerontological Society, St. Louis, Missouri; *Geriatrics,* published by Lancet Publications, Minneapolis, Minnesota. The two leading professional journals in gerontology and geriatrics in the United States.

Lansing, Albert I., ed., *Cowdry's Problems of Ageing: Biological and Medical Aspects,* 3d ed. (Baltimore, The Williams & Wilkins Co., 1952). One of the standard works in American gerontology, although heavily slanted toward the biological and medical aspects.

Pollak, Otto, *Social Adjustment in Old Age: A Research Planning Report* (New York, Social Science Research Council, Bulletin No. 59, 1948). An early but still important review of needed research in problems of aging.

Shock, Nathan W., *A Classified Bibliography of Gerontology and Geriatrics* (Stanford, Stanford University Press, 1951). *Supplement One*—1949–1955 (Stanford, Stanford University Press, 1957). The best bibliography in both fields. Current items are listed in each new issue of the *Journal of Gerontology* under the same classificatory scheme.

Shock, Nathan W., *Trends in Gerontology*, 2d ed. (Stanford, Stanford University Press, 1957). The most recent work on the dynamics of gerontology in terms of its recent findings, leading personages, organizations, etc. An excellent source book.

Early Publications on Longevity

Bacon, Francis, *History Natural and Experimental of Life and Death or of the Prolongation of Life* (London, 1658).

Bailey, John Burn, *Modern Methuselahs or Short Biographical Sketches of a few advanced nonagenarians or actual Centenarians who were distinguished in Art, Science, Literature or Philanthropy* (London, 1888).

Bailey, Thomas, *Records of Longevity with an introductory discourse on vital statistics* (London, 1857).

Cheyne, George, *An Essay of Death and Long Life* (London, 1725).

Cornaro, Louis, *The Art of Living Long* (1558), *a new and improved English version of the treatise of the celebrated Venetian Centenarian* (Wm. F. Butler, Milwaukee, 1903).

Davis, Malcolm B., and Kate C. Jenness, *How to Live a Century* (Boston, 1895).

Durand-Fardel, M., *Handbuch der Krankheiten des Greisevalters* (Wurzburg, 1858).

Flourens, P., *De la Longevite Humaine et de la Quantite de Vie sur le Globe* (Paris, 1815).

Gardner, John, *Longevity, the means of prolonging life after middle age* (Boston, 1875).

Graham, T. J., *The Best Methods of Improving Health and Invigorating Life by Regulating the diet and regimen* (London, 1842).

Hufeland, C. William, *The Art of Prolonging Human Life* (London, 1829).

Humphry, G. M., *Old Age—the results of information received respecting 900 persons who had attained the age of eighty years* (Cambridge, 1889).

Kitchiner, William, *The Art of Invigorating and Prolonging Life by food, clothes, air, exercise, wine, sleep* (London, 1828).

Lathrop, Rev. S. G., *Fifty Years and Beyond; or Gathering Gems for the Aged* (Chicago, 1881).

Medicus, *The Oracle of Health and Long Life or Plain Rules for the attainment and preservation of sound health and vigorous old age; with rational instructions for diet, regimen and the Treatment of Dyspepsy or Indigestion deduced from personal experience and the best authors on dietetics* (London, 1830).

A Physician, *Sure Methods of Improving Health and Prolonging Life; or a treatise on the Art of Living Long and Comfortably by regulating the diet and regimen* (London, 1828).

Rask, Prof., *A short tractate on the Longevity ascribed to the Patriarchs in the Book of Genesis and its relation to the Hebrew Chronology* (London, 1863).

Saffray, *Les Moyens de vivre Longtemps* (Paris, 1878).

Thompson, H., *Diet in Relation to Age and Activity* (London, 1887).

Thoms, William J., *The Longevity of Man* (London, 1879).

2 :

THE AGING POPULATION'S PROBLEMS

We have come to understand:

The old man bent over a cutting table in the garment district of New York City.

The gnarled old farmer who at 82 sold his poultry farm and built himself a new house with his own hands.

The thin, wispy old lady who keeps her slum flat glistening clean and excitedly awaits the monthly visit of a case-worker, virtually the only social time she has all month.

The elderly widow who after her husband's death started a successful home enterprise.

The retired tool and die maker whose garage is almost a metal factory in itself.

The resident of the old age home who has assigned himself the task of cheering his fellow residents.

The bed-bound woman in the nursing home, staring vacantly at the ceilings.

The grey-haired grandmother who darts from the woman's club to samba lessons.

The high-pressure businessman who nearing retirement age suddenly develops choking spells.

These and many others we have come to know and understand. And only out of such understanding can come the programs and legislative measures and alteration of cultural values essential to make life not merely tolerable but affirmatively cherishable for our older people.*

---

* *Enriching the Years,* New York State Joint Legislative Committee on Problems of the Aging (Legislative Document No. 32, 1953), p. 4.

The process of aging has given rise to some of the major social problems facing American society. Our accent is said to be on youth, or as the social scientist would say, our culture is "youth centered." The ready market for nostrums promising prolonged youth and ways of aging successfully and gracefully testifies to the dread millions of Americans have of growing old. Yet this has not always been the position of the aged, nor is it always so today in other societies.

The aged first became a conspicuous problem to themselves and to others in our society during the second and early part of the third decades of this century. Some states began then to notice that families and charitable organizations were failing to give adequate financial aid to those older people being displaced from the industrial economy and to widows and children of deceased older workers. During the economic depression that followed, the number of older, unemployed workers and older women without support became alarming all over the nation. This stimulated passage of the federal Social Security Act, in which the most prominent features were old age insurance and old age assistance.

Since those years the medical profession has relinquished some of its traditional preoccupation with children's diseases, many of which have been brought under reasonable control, and instead is devoting more attention to the chronic illnesses widespread in old age. Both management and organized labor have begun to feel the pressure from older workers reluctant to retire, or who want to return from retirement to gainful employment. Anxiety about economic insecurity in old age and fear of an even greater decline in the employment of old people have led to the establishment of thousands of private pension systems. Social and welfare workers everywhere are receiving increasing numbers of requests for aid in solving the problems of living arrangements, family relations, and leisure-time needs of the aged. Mental hospitals and homes for the aged generally report overcrowded conditions.

The prevailing notion in America until now has been that such problems of aging and the aged are inevitable products of general organic and mental deterioration, beginning in middle life and progressing thereafter at an accelerating rate. Consistent with this notion, little has been expected from or done for older people in distress, and the aged themselves have usually done virtually nothing to better their situations.

Today a new philosophy is slowly but relentlessly emerging, namely, that most problems of aging and the aged are problems in human relations: man-made and therefore controllable. Some physicians, for example, now admit that whereas pediatrics, the care and treatment of infants, is essentially a medical matter, geriatrics, the treatment of the aged, is fundamentally a concern of applied behavioral science. By this they mean that in the course of the life cycle from birth to death the initial priority of biological forces gives way later to the social and cultural factors that influence behavior. This new point of view provides the clue to why problems of aging are acute in some societies such as our own, but not in others. The biology of aging is virtually the same everywhere. But patterns of social relations among the old, the middle-aged, and the young vary as the cultures and social structures of different peoples of the world vary. While some patterns conduce to the development of problems in the aging process, others clearly do not.

A Cross-Cultural Survey of the Aged

Anthropologists, specialists in the study of comparative social life, tell us that in some societies old age is considered to begin relatively early in life, while elsewhere it comes late. Depending on the culture of the society, its coming may be either feared or eagerly welcomed. In some locales old age is regarded a passive, futile period of life; elsewhere it is dynamic and rewarding. It may bring enhancement of status and prestige or deterioration in both respects. Most societies, however, deal with old age somewhere between these two extremes.

It is perhaps an exaggeration to say American society stands at one extreme of the possible patterns of relations between the aged and younger age groups and nonliterate societies at the other. Nevertheless it is true that, in many so-called "primitive" tribes, aging is much less a social problem than in the Western industrial world. Among the Palaung of North Burma, for instance, the aged receive great homage and live happy lives. No one dares step on the shadow of an older person for fear incalculable harm will come. Such an honor is it to be old that as soon as a Palaung girl marries she is eager to appear older than she actually is. The older a woman becomes, the greater the honor she can expect to receive.

Even in the few nonliterate societies where the aged have systematically been put to death, such treatment may actually be a mark of esteem, a special honor expected and actually requested by the aged themselves. Respect for the aged among primitives is ordinarily expressed, however, in ways more palatable and understandable to Western people. As a rule this respect is shown the aged because of particular assets they may have, such as experience, skills, powers of magic, knowledge of folklore, and storytelling ability.

The aged in nonliterate societies are the chief historians and storytellers, and it follows naturally that any prestige associated with old age tends to be reflected in the people's myths and legends. In many of these accounts the leading characters are portrayed as old, wise, important persons. By thus embellishing and glorifying old age, the storytellers understandably have turned the myths and legends to their own advantage. Not only do the primitive storytellers glorify aging characters in their mythology; they even assign the attributes of old age to the deities. Primitive gods are often described as old, wise, and powerful. Never do they appear senile and weak. One may with reason say the aged in primitive societies have created gods in their own image. Unquestionably the mythologies have become instruments to serve the aspirations and ideal roles of the aged.

In those primitive societies where aging is no social problem, old people enjoy active participation in social affairs. Continuing to use their experience, property rights, and religious or magical powers, the aged play important and strategic social roles. This is especially so in their family relations. Among their kin they perform light but essential household chores, instruct the young, and supervise the household economy. Anthropolgists do find that there are some sexual differences in this respect. That is, aged men are better off where there is a patriarchal form of family organization, where herding and agriculture are the principal means of livelihood, and where there is permanence of residence, a constant food supply, and deeply entrenched property rights in land, crops, herds, and goods. Aged women, on the other hand, have optimum conditions of security and prestige in a matriarchal family organization and where the economies are simple food-gathering, hunting, and fishing. An interesting qualification is that wherever among primitives the aged women are respected, most aged men also have considerable honor and prestige. But prestige for aged men offers no assurance of the same for women. If either sex is found to have lost the respect of others in old age, it is more likely to be primitive women than the men. In Western industrial societies, as we shall see in subsequent chapters, the opposite is more likely: the older man deteriorates in status more readily than does the older woman.

Turning from the nonliterate, primitive world to contemporary rural societies in the Western world, we find their social patterns on the whole favorable to the status of the aged. A few basic observations about the nature of rural life may clarify the principal reasons why this could be.

In rural just as in nonliterate communities almost all essential economic activities are ordinarily carried on by the family working as a group, rather than by individuals working alone. The aged are integrated in their tasks with the other persons in the household. And as each member of the family typically consumes goods according to his needs rather than his productivity, the older members enjoy a large part of the goods and services available.

The overwhelming influence of the family in rural life pervades all social relationships as well. This is because the household unit usually embraces the larger kinship group, the extended family: not merely the married couple and their children, but as many as five generations and some collateral relatives. Thus, in a highly rural society the interests of each individual in the family unit, the young, the middle-aged, and the aged, are subordinated to those of the kinship group. The needs, welfare, and activities of the group are of primary importance; those of the individual are secondary. The important point here is that the aged are more than just integral parts of this family group; they are frequently the moving, directing, and controlling agents. If rural familism of this sort did not prevail and if all rural children typically left the family to set up small, independent family units of their own, the rural aged obviously would not enjoy the status they frequently have.

The sheer number in the rural family unit is another reason for the high status of the aged in rural societies in contrast with urban situations. Compared with the urban household, the rural unit is usually much larger. With adequate space to accommodate large numbers, sheltering one or two additional persons presents no critical problem. Similarly, when food and fuel are available at little or no extra expense, and only simple clothing is necessary, the cost of keeping aged parents in the household scarcely resembles the crisis often provoked in the urban family. Indeed, when the rural household includes members of as many as five generations, the presence of a few aged persons can be an asset rather than a liability.

Clearly, the larger and more versatile rural household affords many opportunities for the aged to contribute. With advancing age the rural person is not deprived of his social functions and economic productivity as readily as his urban counterpart. The greater extent to which the aged in rural societies maintain control of property and a dominant role in economic affairs is probably the major reason why their position is high.

Our last reference in this brief cross-cultural survey of the aged concerns modern urban, industrial societies. It is here the status of the aged tends to be lowest, the problems of aging most acute. In all societies, nonliterate and rural as well as industrial, the very young are a problem for adults because they must be supported and trained to assume responsible positions in the community. But during the last few decades in modern industrial life an important change has taken place. While adults still worry about their children, they have also begun to worry about their aged parents.

Nature and Extent of Old Age in Urban Industrial Society

To understand the problems of the aged in a modern society such as the United States, we must first consider what is meant by "old age" in such a society. Typically, an urban industrial society defines old age chronologically: by the number of years lived. This practice stems partly from the influence of private and public pension and retirement systems in our industrial economy. Such systems generally specify normal and mandatory retirement at an arbitrary chronological point, usually sixty-five. Yet it is obvious no such single measure as this accurately identifies and distinguishes the aged from the rest of the population. The disadvantage in so arbitrarily defining old age is that it ignores the wide range of individual differences among human beings in the aging process.

Aging in all living organisms is continuous, proceeding as a series of gradual changes. But from the time of conception onward, in lower animal life and among humans, the *rate* of anatomical, physiological, psychological, and social aging varies. A consequence of these variations is that individuals in their later years differ widely among themselves even though they may be chronologically the same. Aging, in short, is a highly individual matter not very closely related to the number of years one has lived. Everyone is familiar with persons biologically young at seventy and others physically or mentally old in their late forties. Some persons eighty years of age have kidneys that function as well as those of the average forty-year-old person.

Besides these variations between individuals, organs and functions within the same individual age at remarkably different rates. None of us is consistently the same age throughout all parts of our physical constitution. John Doe may have a heart equivalent to that of the average forty-year-old, but kidneys like those of the average eighty-year-old. Such differences suggest why a person's age in years does not, by itself, provide an accurate indicator of what the person is, an accurate answer to the question: "How old is this individual?"

Moreover, we often confuse age changes with many of the changes caused by disease. What we often call "aging" when we observe the human body is not aging at all, but merely the effects of disease. It is quite possible, then, say many gerontologists, that by reducing the damaging effects of disease and improving nutrition we can extend the period of vigor usually associated with youth well into that time of life now regarded as a period of "natural" decline. Much of the cellular atrophy and decreased elasticity and strength of tissue and muscle now considered part of biological aging may not be inevitable.

New experimental research findings suggest that aging of the body is due to the expenditure of its "adaptation energy." According to this concept, the body starts life with a certain reservoir of capability for adapting itself to crises. This is expended by combats with illness, as well as with the normal difficulties of a lifetime, until at length the reserves are exhausted and the body falls victim in its next battle. Evidence of aging owing to the exhaustion of adaptation reserves is found in the greater vulnerability of older animals to diseases induced by stress. Every stress leaves an indelible scar, and the organism pays for its survival after a stressful situation by becoming a little older.

Psychological aging usually follows what has been called a parabolic curve. This means that, on the average, the efficiency of mental, sensory, and perceptual processes increases rapidly until the early or mid-twenties, then very gradually declines until late in middle life, after which the downgrade becomes steeper. Within the averages, of course, there are clear-cut individual differences in the rate of psychological aging. Just as with biological aging, we cannot say all people become psychologically old on reaching a certain age. It is unwarranted to say, for example, that after reaching a specific chronological age a person is "too old to learn" something. Persons of lower mental ability seem to lose learning ability earlier and more markedly than the more intelligent. Perhaps the reason for this is that the intelligent engage in more learning behavior throughout their lives and, by practice, maintain efficiency. The same is true of motor skills. Aged persons who have practiced motor skills for many decades often surpass younger people at learning new skills.

These difficulties in defining old age should suggest why aging poses social problems in our urban industrial society. The arbitrary system of typing people as young, middle-aged, or old chronologically, according to their accumulation of years rather than to specific performance, leads to frustration, despair, and hardship for many persons in the latter two categories. This is particularly true when it comes to getting or keeping a job.

Better to understand the problems of aging in our society, one must also look at the size and distribution of the population considered aged or old. How much of the population is old? What is the trend in this respect? How are the aged distributed geographically?

We have emphasized that we can use no single criterion to determine whether an individual or group is aged or old. The popular chronological definition of old age does enable us, however, to measure conveniently the size of the various age groups in the American population.

As the accompanying Chart 1 clearly indicates, in the year 1960 the number of people sixty-five years of age and over reached almost 16 million out of a total American population of 179 million. Thus, about one out of twelve Americans, or slightly less than 9 per cent, were in the chronologically aged group. Impressive as these figures are, they do not reveal the full significance of the large proportion of people now sixty-five and over. We must further note the profound change in the number and proportion of aged that has accompanied the American population's total growth from 1900 until the present time.

At the turn of the century, there were only three million Americans over the age of sixty-five, or only 4 per cent of the population as a whole. Although our total population has doubled in the ensuing years, the number of persons aged sixty-five and over has increased more than five-fold. Also impressive is the increasing proportion of persons in middle age. In 1900, one person in seven was aged forty-five to sixty-four; today the ratio is one in five. On the other hand, those under twenty years of age have actually declined proportionately from 44 per cent to 33 per cent of the entire population.

During the next generation, population experts estimate, the growth of population will continue to show substantial increases both in the

Chart 1: *Aged Population of the United States, Number and Percentage of Total Population, 1900–1970* *

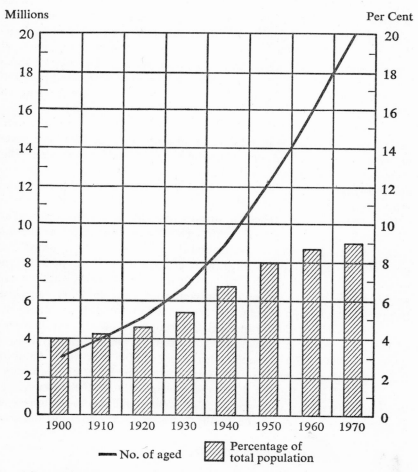

* From *The Aged and Aging in the United States: Summary of Expert Views before the Subcommittee on Problems of the Aged and Aging of the Committee on Labor and Public Welfare, U.S. Senate* (Washington, D.C., U.S. Government Printing Office, June 16–18, 1959), p. 2.

numbers and proportion of older persons.[1] By 1970 those sixty-five and over are expected to swell to about 21 million, or 60 per cent more than in 1950.

Until now the increase in size of the older population has accompanied the trend toward urbanization. In 1900 the American people were still predominantly rural, only about 40 per cent of them living in urban areas. By 1920, however, about half the population had come to live in urban communities; by 1940 almost 60 per cent, and by 1950 almost two thirds of the population. The population sixty-five years of age and over has followed a similar pattern. Since 1930 more of them have been living in urban communities than in rural areas, and by 1950 about 65 per cent of all the aged in the United States were residents of cities.

What accounts for the change in the age composition of the American people, and what is its relation to urbanization? We find the answer in what is often called the demographic or "vital" revolution. This revolution has accompanied the industrial revolution in western Europe and the United States since 1800. High birth rates and high death rates were normal almost everywhere in preindustrial times. Of the many babies born, so many failed to survive that one could properly speak of "islands of life in a sea of death." The "natural increase" in population, the difference between births and deaths, was usually so small that populations hardly seemed to grow at all except by virtue of immigration from other lands. High birth and death rates also gave the Western world, as everywhere, a population young in years. In 1800 American babies at birth had an average life expectancy of about thirty years.

All this changed with industrialization after 1800. The urban way of life accompanying industrialization brought, among other things, a decline in births. For example, for every 1,000 women in 1800 of child-bearing age, twenty to forty-four, there were 1,342 children under five years of age. But by 1950 there were only 517 children under five for every such 1,000 women. With fewer children being born, the average size of the American family between 1800 and 1950 declined from 5.7 to 3.6 persons.

This decline in the birth rate over a century and a half was matched

---

[1] Because of the marked rise in the birth rate since 1940, the proportion of persons over sixty-five in the population has been increasing less rapidly than during most of the first half of the century. Nevertheless the increase at present is still in excess of 400,000 persons a year.

by a decline in the death rate. Medical and hygienic discoveries and inventions in the past 150 years led to the control of most infectious diseases. Lives of millions of persons who formerly would have died in infancy, childhood, or young adulthood are now prolonged many years. Consequently the average life expectancy at birth in the United States today is about seventy, or forty years higher than it was at the beginning of the industrial revolution. Since 1900 life expectancy at birth has increased by nineteen years for males and twenty-two years for females. At the older ages the increase has been less spectacular, but nevertheless substantial: from 11.5 to 13.1 years for white males aged sixty-five, and from 12.2 to 15.7 years for white females aged sixty-five.

It is evident, then, that the impact of urban industrial culture on the birth and death rates has been to magnify the numbers and proportion of the older age group. The lower birth rate until 1940 led to a smaller proportion of younger persons and thus increased the proportion of older people. And the lower death rate has added to this increase, partly because somewhat more older people have been living longer,[2] but primarily because more younger people have been able to survive until old age.

The immigration of about 27 million people between 1875 and 1925 has also contributed to the increase in the proportion of older persons in the American population of today. Most of our immigrants were young adults when they came to America. Those who have survived are now chronologically aged, and sharp reduction in American immigration since 1925 has cut off the influx of young adult immigrants that might have replaced these 27 million.

It is noteworthy that the decline in births, deaths, and immigration has led to more of an increase in aged women than men. Because humans normally give birth to more male than female babies, a lowering of the birth rate cuts deeper into the proportion of males than females in the population. A lower death rate, on the other hand, automatically lifts the proportion of females. They ordinarily outlive males, and a general lowering of the death rate reduces female deaths more than male deaths. Lastly, immigration normally involves more males than females. Reducing immigration, therefore, reduces the proportion of males. And so, although today there are 99 males to every 100 females in the total

---

[2] Although more people are surviving to the later years, old people do not live much longer than they formerly did.

American population, there are over sixty-five years of age only about 90 men to every 100 women. Projections indicate that in 1975 there will be about 138 older women for every 100 older men.

As we would expect, there is a larger concentration of widows in the old age group than widowers. One reason for this is that at all ages the life expectancy of women is greater than that of men. But in addition, a woman tends to marry a man chronologically older than she is. The result is that a married woman today can, on the average, expect to be a widow for ten years before she dies. Typically, then, the older man is married, whereas the typical older woman is a widow. In 1950 more than half the women over sixty-five were widowed, but two thirds of the men were still married. Furthermore, remarriage following death of spouse is more frequent among men than among women. It is not until they reach eighty-five that a majority of men find themselves widowers.

The concentration of the chronologically aged in the United States varies considerably by state and region. The number of persons aged sixty-five and over ranges from approximately five per 100 in New Mexico to eleven per 100 in New Hampshire. The northern states— New England, the West North Central states and the Pacific Coast—have the highest proportions of old people in the country; the lowest are in the South and Southwest. These geographic differences result in part from variations in birth and death rates. In states with high birth rates, and therefore more children, the proportion of older people is likely to be smaller, while in states with low birth rates the proportion is likely to be larger than average for the nation as a whole. To some extent, too, the differences come from interstate migration. Not that the migration of aged persons has been heavy. Except to go to California and Florida, and to a lesser extent to Arizona, Nevada, and Texas, people sixty-five years of age and over seldom migrate. Rather it is the migration of young adults, leaving their aged parents behind, that is changing the age composition in different geographic areas. Even when many older people were moving to California from the Great Plains and the Midwest during the years 1936–40, there were more migrants in their twenties than in any other age group, including the oldest. Mobility is clearly more characteristic of youth than of old age.

But when the aged do migrate, they move not only southward and westward, but also from suburban communities to cities, and from rural areas to villages and nearby cities. The reasons for migration in later life are generally given as follows:

1. The beneficial impact physiologically of warmer climate on aging circulatory systems.

2. Lack or loss of ownership and control of property by the aged in the transition from rural to urban communities, enabling the aged to move from one place and region to another.

3. Lack of a definite place for the aged in the community's social structure, stemming from prejudice against old age.

4. The mass media of communication enabling more people to learn the advantages and disadvantages of various sections of the country.

5. The increase in compulsory retirement and pension programs and the decrease in self-employment, freeing the elderly for migration.

6. The establishment of social security, assuring a modest but steady source of income, without residence requirements.

7. Breakdown of two-generation and three-generation family units, operating to free older couples to migrate.[3]

In summary, the chronological definition of old age in our urban and industrial culture, the increased numbers and proportion of the aged, and the mobility of the American people that separates generations and leaves aged parents stranded provide the general background for the social problems confronting the aged in our time. Out of them have emerged the specific causal factors that have precipitated these problems, and an analysis of these factors concerns us in the section that follows.

Specific Causes of Problems of Aging

1. The Urban Family Structure and Household

Unlike the large, extended, rural family living self-sufficiently in one household, the urban family usually lives in the two-generation household, in which there is neither adequate space nor positive roles for grandparents. Not only does urban housing design fail to provide room for more than two generations, parents and children, but also the hard realities of urban life often conflict sharply with the earlier rural notions of filial duty and respect for the aged. Urban parents seldom feel able to support and house one or both of their aged parents while bringing up their own children.

[3] *Growing with the Years,* New York State Joint Legislative Committee on Problems of the Aging (Legislative Document No. 32, 1954), pp. 31–32.

Thus, 15 per cent of persons sixty-five years of age and over live in their own households, either alone or with nonrelatives. Four per cent of the aged live with nonrelatives but not in their own homes. Three per cent live in institutions and another 3 per cent live in hotels and rooming houses. The remaining 75 per cent are still managing to live with their own families in their own households. The social isolation implied in many of the above domestic arrangements of the aged produces not only feelings of loneliness, bitterness, and a loss of meaning and purpose in life, but also suggests one of the important bases of financial hardship and insecurity in old age: the lack of family support.

2. *The Gap between Life Expectancy and Working Life*

Incongruous as it may seem, it is true that while the life span has been lengthened for millions of people, their working lives have been shortened. As the pattern of self-employment in a rural economy has given way to one of employees working for an employer in our urban industrial economy, the value of older workers has declined. Now that machines have replaced an unusually large number and variety of manual skills formerly acquired during long years of experience on the job, many employers in industry choose to hire for less pay younger workers who can often reach maximum efficiency operating a machine in as little time as two weeks. And as the average age of employed workers continues to rise, it is likely that more and more workers will have difficulty getting or keeping jobs that employers, correctly or not, believe younger men and women can do at less cost.

In 1890 the average age of male workers in the United States was thirty-three; that of female workers, twenty-four. Fifty years later, in 1940, the average age of male workers reached thirty-seven; that of female workers, thirty-one. In 1960 the average age of male workers went up to thirty-nine; that of female workers to thirty-six. At the same time that the entire labor force has grown older, the actual holding of jobs has shown a direct decline with age. In 1950, more than 90 per cent of the men in the forty-five to fifty-four age group worked, as compared to about 60 per cent in the sixty-five to sixty-nine age group and approximately 25 per cent in the seventy-five to seventy-nine age group. The proportion of women participating in the labor force in 1950 declined from 33 per cent at ages forty-five to fifty-four to 13 per cent at ages sixty-five to sixty-nine and 3.5 per cent at ages seventy-five to seventy-nine.

One obvious end result of all this is to lengthen the average number of years in retirement. Thus, in 1900 white males forty years of age had a remaining average life expectancy of slightly less than twenty-eight years, to the age of 67.7. They could expect to remain employable an average of 24.5 years, to the age of 64.5, and then to live in retirement for slightly over three years. By 1950 the forty-year-old white males in this country could expect to live on the average a little more than thirty more years, to the age of 70.8, and since they were employable for possibly twenty-four more years, they could anticipate about six years of retirement. The span of retirement, therefore, approximately doubled in the course of fifty years. The trend since 1950 continues to show a growing gap between working life and total life expectancy.

One way to avoid this pattern in old age is to be self-employed, for unlike employees, the proportion of workers who are self-employed increases with age. For example, in the entire employed labor force in 1954, only 16 per cent were self-employed, but in the age group sixty-five to sixty-nine about one third were self-employed. Among those at work seventy years of age and over, more than 40 per cent were self-employed. Agricultural self-employment accounted for especially large proportions of the employed aged, for along with such others as men in small businesses and members of the professions they can often gradually reduce their work effort with age and they can control their own retirement.

The fact remains, nevertheless, that as of 1960 about 60 per cent of the male population over sixty-five years of age and 90 per cent of the female population over sixty-five were not in gainful employment. Not only is it increasingly difficult to retain work after sixty-five in our industrial economy, but people as young as forty years of age find it difficult to obtain new work, especially in time of economic recession. The best age span for securing employment is between twenty-five and thirty-five.

Yet almost everyone agrees on the right of all, regardless of age, to work for pay. Older workers, it is often argued, give stability to a work force. In loyalty, persistence, knowledge of their company and its tradition, they usually surpass younger employees. A surprisingly large proportion of older workers prefers to continue working rather than retire, especially when inadequate pensions are offered them in the face of rising living costs, and the average social security payments at the beginning of 1960 were no more than $68 a month. Unless they encounter compulsory retirement rules, older workers usually continue working until poor health forces them to stop.'

This reluctance to accept retirement can be verified by several sets of statistics. For example, on January 1, 1950, out of 2,125,000 living workers sixty-five years of age and over who were eligible for federal old age insurance benefits, about two fifths were not receiving such benefits. All but a small percentage of these nonrecipients were workers who had either continued in employment or had returned to work after having once been retired.

The average age of retiring railroad workers has been almost three years beyond the minimum eligible age of sixty-five. Retirement figures of the United States Steel Corporation show that only 40 per cent of those steel employees reaching their "normal" but not compulsory retirement age actually stop working. The Ford Motor Company has revealed that three fifths of those eligible to retire on the company's pension remain in employment.

Of course many workers today lack this opportunity to continue in employment in their older years because they are subject to compulsory retirement systems. For example, in the census year of 1950, 95 per cent of males between the ages of twenty-five and fifty-four and 85 per cent of males between fifty-five and sixty-four were employed, but only 33 per cent of those sixty-five and over had jobs. In contrast, 68.2 per cent of the men sixty-five and over were still employed back in 1890 when much of the American economy had not yet become industrialized and when pensions and compulsory retirement were rare.

3. Discrimination against Older Workers

Discrimination against older workers in retaining jobs as well as attaining new ones arises largely from prejudiced attitudes. The plight of older workers and to a certain extent the plight of all older people in urban and industrial societies has a striking resemblance to that of minorities: the racial, religious, and national or ethnic groups with which the concepts "prejudice" and "discrimination" are usually associated.[4] Sociologists typically define and characterize minorities as follows:

1. They are subgroups within a society, distinguishable from its dominant group, and regarded as inherently so different from the domi-

---

[4] Chapter 3 of this book will develop in detail the theory of the aged in American society as an emerging quasi-minority group.

nant group that they are excluded from participating fully in the life of the society.

2. They are dominated by a ruling group whose ideology sets the norms, the idealized rules or standards of behavior, for the society, and whose position of power enables it to control the actions of individuals or groups.

3. The dominant group "stereotypes" members of the minority group: groups them all as possessing an unvarying set of characteristics. This attitude grows out of their *ethnocentrism,* the belief that one's own group is right and superior, whereas outsiders are wrong and inferior, and their belief in *biological determinism,* the view that explains alleged as well as real differences between one's own group and the outgroup by claiming it is biological. The power of the dominant group over the minority is reflected in the society's laws, which tacitly accept the "validity" of these stereotypes, and in the society's practice of *status ascription,* which arbitrarily places people in certain roles, regardless of ability, on the basis of such traits as color, sex, and age. One of the effects of the dominant group's power is to put the minority group into the condition of *economic marginality:* the status of being "the last ones hired and the first ones fired."

4. Power relations between the dominant group and minority groups are marked by continual conflict, whether open or concealed. On the one hand the dominant group, acting on its ethnocentric beliefs, attempts to suppress efforts on the part of the minorities to assert themselves. On the other hand, the minorities struggle to make their will felt in society, to achieve equality of status with the dominant.

5. In the clash of interests between the dominant group and minorities, the former develops prejudiced attitudes and discriminatory behavior to retain its power.

In many ways these aspects of minorities and dominant groups apply to the aged in their relations with younger adults. Furthermore, many professional observers concede the justice of complaints by the aged that compulsory retirement and the other social and economic consequences of growing old in American society are unfair. They also point out that abrupt termination of active interests and occupations, unless carefully planned and handled, can have disastrous personality effects. Unemployment aggravates existing neuroses and may even reactivate dormant ones. Often the retired employee misses the externally imposed routine of work; he loses familiar landmarks, points of reference, and sense of identity. Suddenly useless and unwanted, deprived of incentive and of the opportunity to continue the accustomed work, such people become restless and dejected. Feeling so, they may develop hypochondria, chronic fatigue, and a resentful, self-deprecating neurotic depression.

4. Lack of Formal Education

Another important specific cause of the problems of aging today is the relatively low level of formal education most older people have had. Two generations and more ago, schooling did not have the significance it has since acquired. Not many boys and girls went on to high school, and college was only for the select few. As a consequence, about one in every five persons aged sixty-five years and over today has had less than five years of schooling; almost half failed to complete eight years of grade school. Only about one fourth have had any high school education, and fewer than one in ten have ever gone to college.

The structure of the urban family, the gap between life expectancy and working life, discrimination against older workers, and the lack of formal education do not comprise all the specific causal factors in the economic, psychological, and social problems of aging. But they do suffice to outline the broad scope of causality for such problems.

The Problems of Old Age

The problems facing the aged in American society stem not only from the failure to satisfy their needs as older persons, but also from the neglect of the needs they have in common with other age groups. All people, regardless of age, need adequate food, clothing, shelter, and maintenance of health. They also need emotional security and affection, social status and recognition, and a sense of worth and self-respect. What, then, are the major problems the aged have in satisfying their needs?

1. Inadequate Income

The family headed by a person aged sixty-five or over is, by and large, a low-income family. If still working, the family head is normally past his peak earning period; if he is retired, his retirement income tends to be low. According to the findings of the Senate Subcommittee on Problems of the Aged and Aging in 1959, three fifths of the men and women sixty-five and over receive less than $1,000 each year in money income. About 11 million men and women over sixty-five receive support from sources other than employment, such as private pensions and social security.

One measure of income adequacy in old age is that provided by the Bureau of Labor Statistics. In 1959, it estimated that an aged retired couple living in their own home in a city would need $1,900 in order to maintain an adequate level of living. Older persons living alone tend to have smaller incomes than families with an older head and would require a different measure or index of income adequacy. A nonworking aged woman living alone in rented quarters, for instance, would need about $1,600 per year.

Spending units headed by persons sixty-five years of age and over save a smaller proportion of their income than those headed by persons in their early and middle adult years. Yet it is not true that the aged are *always* financially disadvantaged when compared with younger groups. For example, total indebtedness, including mortgages, tends to be smaller for spending units headed by older persons. In addition, their net worth tends to be larger. In 1953 the median net worth of spending units headed by people sixty-five years of age and over was $8,400, whereas for all spending units it was approximately half of that, $4,100. Indebtedness of spending units headed by older people was only 4 per cent of net worth, as compared with 13 per cent for all spending units. These differences are related to changes that occur in the spending-saving patterns of people as they age. Older persons are past the time in their lives when relatively large debts are incurred as the result of the purchase of a home and the equipment and furnishings that go with it. They no longer need to save a portion of their income to amortize such debts and to pay premiums on public or private insurance plans providing benefits in old age. Many have completed mortgage payments on their homes and household replacement needs are fewer because home furnishings get less wear with the children grown.

The same qualification applies to the housing of the aged as applies to their total indebtedness and net worth. That is, even though older people own homes of less value than younger people, more of them are mortgage-free. In most cases they have occupied their houses for 10 to 20 years or longer, and depreciation or even obsolescence has reduced the values. Not many persons over sixty-five buy new houses, but when they do they tend to be of low value, partly because of low income, and also because lending institutions may require older persons to make large down payments or amortize mortgage loans over relatively short periods; the result is that some older persons are forced into houses of lower value. Yet 80 per cent of the homes owned by spending units whose head is over sixty-five years of age are free of debt, and the owner's equity tends to be relatively high despite the smaller value of their homes. The reason, of course, is that most older homeowners, as we have seen, have been long-term occupants of their homes and have accordingly had ample opportunity to pay off their mortgages.

These qualifications about the income and financial inadequacy of the aged do not undermine the general picture we have of a seriously disadvantaged group. Their income inadequacies become even more evident when one realizes that the average for the whole age group (sixty-five years and over) is distorted by the relatively high income of those sixty-five to sixty-nine. Incomes of families in which the head is seventy or over are significantly lower than those in the younger five-year bracket because employment drops sharply at the seventy and over level.

What are the major sources of income for the aged? More persons aged sixty-five and over get income from the federal old age and survivors insurance program than from any other single source. As of June, 1956, 45 per cent of these older people were receiving these so-called "social security" benefits, as compared with 29 per cent who were receiving income from employment. Public old age assistance was the third most frequent source of income, benefiting 16 per cent of all persons aged sixty-five and over. About 12 per cent of the older people were receiving benefits under the special programs for veterans and retired railroad and government workers. Between 5 and 6 per cent were receiving payments under private insurance and annuity contracts, and 6 per cent under private retirement plans. An unknown number and percentage were receiving income from investments and contributions from children and other relatives. Still others, primarily widows, had no cash income at all from any source and were living with and being supported by children or other relatives.

Some older persons receive income from two or more sources. Generally speaking, the larger the income, the greater the number of sources from which it is derived. The importance of these sources of income varies with age and size of income. By and large, persons past seventy-five years of age are more dependent upon social insurance benefits, annuities, public assistance, and contributions from relatives, than persons in their late sixties or early seventies, more of whom depend on earnings.[5]

One of the earliest established governmental sources of income for the aged, old age assistance, gives financial aid to men and women sixty-five years old and over who do not have enough income from other sources to provide themselves adequately with food, clothing, shelter, and medical care. Yet the average old age assistance grant provides an amount too modest to help much in providing the basic necessities of life. In June, 1958, the percentages of persons sixty-five and over receiving these payments administered by the individual states ranged from 58 per cent in Louisiana to 3.9 per cent in New Jersey. The national average of such payments was $64 monthly, ranging from $108 in Connecticut and $101 in New York to $29 in Mississippi and $33 in West Virginia.

Old age and survivors insurance, a major feature of the so-called social security program, was enacted into law by the federal government in 1935. The basic idea of this insurance is a simple one: during working years, employers, their employees, and self-employed people pay social security taxes which go into special funds. When earnings have stopped because the worker has retired, died, or is disabled and is fifty years of age or over, benefit payments are made from the funds to replace part of the earnings the family has lost. At the present time, nine out of ten working people are in jobs and positions covered by this insurance under social security law.

As of 1960, about 13.5 million people in the United States were drawing monthly benefits under the program, with payments estimated at $10 billion per year. The plan of financing this insurance program is as follows: Employees pay taxes on their annual earnings up to a maximum amount of $4,800 beginning in 1959. Each employer pays taxes at the same rate on the first $4,800 paid to each of his employees in the year. Year-by-year costs will undoubtedly grow for many years. Therefore the law provides that tax rates will gradually increase from a combined employer and employee rate of 6 per cent in 1960 to an ultimate rate of 9 per cent, to be reached in 1969. The self-employed pay at a rate equal to one and a half times the rate paid by the employee. The contribution rates now scheduled are intended to provide enough income to meet all the costs of the system into the indefinite future. Funds

[5] *Fact Book on Aging* (Washington, D.C., U.S. Government Printing Office, 1957), pp. 28–29, 30–35.

collected in the early years of the program and not needed for immediate benefit payments are invested in United States Government obligations. The interest earnings on these obligations are available to help pay for the larger cost of the system in later years.

The steady rise in tax rates for social security is due, first of all, to the increase in the number of persons in the population who are sixty-five years of age and over and its impact on the number of beneficiaries eligible to receive social security benefits. Since 1950, for example, there has been more than a 400 per cent increase in the number of persons receiving benefits. An even more important reason for the need to increase tax rates has been the easing of eligibility requirements for coverage and benefits under the social security act.

In fact, the whole program covering workers, their families, and disabled workers and their families is vastly different from the one started under the act of 1935. The original legislation provided that retirement benefits would be paid only to retired workers at the age of sixty-five or older, with the first payments to be made in 1942. Congress began changing the program in 1939, moving up the first payments to 1940 and providing benefits for members of families of retired or deceased workers. Further major alterations were enacted into law in 1950, 1952, 1954, 1956, and 1958, all election years.

One result of all these alterations is that a worker who retired from gainful employment in 1940 at sixty-five years of age on the then minimum benefit of $10 a month can now draw $33 a month, even though he earned no further wage credits since 1940. The maximum monthly benefit fixed by law for 1940 was $41.20; in 1960, the maximum reached $127. From no provision under the original law for a worker's family, the program has been altered until a maximum of $254 monthly in 1960 could be paid to a family's members. In the beginning a woman worker was entitled to cash benefits only on retirement at sixty-five years of age or older. In 1960 she could retire at sixty-two with a benefit slightly less than she would receive if she worked until sixty-five.

Widows of deceased workers are entitled to full benefits at sixty-two years of age. Wives of retired workers covered by social security legislation are eligible for reduced benefits at sixty-two. A wife or widow is entitled to benefits at any age if she is caring for a child getting benefits based on the retired or deceased worker's social security account, that is, if the child is under eighteen years of age and unmarried or disabled.

The 1958 amendment of the Social Security Act raised benefits, beginning in 1959, by about 7 per cent over what they had been, to the levels shown in Table 1. But the ravages of inflation have rendered even these increased payments insufficient to provide a suitable living arrangement, a proper diet, adequate clothing, and the other necessities of life. The average monthly payment received in March, 1959, for example, was only $72, and about half of all aged married couples were receiving less than $125 a month. Moreover, the retired worker who tries to earn additional money continues to be penalized by the amendment's failure to eliminate the original act's provision that between sixty-five and seventy-two years of age he shall lose a benefit for any month in which he earns more than $100.

Table 1: *Illustrative Retirement, Disability, and Survivor Insurance Benefits under the Social Security Act, as Amended in 1958*

If average monthly earnings after 1950 were	*$50*	*$150*	*$250*	*$350*
For retirement at 65 or for disability at 50	$33	$73	$95	$116
For retired women workers starting at 62	$26	$58	$76	$92
For widow, or surviving child, or dependent widower, or parent	$33	$54	$71	$87
For retired couple, wife starting at 62	$45	$100	$130	$159
For retired couple, wife starting at 65, or widow and 1 child, or 2 dependent parents	$49	$109	$142	$174
For retired couple and 1 child, or widow and 2 children	$53	$120	$190	$232
Maximum family benefit	$53	$120	$202	$254
Single lump-sum death payment	$99	$219	$255	$255

Private pensions and deferred profit-sharing plans have become increasingly important in supplementing the income of retired workers. With few exceptions, the age selected for normal retirement in both pension and deferred profit-sharing plans is sixty-five in order to coincide with the age at which most benefits become payable under the federal Social Security Act. The first stimulus to these pensions and plans was the Revenue Act of 1942, a war measure that imposed heavy surtaxes and excess profits taxes but permitted employers to deduct from taxable income their contributions to pension and deferred profit-sharing funds qualified by the United States Treasury Department. For employers in the top tax brackets, this meant that the net cost of these contributions was only 18 cents on the dollar, the other 82 cents representing what would otherwise be paid to the government in taxes. During the wage stabilization period of the war years when wage increases were strictly controlled by the government, retirement plans were adopted by many employers as one method of attracting and holding scarce labor. In 1950 this trend toward fringe benefits was greatly accelerated when organized labor in the mass production industries, especially steel and automobiles, began demanding pension plans, and when excess profits taxes were reimposed as a result of the Korean War.

The number of qualified pension and deferred profit-sharing plans has increased from a few hundred in 1942 to more than 50,000 in 1960. A pension plan is a device for accumulating reserves during the period of employment to pay pensions during the period of retirement. The amount set aside for this purpose each year is governed in part by the length of the retirement period. To make this calculation, actuaries must assume a so-called "normal" retirement age. A deferred profit-sharing plan is a device for setting aside a percentage of profits for future distribution to employee participants. This distribution is usually at the time of retirement. "Normal" retirement age in a deferred profit-sharing plan may be the age at which a participant becomes eligible to receive his full distribution. Many employers, especially the larger ones, have adopted sixty-five not only as the *normal* retirement age, but also as the *compulsory* retirement age.

In summary, social security was intended to provide a base on which the individual would plan his retirement income; private pension plans were intended to supplement social security. Individual savings, it was thought, would provide such additional amounts as might be necessary to bring the individual's standard of living up to a decent level. But the realities of life for many retired persons fall short of this ideal. The amount of retirement income provided by social security and private pension plans combined rarely exceeds 50 per cent of preretirement income, and for persons in middle income groups it is more likely to range between 30 and 40 per cent. Furthermore, many people in their early and middle years are reluctant to forego the satisfactions of current consumption by saving for an intangible security in a distant future. Consequently, savings at retirement may be adequate for an emergency, or to provide small amounts of supplemental income, but they are not a substitute for regular paychecks. Lastly, inflation has aggravated the financial problems of persons at or near marginal levels of subsistence, and this inevitably includes many pensioners.[6]

2. Poor Physical Health

A second major problem the aged confront in satisfying their needs is poor physical health. Disease and disability are problems in all age groups, but some are found more in certain age groups than in others. Thus, while infectious diseases are more characteristic of the younger years, chronic disease occurs more frequently among the aged.

More than half of the aged men who are no longer in the labor force retired voluntarily because of health reasons. Only about 5 per cent of those out of the labor force retired voluntarily while in good health. Estimates based on a national sample survey of the prevalence of disabling illness provide comparative data for broad age groups in the population. For the population as a whole, three or four persons out of every hundred has a long-term disabling and chronic illness, defined as any physical or mental impairment that renders the person unable to carry out his regular activities for more than three months. Six out of every hundred persons aged forty-five to sixty-four and seventeen out of every hundred persons aged sixty-five and over had such an illness. Disabilities of a less severe nature limit the activities of a very large proportion of other older persons.

Among persons receiving old age assistance in 1952, the proportion disabled was largest for recipients in the chronologically oldest age groups. About one in every ten aged sixty-five to sixty-nine was bedridden or required the care of others. The proportion of those requiring care increased with advancing years—about one in every eight or nine for those aged seventy to seventy-four, one in every six for those aged seventy-five to seventy-nine, and one in every three for those aged eighty and over. The bedridden were a more or less uniform 20 per cent of those requiring care, regardless of age.[7] Other research findings have led to estimates that nearly 25 per cent of persons who are well at age sixty and 40 per cent of those who are still well at age seventy will develop a chronic ailment within the next five years.

[6] Charles E. Haines, "Economic Aspects of Aging and Employment in Modern Industrial Society," an address at the Southeastern Regional Conference on Aging, Durham N.C., Oct. 6, 1959; see also *Financing Old Age, Survivors, and Disability Insurance,* a report of the Advisory Council on Social Security Financing (Washington, D.C., U.S. Government Printing Office, 1959), 30 pp.

[7] *Fact Book on Aging,* pp. 26–27, 40–43.

Of the chronic diseases, those called cardiovascular-renal are most frequent and deadly. They include heart disease, hypertension, lesions affecting the central nervous system, and inflammation of the kidneys. In the United States they cause more than half of all deaths among people sixty-five years of age and over. Cancer, of course, is another important chronic disease among older people, ranking second as a cause of death. Arthritis and related physical disorders rank low as causes of death, but just below the cardiovascular-renal diseases as causes of disability.

Because many diseases in old age disturb the metabolic processes of the body cells and impair body functioning, they precipitate other diseases. Two or three diseases frequently afflict the same individual. In this respect disease in the aging person often presents a picture different from disease in youth. Ordinarily resulting from infecting organisms, the diseases in youth have an abrupt beginning, obvious symptoms, and specific, easily identifiable causes. They usually run a rapid, self-limiting, and self-immunizing course with few serious consequences. On the other hand, diseases in old age generally do not arise from infections (two exceptions are pneumonia and tuberculosis) but result from multiple and obscure causes. Very frequently these diseases begin in slow, subtle fashion so that the individual is unaware of them until they are well advanced. They progress persistently, and they do not immunize the person. Instead, they make him more vulnerable to other diseases, often with severe consequences. The chronic and disabling illnesses pose problems not only to the individual but to society as a whole. They prevent people from working, create a group dependent on others for their care and livelihood, and make necessary costly nursing homes and other forms of specialized institutional care.

In short, the aged are more frequently attacked by illness, particularly of the chronic variety. When they are afflicted, the disease is likely to last longer and cause more disability than it would to younger persons. The aged have to stay bedridden longer and are more likely to suffer complications and die. If they survive, they must make difficult adjustments to the changes in living resulting from the illness and pose problems to the society as a whole.

Although older persons are more frequently ill than others in the population, they have less money to buy medical care and fewer opportunities to obtain such care on a prepaid basis. At the beginning of 1952, only about one fourth of all persons sixty-five years of age and over had some protection against the cost of hospital care through membership in a Blue Cross or independent plan or through a commercial accident and health policy. In contrast, the same year a little over half of the entire population had such protection. Similar information on the coverage of prepaid medical care or surgical care is not available, but the evidence suggests that it is much smaller than that for hospital care plans.

The infrequency of prepaid care among older persons is due to a variety of reasons. These voluntary plans rely heavily on group enrollment, usually at a place of employment. Most older persons, particularly women, are no longer employed and therefore are not reached by group enrollment. Some prepaid plans, furthermore, either limit the number of older persons enrolled or exclude them altogether. Older persons are also at a disadvantage in the purchase of individually written commercial policies. Some of these policies are cancelable at the older ages. Others require such high premiums that not many older persons can afford them.[8]

[8] In 1960 a bill sponsored in Congress by Representative Forand of Rhode Island sought to provide compulsory health insurance for the aged as an amendment of already existing social security laws. Backers of the bill argued that it was a logical extension of the social security system and the most practical way to satisfy the urgent health needs of the aged. The bill provided for 120 days a year of care, including surgical fees, in hospitals and nursing homes. Hospital care alone would be limited to 60 days a year.

Among the alleged advantages were the following:

1. The insurance would be financed by an extra social security tax of one half of 1 per cent on employers and employees, and three eighths of 1 per cent on the self-employed. This would spread the cost of health insurance widely and assure a strong financial base for the program.

2. Premiums, in the form of taxes, would be payable only by gainfully employed persons and in relation to their earnings. Under voluntary plans, fixed premiums must be maintained regardless of whether there is any income.

3. All employers would be required to share the cost of insurance for their employees. Some, but not all, do so under voluntary plans.

4. Benefits under the bill could not be canceled, and they would be more adequate than most voluntary insurance benefits.

Opponents of the Forand bill contended that its enactment would lead eventually to full-scale socialized medicine. As a result, a compromise federal bill providing medical aid only for the *needy* aged was passed in September, 1960. Most states, with federal support, had already been giving some medical care to persons receiving old age assistance. The new law goes beyond this, for it subsidizes states in offering medical care to the aged who are self-supporting as long as they are healthy but have no funds for medicine or medical services in

3. Mental and Emotional Disorders

Today one third of all persons entering state mental hospitals for the first time are sixty years of age and over. Even more striking, the median age of all psychotic first admissions is about sixty-one years.

At one time most people assumed that the chief mental disorders in old age resulted purely from the inevitable breakdown of the person as an organism. Today, in contrast, the growing belief is that the kind of social relations experienced by the aged, such as isolation and loss of status, help greatly to produce the disorders.[9]

4. Deficient Social Participation and Recreation

Lack of "something to do," especially with others, is one of the most serious problems the aged face in urban communities. When work and family responsibilities are taken away and friends and relatives are lost by death or migration, rest in solitude may not satisfy the psychological and social needs of an aged person. Early highly active lives in a competitive economy often leave the aged unprepared to spend their time pursuing satisfying interests and hobbies.

For a long time the idea has prevailed that the aged are content to sit passively awaiting the grim reaper. Actually, many still want to lead constructive, meaningful lives. They want their activity to be stimulating, informative, even creative. They crave to be recognized as distinctive individuals who count for something. When they fail to achieve these satisfactions they may become bitter and cynical. Yet they frequently do not look for help in these matters, for to do so would be to "lose face," to admit failure and defeat.

Conclusion

Having examined a cross-cultural survey of the aged, the nature and extent of old age in urban industrial society, the specific causes of the problems of aging, and lastly, the major problems of the aged, the

emergencies. Each state, inquiring into the resources of applicants, determines persons needy enough to receive medical aid, the amount of payment, and the extent of coverage.

[9] Theoretical aspects of the social etiology of mental and emotional disorders in old age, with special reference to retirement, will be more fully developed in Section II of this book.

introduction to this book has ended and we are now ready to turn to gerontological theory. Section II that follows will take up on an abstract level some issues on aging that were raised in the introduction, namely, the quasi-minority status of the aged, norms that are proposed to guide their adjustment, and the relationships between work, retirement, and morbidity in old age.

Questions and Research Exercises

1. Present sociological evidence in support of the thesis that American culture is youth centered.
2. How does one account for the fact that problems of aging are not acute in all societies?
3. Compare chronological, physiological, and psychological aging in terms of both resemblances and differences among them.
4. Discuss the importance of the "vital" revolution in creating the change in age composition in American society.
5. Compare life expectancy and working life in American society with those characteristic of a nonindustrial society.
6. In what two ways are the aged found to be not at a disadvantage financially when compared with younger groups?
7. Account for the steady rise in tax rates for social security.
8. Show how disease in the aging person usually presents a different pattern from disease in youth.

Selected Readings

Amulree, Basil, *Adding Life to Years* (London, National Council of Social Service, 1951). A standard work on problems of aging in England by one of the leading figures in English gerontology.

Anderson, John E., ed., *Psychological Aspects of Aging* (Washington, D.C., American Psychological Association, 1956). An important symposium on theory and research methodology concerning psychological and sociological aspects of aging.

Cavan, Ruth S., et al., *Personal Adjustment in Old Age* (Chicago, Science Research Associates, 1949). One of the first empirical studies in contemporary gerontology concerned essentially with the social-psychological problems of aging.

Donahue, Wilma T., and Tibbitts, Clark, eds., *The New Frontiers of Aging* (Ann Arbor, University of Michigan Press, 1957). The proceedings of one of the annual conferences conducted at the University of Michigan; a compilation of recent ideas and research findings in gerontology and geriatrics.

Havighurst, Robert J., and Albrecht, Ruth, *Older People* (New York, Longmans, Green & Co., 1953). A general overview of the conditions of life for older people in the United States, and a report of a study of older people in a small midwestern city.

Sheldon, Henry D., *The Older Population of the United States* (New York, John Wiley & Sons, 1958). An authoritative analysis of the demography of the aged.

Webber, Irving L., ed., *Aging: A Current Appraisal* (Gainesville, University of Florida Press, 1957). The proceedings of one of the annual Southern Conferences on Gerontology and one of the best up-to-date accounts of theory and research findings.

II : Problems in Gerontological Theory

*Aging is like a game of chess,
in which individual pieces may be captured,
but in which a few potent figures can still hold the field
and even regain a new and powerful position.*

MARTIN GUMPERT

3 :

THE AGED AS A QUASI-MINORITY GROUP

Employers, whether public or private, whether in Nicaragua, New York, or New Zealand, are generally not eager to hire older workers. Nowhere in the world do employers generally equate the plus-factors of age, such as experience, judgment, know-how, with the energy, adaptability, growth prospects of younger job seekers.

In seeking a job, the older person finds himself at a disadvantage vis à vis the younger person, whether he be in the Orient or the West, whether in a statist economy or free enterprise economy or mixed economy, whether he be in a full-employment or a labor shortage environment.

There is no evidence available that indicates that anywhere in the world employers generally are free from prejudice against the hiring of older workers. On the other hand, clear and unmistakable evidence exists that even in areas of labor shortage, employers are reluctant to hire older workers.

The intensity of the reluctance to hire older workers varies from country to country and within countries from region to region, from time to time. Variations in intensity may be cyclical, depending in part on the ups and downs of labor supply in relation to labor demand; it may be due to such mechanistic factors as societal-sponsored propaganda campaigns; it may be due to variations in the degree of industrialization, or to basic cultural conditions.

We learn of the move in Belgium to reduce the age of retirement from 65 to 60 in order to take oldsters out of the labor market, of Iran's work permits for the elderly designed to control their entry into the labor force, and of Italian labor unions' drive against older workers to aid young people seeking jobs.

We see, too, significant patterns of social action aiming to improve the older person's position in the labor market in some countries, such as Holland, where a joint government-union-employer educational campaign attempts to widen job opportunities for senior citizens; or England where pension bonuses are offered for continuation at work past normal retirement age; or France, where dismissals are subject to strict governmental control; Canada, where specialized counselling and placement service is made available to older job seekers; the United States, where special counselling and placement efforts in the public employment service offices are just beginning, where a few states have attempted by law to ban discrimination against older workers, and where voluntary group action by overage job seekers has helped combat discrimination.*

For the most part, sociological research on problems of aging has been vigorous in gathering facts but weak in arranging facts abstractly into theoretical frameworks. In this chapter we will develop the possibility suggested in the previous chapter of studying and analyzing the aged in American society as an emerging quasi-minority group. We will attempt to demonstrate that both the social psychology of older people at work and retired from it and to a large extent their whole situation in urban industrial life resemble those of the ethnic groups we usually call minorities. To regard the aged thus as an emerging quasi-minority group may well enlarge our understanding of the problems of aging and the aged and hasten their resolution.[1]

A fundamental question, of course, is whether it is sociologically valid to consider the aged a quasi-minority rather than a genuine minority. Why, we may ask, should they be confined conceptually to the quasi-minority level? Are they not, like authentic minorities, stereotyped by other groups (in this case, the younger age groups), and do they not suffer from subordination, prejudice, and discrimination? Is it not true that they demonstrate such typical minority group feelings as hyper-

---

* Albert J. Abrams, "Discrimination in Employment of Older Workers in Various Countries of the World," in *Age Is No Barrier*, New York State Joint Legislative Committee on Problems of the Aging (Legislative Document No. 35, 1952), p. 70.
[1] It is possible such a theoretical point of view of the aged may even contribute new insights for the fruitful examination of the traditional minorities.

sensitivity, self-hatred, and defensiveness in reacting to their distinctive trait, old age?

Some scholars [2] say emphatically that minority and majority characteristics and experiences are not confined solely to ethnic groups. They argue, for instance, that most of the essential defining aspects of majority-minority group interaction apply as readily to women in our society in their social relations with men as to intergroup relations between American Negroes and whites.[3] Therefore, they claim, it is unwarranted to think of minorities and majorities exclusively in terms of racial, religious, and nationality groups.

In criticizing this argument, however, we may say it is not enough to show that women and the aged share the traditional minorities' experiences of subordination and exclusion from equal participation in those opportunities American society theoretically extends to all its members. Unlike the traditional minorities, neither women nor the aged are socially organized as independently functioning subgroups in American society. On the contrary, they live as individuals within the very families of the alleged majorities, so that we cannot accurately say they are engaged in intergroup relations in the full sense of that term. Hence, our preference for the quasi-minority over the minority concept certainly seems justified in the case of the aged as well as in that of women.

We should make another basic distinction between the aged as a quasi-minority on the one hand, and as members of interest or pressure groups on the other. Like the membership of other minorities, quasi-minorities, and even majorities, some of the aged have organized themselves into pressure groups, the most conspicuous of which are the Townsend and McLain movements. Pressure groups are seldom identical with the larger groups from which they are derived, although as they contend for influence, directing their pressure at whatever centers of power may exist, governmental and otherwise, they seek to represent those larger groups.

[2] See, for example, E. K. Francis, "Minority Groups—a Revision of Concepts," *British Journal of Sociology* (Vol. 2, 1951), pp. 219–30.

[3] H. M. Hacker, "Women as a Minority Group," *Social Forces* (Vol. 30, 1951), pp. 60–69; Gunnar Myrdal, *An American Dilemma* (New York, Harper & Brothers, 1944), Appendix 5; Bernhard J. Stern, "The Family and Cultural Change," *American Sociological Review* (Vol. 4, 1939), pp. 199–208; J. J. Williams, "Patients and Prejudice: Lay Attitudes toward Women Physicians," *American Journal of Sociology* (Vol. 51, 1946), pp. 283–87.

Majority Attitudes and Behavior toward the Aged

We can easily discern prejudice, stereotyping, and discriminatory behavior against the aged by the majority group of younger adults. One student of the American labor force has even asserted that older workers are the group in the labor market most vulnerable to discrimination. "Many persons," says Bancroft, "can live out their working lives untouched directly by the factors that adversely affect the employment of women, of Negroes, of the foreign-born, or other minority groups, but none can escape the effects of age—as it influences both his own employment and that of someone to whom he is closely related." [4]

1. Fears the Aged Are a Menace

We find an extreme yet useful illustration of majority fears of the threat and menace posed by the aged quasi-minority in the following statement:

The new class war between the young and the old will manifest itself in several ways. First, there will be heavy pension taxes that may eventually absorb more than one-fourth of the income of both workers and employers. This new class war may progress so far that we will see workers and employers standing shoulder to shoulder against the hard-driven politicians who promise our senior citizens impossible pensions and encourage the older worker to exploit the younger worker, the older farmer to exploit the younger farmer, the older businessman to exploit the younger businessman, the older professional man to exploit the younger professional man. . . . Let us remember that these pension leaders will soon have the votes. Karl Marx and others have taught us that mass movements are rarely rational: they spring from broad social changes. These basic changes in the population pattern started recently and slowly; the resulting mass movement has not yet matured. Townsendism may be as important in the next fifty years as were the doctrines of Karl Marx during the last half century.

May I put the proposition quite bluntly? "Cradle to the grave" is a scheme whereby those close to the grave would fasten themselves on the pay-checks of those closer to the cradle, and ride piggy-back (or piggy-bank) to the grave. Has our aging population condemned us or entitled us to an age-conscious future rather than a class-conscious future? Will the increased voting power of older people be used to exploit youth to such an extent that

[4] Gertrude Bancroft, "Older Persons in the Labor Force," *The Annals of the American Academy of Political and Social Science* (Vol. 279, 1952), pp. 52–61.

a revolt of youth will become inevitable? Should the state constitution be amended to provide a maximum voting age? [5]

The aged have so far provoked relatively few public statements as hostile or fearful as this. Fear of the aged by younger adults is today still subdued, and the majority acts much less drastically than suggested in the quotation above. This fact is illustrated by the following statement of an oil company defending its practice of compulsory retirement and rationalizing its program of preretirement counseling:

All of the working population over sixty-five, and to a lesser degree those who have passed the forty-five-year mark, are conscious of the idea of compulsory retirement. They are aware of the difficulty in obtaining employment and are doubly concerned about their uncertain future. If a sizable portion of this group were to band together, the weight of their combined support would be the most powerful political force the country has ever known. . . .

There is another possibility inherent in this problem, however. Conservatism and age are companions. Thus it is possible that the peak of political support for radical changes in our government's economic system has been reached. Preservation of property rights and individual security are of more personal importance to the elder citizen than experimental radicalism. If industry can convince the aging industrial population that it is doing something concrete about their uncertain future, socialistic remedies might well wither for lack of support.

This situation also holds the possibility of unfavorable repercussions for industry. Consider the community aspects. If a man is retired from business and goes into the community feeling that he is no longer useful to himself, to industry or to anyone else, his degeneration tends to be rapid. . . . A defeated, apathetic attitude on the part of retired individuals soon permeates the community and it is not very long before members of the community point to the company from which Jones was retired with such statements as "They certainly killed poor Jones retiring him like that." The cumulative adverse effect of such reaction is obvious.

This company feels that retirement is something earned by faithful service, a form of "graduation" into a new phase of life rather than a "casting out" process. Retirement should be the opportunity for the employee to enjoy the fruits of his labors in freedom, leisure and relaxation as well as

[5] F. G. Dickinson, "Economic Aspects of the Aging of Our Population," in *Problems of America's Aging Population: A Report on the First Annual Southern Conference on Gerontology* (Gainesville, University of Florida Press, 1951), pp. 79 ff.

an opportunity to serve himself, his family and his community in ways not open to him during his working career.

In seeking to help its employees approach retirement in this way, the company feels that individual counselling and help are basic prerequisites. . . . Thus the concept developed of a seminar or discussion-type approach, wherein a group of employees approaching retirement is offered the opportunity to gather and explore some of the problems and requirements of a successful retirement.[6]

2. Employers' Rationalizations for Discrimination

Many of the reasons employers give for discriminating against older workers in hiring and retirement policies involve the same process of stereotyping that is an integral part of prejudice against ethnic minorities. Pigeonholing, premature generalizations, and unwarranted economy of thought are found in the reasons given for arbitrary retirement and the reluctance to hire older workers. For example, a survey of 94 employment agencies in New York City in 1952 uncovered the unsubstantiated belief held by these agencies that the older job-seeker is "his own worst enemy," destroying his chances for employment by such alleged personality deviations as "talking too much, being hard to please, too set in his ways, and lacking poise and grooming." [7]

Before considering the reasoning of employers, we should note that the advice of insurance companies to employers underlies many of such discriminatory policies. Insurance companies warn employers that to hire men over forty-five years of age and women over forty, or to retain employees beyond sixty-five, would require the companies to request payment of higher premiums for workmen's compensation and such other forms of insurance carried by the employing firm as disability and accident insurance. Another underlying factor is the development of pension plans. If a company is committed to paying a pension at a fixed age, such as sixty-five, it will probably refrain from hiring people fifty or fifty-five years of age. If it hires these people, the company must then set aside enough money to pay them pensions comparable to those going to employees whose service in the company has extended over a greater number of years.

Aside from the arguments that younger workers need to be given a chance to advance into better jobs and that "the organization needs

---

[6] *Preparation for Retirement,* a brochure published by Esso (Standard Oil Company of New Jersey, New York, 1950).
[7] *The New York Times,* July 31, 1952.

new blood," there are eight reasons given by employers for retiring older workers and refusing to hire them. They are as follows:

1. Older workers are less productive. But such facts as are available do not bear this out. Surveys generally show that the quantity and quality of work by older workers are equal to or superior to those of younger employees.

2. They are frequently absent. Yet a 1956 survey by the United States Labor Department showed that older workers had an attendance record 20 per cent better than that of younger workers.

3. They are involved in more accidents. Yet the same survey by the Labor Department showed that workers forty-five years of age and over had 2.5 per cent fewer disabling injuries and 25 per cent fewer non-disabling injuries than those under forty-five.

4. They do not stay on the payroll long enough to justify hiring expenses. Yet studies show that separation rates for older workers are much lower than for younger employees.

5. It is too costly to provide them with adequate pensions. But this is an easy generalization that is rarely based on a careful scrutiny of the company pension plan to see just what the impact of hiring the worker will be. It often depends on the type of plan.

6. Older workers cause major increases in employee group insurance costs. But here again the costs all depend on the nature of the plan.

7. They do not have needed job skills. However, on the contrary, the facts show that the older worker is likely to possess more skills, training, and know-how than younger job hunters.

8. They are inflexible and unimaginative and have trouble getting along with younger workers. It is hard to imagine a generalization more susceptible to contradiction by the individual case than this one. The practical experience of many companies indicates that this factor is seriously overrated.

That discrimination based on such reasoning as we have described decreases during time of war further argues the propriety of classifying the aged as a quasi-minority. It is a widely held theory that whenever there are serious external threats to a nation's military security, internal social distinctions are reduced, and discrimination against minorities is held in some abeyance. How precisely this theory applies to the aged is still uncertain, but there is little doubt that the urgent need for industrial manpower during recent wartime emergencies caused a noticeable relaxation in the otherwise stringent restrictions against the hiring or retention not only of ethnic minorities, but of older workers and women as well.

Minority-Group Reactions of the Aged

To be properly categorized as a quasi-minority group, the aged, especially older workers, should exhibit typical minority-group reactions. These include such things as marked self-consciousness, sensitivity, and defensiveness about their social and cultural traits, accompanied by self-hatred. Williams asserts that militant forms of these reactions are most likely when the group's position is rapidly improving, or when the position is rapidly deteriorating, especially following a period of improvement.[8] Young has suggested the hypothesis that the harder minorities are pressed to earn a living, the more likely they are to be defensive about their minority qualities and traditions.[9] This hypothesis is likely to hold true only when minority persons find it impossible to "pass" and identify with the majority.

The bitterness, resentment, and self-hatred of older workers who experience discrimination in employment and reëmployment are minority group reactions. Consider, for example, the following comment of a Midwesterner:

I am in my middle fifties and want to state that I regard myself a pretty good person and able to do a good day's work, a veteran of World War I. Some of the punishment I go through from persons twenty years up regarding my age is sickly. Such remarks as "you old S.O.B., you're all washed up" at times makes me want to do some harm. I am the oldest in my department. I help the new employees who lack experience with my knowledge of certain types of work, and after they gain the experience, they give you the brush. One thing I notice when a younger person has authority over an older person, there seldom is any consideration.

A Southerner writes:

I am a construction man and have handled thousands of men as a general labor foreman. But what's killing off the elderly people is being

[8] Robin M. Williams, Jr., *The Reduction of Intergroup Tensions* (New York, Social Science Research Council, Bulletin No. 57, 1947), p. 61.

[9] Donald Young, *Research Memorandum on Minority Peoples in the Depression* (New York, Social Science Research Council, Bulletin No. 31, 1937).

told "you're too old." The government and the employer are to blame. When a man reaches the age of forty, from then on there is the same tune until sixty-five. Right here in the U.S.A., think of the millions of men who are willing to work but cannot get work. It rings in their ears, "you're too old."

A Westerner says:

No one, except a man who has worked regularly for thirty or forty years at one kind of work and very suddenly at the age of sixty-five is thrown out of work on one-third his regular pay, can realize or understand the depressive mental effect or the worry brought by the fact that he is old and not wanted in a country he worked so hard to build. Eleven months ago at the age of sixty-six and in good health after forty-eight years of railroad work I was taken out of service. I accepted my annuity, $97.31 per month. By living conservatively the wife and I could get by on $160 per month. I have tried many times to secure work with no success. I would be glad to work. Retirement as it is today is a death sentence, by worry, depressive feeling of being useless and an insufficient annuity. I was compelled to drop my lodge dues. I may drop my insurance. I worry almost continually and sometimes feel that I'd be glad to know that I will not awaken tomorrow to a useless and idle life.

Legislation against Discrimination

Increasingly, the reaction of American society to majority discrimination against minority groups is to enact legislation intended to punish or deter such behavior. Some states have enacted not only "fair employment practices" laws against ethnic discrimination, but also similar legislation against age discrimination, a course other states show signs of imitating. This fact supports further the propriety of viewing the problems of the aged as occurring in a modified majority-minority group framework.

Until the McGahan-Preller Act became effective in New York State July 1, 1958, there had been three main types of laws against age discrimination enacted previously. One was a ban on discrimination in hiring based on age (Rhode Island and Pennsylvania); a second was a ban on hiring and rehiring based on age (Louisiana, Colorado, and Massachusetts); a third was a ban on discrimination based on age for public employees or civil service applicants only (New York).

Massachusetts and Rhode Island limit coverage of their respective laws to ages forty-five to sixty-five, Pennsylvania to forty-five to sixty-two, Colorado to eighteen to sixty, and Louisiana and New York's laws mentioned no specific ages. Exempted from most of the laws were jobs for which age is a "bona fide occupational qualification."

The best known of all of these early laws was that of Massachusetts, passed by the legislature in 1937. The law included virtually no enforcement provisions, however, with the result that virtually no cases of discrimination were brought before the Massachusetts authorities during the first 13 years of the law's existence. In 1950, however, the state enacted into law a bill that included age in the coverage of its Fair Employment Practices Act protecting ethnic groups that had been in existence since 1946. The agency administering the law tries to "conciliate and persuade" between the parties involved in the violation or alleged violation. If this fails, a penalty up to $300 for a violation may be exacted. The law also provides that the victim of discrimination may secure from the violator between $100 and $500 in payment for the damage of discrimination. One outgrowth of this law is that the Massachusetts Commission against Discrimination has ruled that pension plans with a compulsory retirement age of less than sixty-five are inoperative and in violation of the state law. In contrast with the early inactivity in law enforcement from 1937 through 1950, the Massachusetts Commission against Discrimination from 1953 through 1958 handled over 300 cases of age discrimination in employment. Not a single case went to the courts, being settled in the traditional pattern of "fair employment practices," namely, by conciliation and negotiation.[10]

The generally mixed experience of both success and failure in banning age discrimination by law, prior to the enactment in New York State in 1958, is best expressed by the following list of pros and cons gathered by the New York State Joint Legislative Committee on Problems of the Aging after examining the happenings in other states:

1. Pros
   a. Removes the sanction of discrimination.
   b. Forces reëxamination of unrealistic personnel policies.
   c. Enables power and prestige of the government to be used to "educate" employers.

[10] K. J. Kelley, "Massachusetts Law against Age Discrimination in Employment," in *No Time to Grow Old*, New York State Joint Legislative Committee on Problems of the Aging (Legislative Document No. 12, 1951), pp. 173–75; *Good News for Later Life*, New York State Joint Legislative Committee on Problems of the Aging (Legislative Document No. 8, 1958), pp. 23–24; Federal Security Agency, *Aging* (Vol. 3, 1953), p. 5.

    d. Reduces overt symbols of discrimination such as age limitations in help wanted ads and job orders.

    e. Provides an agency before which older workers may air their grievances.

    f. Permits olders workers at least to gain access to personnel managers and employment office.

    g. Proclaims a state policy.

2. Cons

    a. Does not materially affect basic conditions of the labor market, which primarily determine hiring of the forty-plus.

    b. Does not wipe out stereotypes and prejudices about older workers.

    c. Does not result in placement of more older workers in jobs.

    d. Evasion is simple, widespread, and enforcement most difficult.

    e. Does not strike at employer concern with increased costs of pensions, insurance, nor with personnel policies of promotion-from-within.

    f. Falsely raises hopes of older workers.

Undeterred by these mixed findings about age discrimination laws elsewhere, New York State amended its already existing law against ethnic discrimination, effective July 1, 1958, to prohibit employers and unions from discriminating against workers forty-five to sixty-five years of age on the basis of age, and to prohibit "help wanted" advertisements and application forms that discriminate against anyone on the basis of age, unless based on a bona fide occupational qualification.

Enforcement of New York State's law is a responsibility of the State Commission against Discrimination, an agency created in 1945 to enforce laws prohibiting discrimination in employment, public housing, and public accommodations based on race, religion, and national origin. The Commission acts on complaint. A cease and desist order by the Commission is enforceable in the courts, but the Commission attempts to effect conciliation before the proceedings reach the enforcement stage.

The rules of the Commission permit any employer or employment agency to obtain age information for *nondiscriminatory* purposes, such as the gathering of statistics, the preëmployment medical examination, eligibility for OASI disability and retirement benefits, and fringe benefits. Also, consideration may be given to age as a bona fide occupational qualification in circumstances such as the following: where age is a bona fide requisite to job performance, as for a person to model clothes for teen-agers; where age is a bona fide requisite to the provisions of a career system for particular jobs, as for jobs filled by upgrading from lower ranking positions; and where age is a bona fide requisite to an apprentice training or on-the-job training program of long duration.

Evidence of some success in achieving the purposes of the New York State law was clear within a year following its passage. For example, placement of nonagricultural workers forty-five years of age and over by the New York State Employment Service increased from 21 per cent of total placements in the first six months of 1953 to 29 per cent in the corresponding period in 1958 and 30 per cent in 1959. There has been a precipitous drop in age specifications in advertising. During the first year of the law's operation, a total of 148 complaints were filed with the New York State Commission against Discrimination; employers were named as respondents in 73 per cent of the complaints, employment agencies in 17 per cent, and labor unions in 10 per cent. Fifty-four of the 148 complaints had been closed by the end of the first year of the law's operation. Charges of discrimination were sustained in nine cases, dismissed for lack of jurisdiction in 28 cases, dismissed for lack of probable cause in 15 cases, and dropped by complainants in two cases. Clerical workers comprised 38 per cent of the complainants; professional, semiprofessional, and managerial workers, 22 per cent; skilled, semiskilled, and unskilled workers, 27 per cent; service workers, salesmen, sales clerks, 13 per cent.

That age discrimination legislation will continue to be adopted elsewhere is a safe prediction to make. Following the precedent established by such pioneering states as Massachusetts, Rhode Island, Pennsylvania, and New York, age discrimination bills were introduced in the 1959 and 1960 legislatures of Connecticut, Oregon, Maine, Kansas, Michigan, Montana, Wisconsin, California, Washington, Nevada, Texas, South Carolina, Ohio, Minnesota, and in the Congress of the United States.

Summary and Conclusion

We have seen that although the aged in urban industrial society are not an independently functioning subgroup, they do meet many other of the criteria for a minority defined in sociological theory concerning majority-minority group interaction. We have presented evidence that in the outgroup of younger adults they are sometimes looked upon as a threat to the present power structure. Prejudiced attitudes against the aged are common. Stereotyping and the reasoning behind discrimination by younger adults are similar to those applied against ethnic minorities. When employer discrimination against ethnic minorities abates in time of war, it also lessens against older workers. The aged have many of the reactions of a minority group. Lastly, legislation against discrimination has begun to be enacted on behalf of the aged, paralleling that for the protection of ethnic groups.

One may conclude, therefore, that there is considerable justification for employing the theory of the aged as a quasi-minority group in collecting and analyzing data on problems of aging in urban industrial societies.

Questions and Research Exercises

1. Compare the aged, Negroes, and women in American society with regard to the extent they satisfy the requirements of a minority group.
2. Make a study of the Townsend Plan and the social movement based on it, showing its social setting, its growth pattern, and its organizational structure.
3. What are the reasons given by employers for refusing to hire or retain older employees and show why they are often called myths by critical observers.
4. Self-hatred, according to social psychologists, results when minority group members internalize the hostile attitudes directed against them by the dominant group. Show how this takes place among some of the aged.
5. Compare the Massachusetts law against age discrimination with the one legislated in New York state in terms of coverage, sanctions and accomplishments.
6. What are the pros and cons of age discrimination legislation?

Selected Readings

Abrams, Albert J., "Discrimination against Older Workers in Various Countries," in *Old Age in the Modern World* (Edinburgh, E. and S. Livingstone Ltd., 1955), pp. 291–95. An excellent, brief survey of older workers' difficulties in attaining and retaining work throughout the world.

Barron, Milton L., "Attacking Prejudices against the Aged," in *Growing with the Years,* New York State Joint Legislative Committee on Problems of the Aging (Legislative Document No. 32, 1954), pp. 56–58. An attempt to substantiate through research findings the theory of the aged as a quasi-minority, and a classification of types of action to reduce prejudice and discrimination that are transferable from the traditional minorities to the problems of the aged.

Hacker, H. M., "Women as a Minority Group," *Social Forces* (Vol. 30, 1951), pp. 60–69. One of the better efforts to apply minority group criteria outside the ethnic context.

Simpson, George Eaton, and Yinger, J. Milton, *Racial and Cultural Minorities,* rev. ed. (New York, Harper & Brothers, 1958). The standard textbook in the sociological analysis of American prejudice and discrimination.

Williams, Robin M., Jr., *The Reduction of Intergroup Tensions* (New York, Social Science Research Council, Bulletin No. 57, 1947). A useful, sophisticated critique of the bases of action programs in intergroup relations.

4 :

NORMS FOR THE AGED

When Alice Langhorn, a trim little dynamo at 60, retired as manager of one of Chicago's leading fashion shops, she too thought retirement was going to be a cinch. "I'm sure going to enjoy the rest," she said. "Getting up late for breakfast. No pell-mell rush to work. No customers or board of directors to hound me. What a life it's going to be."

And at first, her optimism seemed justified. She'd listen to the alarm clock jangle at 8 A.M., then smilingly shut it off, turn over and go back to sleep. She got a lot of things done that she had put off for a long time, like redecorating her living room and visiting her niece in Dallas. "My only responsibility," she said smilingly, "is keeping the percolator from boiling over."

But as the weeks were swallowed up into months, she began to get as restless as a caged fox. The hours of the day stretched out interminably. She missed the old gang at the office, and felt "out of things." She was very lonely. And before long her normally happy disposition was marred by spells of depression. She began to wish she had never retired.

"You've got to know how to retire," she admitted. "And I guess I wasn't prepared for it." *

Gerontologists find in their studies that traditionally almost all human societies have deemed the long, active years of young and middle adulthood the only life periods worthy of systematic, intensive prepara-

* Thomas C. Desmond, "Retirement Is a Trap," in *Never Too Old,* New York State Joint Legislative Committee on Problems of the Aging (Legislative Document No. 32, 1949), pp. 171–72.

tion and planning. The techniques may vary from informal apprentice-ship and involvement in family and household chores to the formal education characteristic of the modern world. Old age, on the other hand, has typically been regarded by most cultures, especially in the Western part of the world, as a brief and static period, "a time when the individual's development has been halted and his potentialities dis-sipated by the blight of age, during which he can only await his ultimate dismissal from life." [1]

A New Philosophy of Life

In the United States a new philosophy of life, which gerontologists and geriatricians have helped formulate, is challenging this traditional view. The new philosophy has developed largely from a recognition of two facts. One is that during the past half century the average life ex-pectancy has increased, and the average length of working life de-creased, sufficiently to double the span of retirement. Secondly, more and more of us are coming to view life as a continuously changing process, the arbitrarily defined periods of which, including that of old age, require people persistently to adapt to new conditions. No period of life is exempt from change and the need for people consciously to reorient themselves.

In short, the new philosophy holds that preparing and planning for the years of "later maturity" may be just as important and complex as for the earlier years of life. The major purpose of preparation in each case is to enable a person to explore and develop his potentialities in the years ahead, and to achieve and retain meaningful economic and social roles.

Yet only a small proportion of people appear to be acting on this philosophy by actually preparing and planning for old age. For exam-ple, a nationwide survey, conducted in the United States by Cornell University in 1952 and 1953 of a representative cross-section of the urban population sixty years of age and over, revealed that the majority of older people do not plan ahead adequately even for the immediate future.[2] The survey respondents were asked: "How much do you plan ahead the things that you will be doing next week or the week after?

[1] Wilma T. Donahue, "Education's Role in Maintaining the Individual's Status," *The Annals of the American Academy of Political and Social Science* (Vol. 279, Jan., 1952), p. 115.
[2] Chapter 7 of this book presents a more comprehensive analysis of the survey findings.

Would you say you make many plans, a few plans, or almost none?" Over half, 57.6 per cent, replied they made almost no plans; 27.4 per cent made only a few plans; and only 14.5 per cent claimed to make many plans. These answers alone, of course, are not conclusive evidence that older people fail to prepare for the future. But the significance of the answers is heightened by their consistency with those given to other survey questions directed more pointedly at the issue.

The employed respondents were asked: Have you made plans for anything you would like to do after you stop working?" Only 23 per cent of them said "yes," whereas 76.7 per cent said "no." Employers in preparing elderly employees for retirement are even more negligent, for the employed respondents were also asked: "Has your company or employer tried to do anything to help you prepare for retirement, aside from pensions?" The overwhelming majority, 83.7 per cent, denied they had received any help, and only 15.4 per cent could say they had. Most convincing that preparation is infrequent were the replies to the following question, asked of those respondents no longer working: "Before you stopped working, did you make plans for anything you would like to do after you stopped working?" Eight out of ten asserted they had made no plans for their retirement. The 20 per cent who claimed they had made plans were asked further: "Well, did you carry out these plans or not?" Only 38 per cent could answer "yes"; 23 per cent said "partly"; and 38 per cent replied "no." The over-all picture for older people in the United States then, as indicated by this survey, is one of gross negligence in preparing for old age.

Before we deplore this situation, we should ask why it has occurred. Undoubtedly, several causes are involved. First of all, as gerontologists point out, there are still no clear-cut roles in our culture for aged adults, particularly for those in retirement. The status of old age is largely "cultureless." For what shall older people be prepared? Many professional educators frankly admit they do not know the answer, and understandably, they are reluctant to develop programs preparing for retirement until the roles of the aged and retired in American society are more clearly delineated.

Secondly, we know very little about the most efficient methods of educating older people. As Donahue has pointed out:

Research has not been done on such questions as whether older people learn better in mixed-up age groups or in peer groups, whether smaller assignments are indicated, whether more time should be allowed for discussion, and whether the lecture technique is better suited to classes of older students than, for example, are group project techniques. Other questions which need to be probed include: What and how much visual aids material will be of value in the instruction of people whose visual and auditory acuity is diminishing? Do special materials need to be prepared? What type of leader is best suited for instructing older people; that is, how important are age and prestige factors in speakers? [3]

A third cause of negligence in preparing and planning for old age is the considerable evidence that many people, especially industrial workers, think retirement economically impracticable, and preparing for such an experience, unrealistic. Retirement is something many of them feel they cannot financially afford. Consequently, they are convinced it must be deferred indefinitely, if possible. Why should one prepare for an experience that is financially not feasible?

Middle-Class Norms

It is on a fourth factor that we shall dwell most, however, for with it we touch a most crucial weakness of gerontology and geriatrics. Negligence in preparing and planning for old age stems from the fact that whatever norms today determine what is desirable for the aged and govern the nature of such preparation and planning have been formulated mostly by professional educators, physicians, clergymen, social workers, and industrial and business personnel; that is, by typically middle-class spokesmen. These norms, taking substance in such activities as hobbies, avocations, club activities, and other nonvocational pastimes, offer, as should be expected, more meaning and appeal to older people of the middle classes than to those of lower economic, social, and educational strata.

In support of this last point is Noetzel's observation that, in some counseling programs for older people, the foreign-born and semiskilled manual workers react negatively to any discussion of hobbies.[4] To them the word has the connotation of "make work," "childishness," or "futile play." Indeed, we have reason to believe the very concepts of "preparation," "life planning," and "adjustment" are more intimately associated with middle-class psychology than with the psychology of

[3] Donahue, *op. cit.*, pp. 117–18.
[4] Arthur Noetzel, *Preparation of Industrial Workers for Retirement* (Pittsburgh, Health and Welfare Federation of Allegheny County, 1952), pp. 12–13.

industrial workers. Sociological studies of class structure clearly indicate that middle-class people value and practice foresight (implicit in preparation and planning) and conformity (both a means to and end of adjustment) more than do people in the lower social classes.[5]

This middle-class bias is particularly significant in the face of research evidence that indicates that the aged in American society are more inclined to identify themselves as belonging to the "working" classes than to any other social stratum. This self-identification not only helps explain the general state of negligence in preparing and planning for old age, but also suggests why much of the counseling that does take place is ineffective.[6] Working-class oldsters may not respond to middle-class advice. A careful study by Special Surveys in Cleveland supports this point, for it casts doubt on the middle-class assumption that those who plan and prepare for retirement inevitably reap advantages. The investigators, interviewing 483 men retired for one to five years from six Cleveland companies, found that of those who had not made retirement plans, the proportion seemingly well adjusted (36 per cent) was nearly as great as that of all those who had. They also found that "keeping busy" was no guarantee of contentment in retirement, and that having a hobby was a very minor factor in securing satisfaction. Only 5 per cent of those most contented with retirement, for instance, spent much of their time on a hobby; and many spurned this word to describe their activities, protesting that "hobbies are only for children or sissies."

Gerontologists and geriatricians are not alone in misapplying middle-class norms and concepts to what is largely a working-class group. A great number of educators, social scientists, and social workers commit the same mistake. For example, in their empirical studies of the adolescent, social scientists have constantly employed middle-class norms to evaluate the behavior of their usually working-class subjects. Habituated to this approach, some go even further than do gerontologists and geriatricians. Gesell in his studies of the infant, child, and most recently, the adolescent, assumes we should properly look at middle-class chil-

[5] The relation between adjustment and conformity appears to be close indeed. The *Dictionary of Sociology*, Henry Pratt Fairchild, ed. (Ames, Iowa, Littlefield, Adams & Co., 1955), p. 152, in defining individual adjustment, does so almost entirely in terms of conformity: "Individual adjustment is the process by which an individual consciously modifies a socially acquired characteristic in order to make it conform to a desired standard or norm."

[6] See Perrin Stryker, "When Should Workers Retire?" *Fortune* (Sept. 1952), p. 160.

dren to find the criteria for "normal" behavior, but at working-class children to find the criteria for "deviant" behavior, particularly juvenile delinquency.[7] No gerontologist would dare postulate such an extreme position in locating his subjects for study. The fact remains, however, that middle-class norms do influence his research too and prejudice his selection of the criteria by which he evaluates his findings. Geriatricians similarly have, with few exceptions, based their programs of service to senescent individuals and groups on dubious middle-class grounds.

Conclusion

The most credible explanation for this is that social scientists and social workers commonly tend to assign to behavior a significance measured by the researcher's or worker's own cultural norms. Since the norms of educators, legislators, physicians, clergymen, social workers, and social scientists are largely middle class, we should not be surprised that the definitions of problems and efforts at solutions affecting young and old people have taken their currently prevailing middle-class forms.

When gerontologists and geriatricians free themselves of this deeply ingrained misconception, they shall then have cleared the way for a more realistic application of norms in the next generation. A greater participation by labor unions in defining and solving the problems of aging could well speed the development of such realism. Until now their representatives have not only failed to contribute, but often have even actively opposed many geriatric programs because of the initiative taken by managerial representatives. As long as the labor unions range from indifferent to hostile in their attitudes to techniques other than pensions for improving the lot of the aged, the misapplication of middle-class norms will likely continue to plague gerontology and geriatrics.

Questions and Research Exercises

1. Account for the emergence of a new philosophy regarding the need to prepare and plan for old age.
2. Why do research findings show that few older people actually do prepare and plan for old age?

[7] See Arnold Gesell, Frances L. Ilg, and Louise Bates Ames, *Youth: The Years from Ten to Sixteen* (New York, Harper & Brothers, 1956).

3. Illustrate what is meant by a middle-class norm in gerontology and geriatrics.
4. In what way did the Cleveland Study refute the assumption that preparation and planning for retirement inevitably lead to beneficial results for older people?
5. Show how Gesell in his studies of younger people used the same middle-class bias as do gerontologists.
6. What can labor unions contribute to the correction of middle-class biases in gerontology and geriatrics?

Selected Readings

Barron, Milton L., "Preparing for Retirement," in *Proceedings of the National Council on Teacher Retirement* (St. Louis, National Education Association, 32d Annual Meeting, 1955), pp. 67–76. An analysis of the different norms that apply to the retirement of employees of different social classes.

Donahue, Wilma T., "Education's Role in Maintaining the Individual's Status," *The Annals of the American Academy of Political and Social Science* (Vol. 279, January 1952), pp. 115–25. The new philosophy behind education for old age.

Noetzel, Arthur, *Preparation of Industrial Workers for Retirement* (Pittsburgh, Health and Welfare Federation of Allegheny County, 1952). Description of a preretirement program and the difficulties it faces because of unrealistic norms.

Palmer, Edward N., "Toward a Sociological Definition of Old Age," *American Journal of Sociology* (Vol. 59, July 1953), pp. 28–29. An attempt toward a more critical use of terms and concepts than the usual middle-class ones.

Schmidt, John Frank, "Patterns of Poor Adjustment in Old Age," *American Journal of Sociology* (Vol. 57, July 1951), pp. 33–42. A prime example of the uncritical use of the concept of adjustment in social gerontology.

5 :

WORK, RETIREMENT, AND MORBIDITY

John Timothy was foreman at the LaSalle Button Company for thirty years, and when he got so feeble he couldn't do his work, he reluctantly decided to retire. A month after he left the concern, he came back and pleaded with his old boss, "I'm going crazy with nothing to do. I know I can't get around the plant like I used to. But give me some job I can do. Get me a stool and I'll run the freight elevator!" So John went back to work.

Talk to the wife of big, bluff Ed Horkan, a high-pressure insurance salesman. She'll tell you what happened when Ed was retired last year. "Ed's always been too much of a work horse to enjoy doing nothing," she says. "He got so he hated hanging around the house all day. He didn't like puttering around with flowers, or killing time. He began to get under my feet around the house. And as he became more irritable, we began to snap at each other. Finally, he exploded one day, 'I can't stand this moping around any longer. I'm going downtown and see if I can buy an insurance agency.' Today, Ed's once more in the business saddle and happy as a well-fed baby. And me? I'm glad he's out of the house during the day so I can get my housework done." And Ed says determinedly: "I learned my lesson. I'm going to keep going as long as I can."

John and Ed may have added years to their lives by refusing to stay retired. Dr. Roger I. Lee of Boston, former President of the American Medical Association, states emphatically, "Death comes at retirement." One of America's outstanding experts on aging, Dr. Edward J. Stieglitz, maintains that "premature retirement while still vigorous, ambitious, and anxious to serve can be a major disease." The dean of a great college said recently he was struck by the fact that whenever a member of his faculty retired to live "the life of Riley" he soon died.

Many doctors say that soon after retirement, men and women apparently in the best of health begin to rush to their physician's office with groaning complaints about vague aches and pains. "A banker who is a patient of mine," notes one doctor, "is suffering from nothing organic, but from 'retirement shock.' As he sat around with time hanging heavily on his hands, whether on his yacht or at his home in Palm Beach, he began to worry about himself, and his worry sprouted into full-fledged pains, and actually led to invalidism." *

As the preceding chapters have intimated, an older person who retires from work in American society generally risks getting involved in one or more serious problems. The greatest risk he faces is a drastically reduced income with all this implies, especially the difficulty of meeting ongoing expenses and the agonizing readjustment to a new, lower standard of living. In addition there may be many less obvious but nonetheless vital repercussions in not only the retirant's social life, but in his psychological, emotional, and possibly even his physical make-up as well.

To comprehend the nature of retirement and the problems attending it, we need first of all to analyze the various meanings people attach to work. In this chapter we shall outline and discuss these theoretical meanings of work and thus establish a basis for considering some theoretical propositions about the morbid consequences of retiring from work.

Theory of the Meaning of Work

Gerontologists at the University of Chicago, generally acknowledged as the pacesetters in studying the meaning of work in terms of its implications for retirement, have developed a threefold theory comprising

* Thomas C. Desmond, "Retirement Is a Trap," in *Never Too Old*, New York State Joint Legislative Committee on Problems of the Aging (Legislative Document No. 32, 1949), pp. 171–72.

(1) five universal functions of work; (2) the process of assigning meanings to these functions; and (3) the noneconomic meanings of work.[1]

1. Five Universal Functions of Work

The first part of their theory is that work serves the following universal functions:

1. It provides income.
2. It regulates life activity.
3. It offers status or social identification.
4. It permits association with others.
5. It makes available a meaningful life experience.

One cannot seriously disagree with this formulation by the Chicago gerontologists so far as it goes; we can readily and daily observe that work does indeed have these functions. In further research it may be worthwhile to ask, however, whether these are the only functions of work in American society. For example, is it not a function of work to provide social power? Is it not possible, too, to think of work as a means to acquire higher social status, security, and even the anticipated benefits of retirement itself? It can be argued, of course, that power and these latter goals are included in the first general function of work, the provision of income. But for gerontological research it should prove fruitful to be more specific about these allegedly supplementary functions of work.

We also need to ascertain whether work has functions less obvious than those considered so far. For instance, work may perform a function of health maintenance far beyond our ordinary estimation. It may also serve as health therapy, as escape, as fulfillment of emotional needs, and as a satisfactory outlet for compulsive personality traits.

2. Assigning Meanings to Work

The second part of the theory of work holds that to the extent the worker recognizes or defines the five functions of work, he has assigned meanings to his work. When he loses these meanings or replaces them unsatisfactorily, he confronts a major problem of maladjustment.

[1] See Eugene A. Friedmann and Robert J. Havighurst, *The Meaning of Work and Retirement* (Chicago, University of Chicago Press, 1954).

To refine this part of the Chicago theory, it would be useful to develop a social psychological explanation of the process by which the worker comes to attach meanings to work. Undoubtedly the attitudes of the group (especially what the sociologist calls the "reference group," that is, those people who are "meaningful others" to the person) toward the worker and his work influence both his attitudes toward himself and the meaning he attaches to his work. But exactly how this process oper-ates is unknown and deserves intensive research.

We may gain further insight into the meaning of work and its im-pact on adjustment to retirement by investigating the meaning a workei attaches to "nonwork"; that is, to all kinds of economic inactivity during his lifetime. This refers to experiences he may have had such as un-employment, being "laid off," strikes, leaves of absence, illness, vaca-tions, holidays, leisure, and travel. To question the meaning of nonwork raises specifically the following two hypotheses:

1. A worker's experience of economic inactivity between jobs and the type and duration of such inactivity influence his adjustment to terminal retirement.

2. Psychological morbidity results from retirement more frequently in the lower than in the upper classes because the former, having more often associated economic inactivity with unemployment, being laid off, illness, and reduced income, regard inactivity negatively. On the other hand, people in the upper social strata, having more frequently in their lifetime experiences associated economic inactivity with vacations, education, avocational and leisure-time pursuits, are inclined to evaluate it positively.[2]

A further suggestion is that we should not view the meaning of work and the meaning of nonwork or economic inactivity as being mutually exclusive. For instance, it is likely some people are reluctant to retire because they fear they would lose thereby the status that working affords. Yet others may be unwilling to continue working for precisely the same reason: they fear that in an inevitably losing struggle to compete with younger, more aggressive workers, they will suffer a decline in status. To retire, therefore, may be to "save face," permitting older people to

[2] The psychologically morbid effects of retirement will be given considerable elaboration in the last section of this chapter.

depart from an arena of intense, hopeless competition, to enter a situation in which differences in efficiency are of no importance.

A last recommendation regarding the second part of the theory of the meaning of work is that we consider the American belief, usually linked with what Thorstein Veblen called "the Protestant ethic," that work is an end and has meaning in itself. Although this view of work as something having intrinsic, unqualified, and absolute worth has undoubtedly lost a great deal of the potency it enjoyed when linked with an agrarian social structure and when the independent farmer and the small businessman were leading occupational types on the American scene, it still may have a tenacious hold on the older members of our population and therefore merits serious consideration in the search for the causes of morbidity in retirement.

3. Noneconomic Meanings of Work

In the third and final part of the theory of the meanings of work, the Chicago gerontologists pose four testable hypotheses:

1. Work has meaning other than that of earning a living.[3]
2. The noneconomic meanings of work are stressed to a greater extent by members of the more highly skilled occupations.
3. Those persons who regard work primarily as a way of earning a living will prefer to retire at age sixty-five, or whatever else happens to be the normal retirement age.
4. Those persons who stress meanings of work other than that of earning a living will prefer to continue working past the normal retirement age.

At first glance the astute reader may conclude there is a contradiction between these hypotheses and the two hypotheses about the meaning of nonwork stated in our discussion of the second part of the theory.

[3] This is admirably illustrated in the following passage of a novel describing the hero, a retirant: "That was what Munsey Wills missed most—the sense of orderly procedure, the pattern for getting through a day. . . . There was no substitute for work. It wasn't enough to feel oneself useful, at least not if one's life was small and unimportant. Then it became necessary to be thought useful by others, necessary to stand approved in other eyes. If you had a job, you had your self-respect—it was as simple, and as difficult, as that." See Josephine Lawrence, *The Web of Time* (New York, Harcourt, Brace and Co., 1953), pp. 227, 238.

In the former case it is postulated that the working classes should be less adaptable to retirement than the upper classes because of the different meanings they attach to economic inactivity. In the latter case it is suggested that the upper classes are "better off" working than the working classes and have a greater reluctance to retire because of the greater variety of meanings they attach to work. But in actuality there is no contradiction, for the two sets of hypotheses merely assert that the upper strata are more adjustable to either work or nonwork than the lower classes because they are in each situation more versatile in attaching meanings.

Hypotheses 3 and 4 in this final part of the theory invite special attention because both employ the word "prefer" in somewhat ambiguous and unrealistic fashion. In testing these hypotheses, different responses are likely to come from the same respondent, depending on the type of conditional clause that accompanies a researcher's solicitation concerning preference for working or retiring after sixty-five. If workers are asked what they prefer, with the understanding their income in retirement would be maintained at or near the present level, the answer will be different from the answer if their understanding is that retirement income will be drastically curtailed. Many workers who "prefer" to retire at age sixty-five under the first condition nevertheless may "prefer" to work if retirement means subsisting on small, fixed pensions in a time of spiraling costs.

We can direct still other critical comments against these hypotheses, for there may be only a spurious, not a genuine cause-and-effect relationship between the meaning a worker attaches to his job and his preference either to continue working or to retire. Because some people regard work primarily as a way to earn a living does not necessarily lead them to choose to retire at the normal retirement age. Nor does it unalterably follow that other people who find and stress noneconomic meanings in their work will want to continue working. They may also find noneconomic meanings in retirement.

A final set of critical questions about the noneconomic meaning of work in terms of its implications for retirement revolves about the significance of such variables as marital status and sex. Do unmarried workers stress the noneconomic meaning of work more than married workers? If so, do they do so in order to compensate for the marital gap in their lives? Do male workers attach the noneconomic meanings to work more than female workers, or is it the other way around? Answers to questions such as these can add considerably to our understanding of the patterns and reasons for success and failure in retirement.

Retirement Morbidity

To achieve a comprehensive theoretical understanding of the potentially morbid consequences of retirement depends not only on an analysis of the meaning of work and nonwork but also on some insight into the social psychological processes involved in growing older in American culture. The theoretical ideas of Mead, Waller, Cottrell, and other leading social psychologists jointly stress that the individual personality may fruitfully be viewed as a "social self"; it internalizes in the course of its development not only society's or the group's normal attitudes but also the group's confusions and frustrations.[4] Society's tensions and cultural inconsistencies contribute to the conditioning of the self. When the self is mentally and emotionally disordered as well as physically ill, the family, the neighborhood, or society itself may be the cause. The inability of people to cope with their social environment sets up emotional disturbances that frequently translate into physical symptoms.[5]

Social psychological and psychosomatic interpretations such as these are supported by the observation that aging is less disturbing in a culture that accords reverence and high status to older people simply because they are aged.[6] In contrast aging is more disturbing in a society whose culture provokes irreverence toward the aged, and where economic competition works to their disadvantage.[7]

Two of the primary mental disorders in later life, senile dementia and psychosis with cerebral arteriosclerosis, are assumed in standard texts in abnormal psychology to result from organic deterioration. Yet

[4] George H. Mead, *Mind, Self and Society* (Chicago, University of Chicago Press, 1934); Willard Waller, *The Family* (New York, The Dryden Press, 1938); Leonard S. Cottrell, Jr., "Some Neglected Problems in Social Psychology," *American Sociological Review* (Vol. 15, Dec. 1950), pp. 705–12.

[5] Flanders Dunbar, *Mind and Body: Psychosomatic Medicine* (New York, Random House, 1947), pp. 19–20.

[6] See the section, "A Cross-Cultural Survey of the Aged" in Chapter 2 of this book, and Leo W. Simmons, *The Role of the Aged in Primitive Society* (New Haven, Yale University Press, 1945), pp. 50–81.

[7] Bela Mittelman, "Psychosomatic Medicine and the Older Patient," in O. J. Kaplan, ed., *Mental Disorders in Later Life* (Stanford, Stanford University Press, 1945), p. 350.

an organic interpretation fails to explain the differing frequency of these disorders according to the variables of rural-urban, sex, nativity, racial, social class, and regional distribution of population. Conceivably the sociopsychological theory summarized above may succeed in explaining such variations where the organic interpretation alone has failed.[8] For in considering the health and illness of older persons the theory requires that social and cultural factors, which often determine what the aged can do and how they can do it, be weighed carefully.[9]

Several studies have already pointed out that the kind of social relations older persons engage in is a crucial factor in the causation of their mental disorders. Such social relations have been characterized by concepts like Durkheim's "anomie," Jung's "loss of significance," and Faris and Dunham's "isolation." [10] For example, studies at Washington University have revealed that certain mental patients participate very little in social activity before hospitalization. The relationship between mental disorders and social participation undoubtedly operates in the reverse, too, for a mental breakdown excludes the patient from much social participation.[11] In England, Lewis and Goldschmidt sought to discover the common social causes of disorders that require placing the aged in mental hospitals. They found that "failure to retain a place in the community, to be a member of a family, to have an appreciated share in the life of some household or working group has been common in patients studied." Their conclusion was that lack of social integration was the over-all sociogenic factor in disorders of mental health.[12] Beard and Wagner suggest that forgetfulness, hallucinations, feebleness, dizziness, and pain may be unconscious mechanisms used by old people to attract attention, avoid boredom and unpleasant reality, and escape from the perplexities and disappointments of life.[13]

[8] Ivan Belknap and Hiram J. Friedsam, "Age and Sex Categories as Sociological Variables in the Mental Disorders of Later Maturity," *American Sociological Review* (Vol. 14, June, 1949), p. 367.

[9] Ollie H. Randall, "The Essential Partnership of Medicine and Social Work," *Geriatrics* (Vol. 5, Jan.–Feb., 1950), p. 46.

[10] See Belknap and Friedsam, *op. cit.,* p. 368.

[11] Stuart Queen, "Social Participation in Relation to Social Disorganization," *American Sociological Review* (Vol. 14, April, 1949), p. 258.

[12] Aubrey J. Lewis and H. Goldschmidt, "Social Causes of Admissions to a Mental Hospital for the Aged," *Sociological Review* (Vol. 25, July, 1943), pp. 86–98.

[13] Belle Boone Beard, "The Army of the Aged: A Sociomedical Problem," *Geriatrics* (Vol. 1, July–Aug., 1946), p. 303; Margaret W. Wagner, "Mental Hazards in Old Age," *The Family* (Vol. 25, June, 1944), pp. 132–37.

The aforementioned theory appears to be especially useful as a means to analyze the problem of retirement morbidity in old age. It interlocks nicely with Cameron's following theoretical speculation about the bases of neurosis as a consequence of abrupt retirement:

The abrupt termination of one's active interests and occupation, unless carefully handled, can have disastrous personal effects. Unemployment aggravates existing neuroses and tends to reactivate dormant ones. . . . The retired worker, businessman, professional man, or homemaker misses the externally imposed routine. He loses his familiar landmarks, his points of reference, and with them his sense of personal identity. . . . The experience of being all at once unnecessary and unwanted, with the deprivation of incentive and of an opportunity to continue one's accustomed work, may precipitate restlessness, weariness, and dejection that leads over into hypochondria, chronic fatigue states, or neurotic depression with resentment and self-depreciation.[14]

Some Propositions about Retirement

For facilitating research on the personal and social disorganization of retirement, it is appropriate that a number of propositions or working hypotheses be devised. The propositions that follow have been, for the most part, supported by few systematic and empirical data. They are merely a sample of the many "educated guesses" requiring confirmation by research.

1. Retirement and Social Relations

(*a*) The greater the dependence of the individual on his co-workers for the satisfaction of social needs, the more intense is his morbidity in retirement. (*b*) Retirement, by reducing income and disrupting the interaction pattern that accompanies gainful employment, tends to isolate the retired worker. Isolation, in turn, is conducive to introspection and functional symptoms of illness. (*c*) The more autocratic the family structure of the retirant, the greater is the deterioration of his status and the more intense is his morbidity in retirement. (*d*) Retirement is generally a greater social problem for unmarried than for married people because the former depend more on their work for gratification of their social and emotional needs than do the latter.

[14] Norman Cameron, "Neuroses of Later Maturity," in Kaplan, *op. cit.*, pp. 160–62.

2. Retirement and the Meaning of Work

(a) The higher the level of job satisfaction and the more recent the attainment of symbols of job success, the more reluctant one is to retire and the more difficult it is to adjust to retirement. (b) Retirement is generally a difficult experience to accept, for it represents a sharp cleavage in the life continuity of a working person who in the course of time usually comes to identify himself with his occupation. (c) Some old people are reluctant to retire and cannot adjust to retirement because they are unable to keep busy for long with anything other than what is systematically required of them, namely, the demands of their work. (d) No activity, such as a hobby, can replace gainful employment for a retirant unless it takes on values and meanings, such as being an actual or potential source of income, creativity, or identification with a group, similar to those of gainful employment.

3. Retirement and the Life Cycle

(a) By disrupting the daily life pattern of the individual, retirement may disturb his physiology sufficiently to induce organic illness and premature death. (b) Expectations of physical and mental morbidity and impending death are so dramatically intensified by the formality of retirement that they become "self-fulfilling prophecies," expressed in hypochondria and functional symptoms of illness.

Questions and Research Exercises

1. What are the shortcomings of the theory that work serves "five universal functions"?
2. Show how the reference group of an older worker can mold the meaning he attaches to his work.
3. What effects, if any, will the new "mass leisure" have on the Protestant ethic as well as on the meaning of work and retirement in American society?
4. By interviewing a small sample of older workers, determine what meanings work has other than that of earning a living.
5. Senile dementia has been assumed for a long time to be the consequence of organic deterioration. What evidence is there to suggest that this is not true?
6. What does research show concerning the relationship between mental disorders and social participation in old age?

Selected Readings

Belknap, Ivan, and Friedsam, Hiram J., "Age and Sex Categories as Socio-logical Variables in the Mental Disorders of Later Maturity," *American Sociological Review* (Vol. 14, June 1949), pp. 367–76. One of the first studies dispelling organic interpretations of mental disorder in favor of cultural interpretations.

Dunbar, Flanders, *Mind and Body: Psychosomatic Medicine* (New York, Random House, 1947). A clear, popular explanation of psychosomatics.

Friedmann, Eugene A., and Havighurst, Robert J., *The Meaning of Work and Retirement* (Chicago, University of Chicago Press, 1954). The standard work in gerontology on the meaning of work.

Hurff, George B., ed., *Economic Problems of Retirement* (Gainesville, University of Florida Press, 1954). The proceedings of the annual Southern Conference on Gerontology; a comprehensive analysis of the economic problems of retirement.

Kaplan, Oscar J., ed., *Mental Disorders in Later Life* (Stanford, Stanford University Press, 1945). The standard work in gerontology on mental illness.

Mathiasen, Geneva, ed., *Criteria for Retirement* (New York, G. P. Putnam's Sons, 1953). A conference attempt to understand the effect of compulsory age retirement upon the lives of individuals and upon the responsibilities of the community.

III : Gerontological Research

To me, old age is always fifteen years older than I am.

BERNARD M. BARUCH

6 :

SURVEY OF ATTITUDES TOWARD RETIREMENT

As George Kirk shuffled out of the employment office, his disheartened appearance expressed far better than a thousand words could the result of the interview.

He had seen an ad in the local newspaper. The largest manufacturing concern in town was looking for skilled help. George was delighted, for he had machine skill and experience in abundance. For 30 years he had worked for a tool and gauge company which sold out to a textile concern after the lush war years.

George was at the factory gate early on a cold and bleak morning. It wasn't long before his application blank was completed, and he was sitting opposite the personnel manager. Yes, George seemed to have the qualifications. There was little doubt about that. But wait! The interviewer's eyes fastened for a moment on the shortest space in the application form, where George Kirk had given his age as 63. He looked far younger. The ad hadn't even mentioned age. But he was made to feel now as though he should have known better; like a child who tried to steal a cookie, and was caught at it. The interview ended abruptly.

George was troubled as he started that long walk back to his room. He was worried. After all, a man can't get along without an income. But even more, he was puzzled. Hadn't old Doctor Wheeler told him just a few weeks ago that he was as sound as a dollar? Hadn't he said that a man's health and ability can't be judged by his number of birthdays? How old is "old" anyway? Doesn't industry know or care what the medical men say?

Some of these questions which George Kirk pondered over are at the core of the employment problems of the elderly. And the answers are not simple. Our geriatricians, specialists in aging, are doctors whose chief interests are prolonging life and promoting physical well-being through better health. They cannot be expected to know just how industry operates, and what it has to do to show black ink instead of red at the end of the year. On the other hand, the personnel manager knows and cares little about the physical and mental structure of the human body, and what happens to it as it grows older. His company is in a competitive market for profit, and he naturally does what he believes will result in the greatest return per labor dollar spent.*

Every scientific endeavor attempts to go beyond hypotheses or "educated guesses" to the testing of hypotheses in empirical research. In this chapter, then, and in the two subsequent chapters of this section, we shall examine the fact-gathering research that has sought to lend some substance to the hypotheses and theories about aging that comprised the content of the previous section. A good starting point in research on aging is the *attitude* toward work and retirement. What do people in American society actually think about the age of retirement and compulsory retirement?

Attitudes toward Retirement in the Nation

One source of such data is the nationwide public opinion survey conducted by the American Institute of Public Opinion in 1955. It revealed, among other things, that although sixty-five is the most popular age at which to retire in the United States, a majority of the American public believes that a business firm should not insist on an employee's retirement at that age. That is, in answer to the question: "Some companies insist on a man retiring when he reaches the age of sixty-five. Do you think this is a good idea, or not?" over half (51 per cent) of all adults in the survey responded that it is not a good idea. Of the remainder, 46 per cent thought it is a good idea to insist on retirement at age sixty-five, and 3 per cent had no opinion.

Of interest is the fact that the strongest sentiment against the

---

* Thomas C. Desmond, "Let's Give the Older Worker a Chance!" in *Never Too Old*, New York State Joint Legislative Committee on Problems of the Aging (Legislative Document No. 32, 1949), p. 150.

"forced retirement" policy came from those persons who were themselves sixty-five and older. The weight of sentiment among younger persons between the ages of twenty-one and thirty-four was that this is a good idea.

When asked: "At what age do you plan to retire?" the respondents revealed answers consistent with those given in answer to the first question, for more than half indicated they did not plan to retire at sixty-five years of age. Seventeen per cent said they planned to retire at sixty-four years of age or younger, another 17 per cent indicated they would never retire, 13 per cent had no plans, 6 per cent were going to retire at sixty-six years of age or older, 8 per cent were already retired, and 39 per cent planned to retire at age sixty-five.

Attitudes toward Retirement in the Community: A Pilot Study

To discover in what way the variables in old age affect and are affected by retirement, a more intensive survey of attitudes toward retirement took place in the community of Elmira, New York, in 1951 under the auspices of Cornell University. The researchers designed a schedule of questions to be asked of a representative cross section of the adults in the community, involving a total of 418 respondents, and we may profitably analyze here some of the survey's more significant findings.

One of the questions asked was: "Who do you think should make the decision as to when a person should retire?" The majority response (60 per cent) was that "the person himself" should make the retirement decision, with other preferences, in declining order, given to "the doctor" (29 per cent), "the employer" (15 per cent), "a governmental agency" (5 per cent), "a local union-management committee" (2 per cent), and "someone else" (1 per cent). Six per cent of the respondents gave no answer to the question.[1]

To judge from these responses, the adults of the community repudiate the system of compulsory or involuntary retirement. The number of respondents believing the worker himself or his physician should decide when a person should retire is much greater than that of those who would grant the decision to the employer. Furthermore, the age of the respondents appears to be highly significant in accounting for their

[1] The proportionate responses total 118 per cent because some respondents gave more than one answer.

answers, whereas such variables as sex, education, occupation, and source of income are not. That is, the youngest respondents (those up to thirty-seven years of age) showed a far greater preference for the employer's and the doctor's decision than did the oldest respondents (those fifty-eight years of age and over). On the other hand, there was little in the distribution of preferences to distinguish between males and females; among the grammar school, high school, and college educated; among self-employed, managerial, professional, white collar, skilled, and semi-skilled workers, retired and employed, and housewives; or among those living on salary, wages, profits, and pensions.

The survey revealed an interesting personality differential in that those respondents believing the person himself should make the decision to retire were more trustful of people in general than those choosing the doctor or employer. This was apparent in answers to the question: "Some say that you can't be too careful in your dealings with people, while others say that most people can be trusted. From your own experience, which would you agree with most?" Of those who would leave retirement for the worker himself to decide, 64 per cent felt people can be trusted; whereas 53 per cent of those choosing the doctor and 52 per cent of those favoring the employer for the retirement decision were trustful.

Another question concerning retirement was: "Do you agree or disagree with the statement: 'Workers should be *encouraged* to retire at sixty-five'?" The majority (56 per cent) of the respondents agreed and the minority (44 per cent) disagreed. While this seemed to indicate popular support for the prevalent pattern of retirement at sixty-five, it must be stressed that the question concerned "encouragement" to retire rather than coercion to do so. Furthermore, it still cannot be ignored that a sizable proportion objected either to retirement or to the sixty-fifth year as the age of retirement. The youngest respondents (those up to thirty-seven years of age) believed that workers should be encouraged to retire at sixty-five to a far greater extent than did middle-aged respondents (thirty-eight to fifty-seven years of age) and the oldest respondents (fifty-eight years of age and over). That is, 71 per cent of the youngest agreed, but only 54 per cent of the middle-aged and 40 per cent of the oldest agreed on the acceptability of retirement at sixty-five. As one might expect, older respondents tended to identify themselves with the problems of retirement much more than did younger respondents.

What happens when a comparison is made between the findings on the latter question and those of the earlier question regarding the decision-making role about retirement? Those who were found to choose the doctor and employer for the retirement decision were more likely to agree that a person should be encouraged to retire at age 65 than were those who would leave the decision to the person himself.

A third question, not ostensibly related to retirement at first glance, was: "Do you agree or disagree that old people demand more consideration than they have a right to expect?" This had been thought to be a prejudice-evoking question, useful for purposes of probing the feasibility of a majority-minority group schematization for the study of retirement. Yet only 23 per cent of the respondents agreed that old people are too demanding, with 77 per cent in disagreement.

Hypothetically, one would expect that an age breakdown of the respondents to this question would have revealed that the younger people were more "prejudiced" against old people than the older respondents themselves. However, this was not found to be the case. Only 14 per cent of the youngest people (up to thirty-seven years of age) agreed with the statement as compared with 26 per cent of the middle-aged group (thirty-eight to fifty-seven years of age) and 36 per cent of the oldest respondents (fifty-eight years of age and over). On the other hand, one's hypothetical expectation actually is confirmed that those who engage in the least amount of stereotyping of minority groups such as Negroes and Jews are less prone to agree with the allegedly prejudiced statement against older people than are those who stereotyped ethnic minorities the most. Only 13 per cent of the least stereotyping respondents agreed that old people demand more consideration than they have a right to expect, as compared with 41 per cent of the most stereotyping respondents who agreed with the statement.

How is it that in one respect, age, we find prejudice against old people where we do not expect it, but in another respect, degree of ethnic stereotyping, the hypothetical expectation of prejudice against old people is confirmed? One possible explanation is that younger people may generally *express* less prejudice than older people, regardless of the object of prejudice. In this case they may stereotype and be apparently prejudiced against ethnic groups less than older people, and at the same time express less prejudice against older people than do the older people themselves.

This explanation finds support when one correlates the respondents' age, degree of stereotyping, and agreement or disagreement with the statement. In doing so, we find that only 9 per cent of the least stereotyping and 19 per cent of the most stereotyping among the young respondents agreed that old people demand more consideration than they have a right to expect. This stands in contrast to the finding that 37 per cent of the least stereotyping among the oldest respondents and 44 per cent of the most stereotyping among the same age category agree with the statement.

Conclusion

All this leaves one problem unsolved. If older respondents are found to be more prejudiced against old people than are younger respondents, at least in terms of a higher percentage of agreement with the statement that old people demand more consideration than they have a right to expect, how can one account for the finding that older respondents are less arbitrary and more individualistic than younger respondents about the decision and age of retirement? Here is but one interesting differential judgment that calls for further investigation. We need to know more about what and how the aged feel, think, and behave than gerontological research has heretofore revealed.

Questions and Research Exercises

1. Compare the findings of the nationwide public opinion survey on attitudes toward retirement with the Elmira study's findings. What were the resemblances and differences between the two?
2. Of what importance is the age of the respondent in determining his attitude toward retirement?
3. What personality differential appears in research findings concerning differential choices of the agent of the retirement decision?
4. Formulate some prejudice-evoking questions, other than that used in the Elmira study, that you think could be used in a community study of attitudes toward old age.

Selected Readings

Burgess, Ernest W., ed., "Aging and Retirement," *American Journal of Sociology* (Vol. 59, January 1954), pp. 301–90. An entire issue of a leading sociological journal devoted to attitudinal and other aspects of retirement.

Fried, Edrita G., "Attitudes of the Older Population Groups towards Activity and Inactivity," *Journal of Gerontology* (Vol. 4, April 1949), pp. 141–51. One of the earliest empirical studies of the attitudes of older people toward work and retirement.

Moore, Elon H., *The Nature of Retirement* (New York, The Macmillan Co., 1959). A sociologist's various findings on retirement published posthumously.

Tuckman, Jacob, and Lorge, Irving D., *Retirement and the Industrial Worker* (New York, Columbia University, Teachers College, 1953). One of the best empirical studies of attitudes toward work and retirement.

7:

SURVEY OF THE URBAN AGED

We wish to point up the main problems that confront our elderly by citing specific cases of older persons who have difficulties which are most common among older persons. Here are nine such elderly with acute problems:

1. After 50 years as bookkeeper for a chain store, Miss L. H. was "retired" with two weeks pay, a $500 check from the company, and a wrist watch. Two years later, her savings exhausted, she shows signs of acute nervous exhaustion, melancholia, because of the prospect she will have to go on old age assistance rolls, to supplement a small social security check.

2. Mrs. E. M., 72, has been getting very forgetful and showing signs of eccentricity such as sleeping with clothes on. Her daughter doesn't want to send her to the state hospital, but has no room for her. The situation is a strain on all.

3. A. C., 74, is on old age assistance rolls. He wants work, not relief. But he can only work part-time and at light work.

4. Mrs. H. D., a lonely widow, 68, sits all day looking out her window. Her mind is rusting away. She faces the future with terror in her heart.

5. T. A. is a retired banker who misses his old work, the routine of his job, the dignity and status of his old position; he is suffering from "retirement shock" and has slipped into melancholia.

6. Mrs. A. V., 72, can't get along with her son-in-law, with whom she lives. Tensions in the family are terrible. If the son-in-law makes good his threat "to throw the old crab out," she doesn't have a place to go, anyone to support her.

7. E. P., 67, suffered a stroke recently. He needs care during his convalescence, but can't afford expensive nursing home service, hospitals don't want long-term care patients, the few old age homes which take "chronics" have long waiting lists.

8. A. K., 66, spinster, lives alone in a slum room, gas burner, and "bathroom downstairs." She gets along on $40-a-month social security check by eating one meal a day. She is anemic.

9. X. O., 86, widower, lives in his big, rambling old house, which has become a ramshackle rural slum. When he took ill recently, there was no one to care for him; neighbors took turns buying food.

But many senior citizens who have acute problems do find solutions to them. Here are some cases of old folks who managed to extricate themselves from their difficulties:

1. Tom H., 71, found that his hobby paid off. When he was laid off as a clerk in a bottling company, job counsellors at state employment service giving special attention to older job seekers, urged him to find work operating a lathe in a defense plant. He now earns more than he did before.

2. When Mrs. C. L. T. faced the prospect of moving in with her son and his family, she decided she did not want to burden them and wanted her own freedom; she rented a room near her son, eats with him occasionally, serves as baby sitter from time to time. This way intergenerational tensions are eased. Though her room isn't much, it's enough to give her freedom, yet close to her son and his family—helpful in case she needs help.

3. Mr. K., an aged amputee, whose children rarely visited him and who had problems of their own, was left a widower. He couldn't take care of himself. A private welfare agency helped him get placed in a private foster home.

4. Ed V. was smart. He knew his company would pension him off at 65. So he prepared for it. He prepared a plan, tried it out on a small scale during vacations, was all set when he got the "watch" at his retirement party at the plant.

5. Mrs. Edward H. rented a rooming house in her later years; makes enough money to get by, the business keeps her in touch with

people, useful and active; she can "slow down" without reducing her income materially.

6. Herbert T. at 77 doesn't worry about his health. He gets a comprehensive physical exam periodically, eats a balanced diet, doesn't "overdo," avoids worry, and keeps his mind busy. He's so active serving the Red Cross, the Community Chest, and other good causes, he doesn't have a chance to grow old.*

As the previous section on gerontological theory frequently indicated, the effects of occupational retirement in comparison with the effects of other occupational roles in old age has long been a controversial question in American society. On the one hand, there are those who claim that retirement generally has a negative impact on the health and longevity as well as on the economic, psychological, and social adjustment of older people. As supporting "evidence," accounts are cited of specific individuals who died within a year or two after retirement had removed them from the labor force. Similar use is made of the finding that there is a high death rate in the first year of retirement among the beneficiaries of old age and survivors' insurance.

On the other hand, there are those who are, at least, skeptical of this position. Tibbitts, for example, grants there may be "premature deterioration when retirement deprives the organism and the mind of activity," but, he points out, "declining health is generally a predisposing factor in retirement rather than a consequence. There is a marked inflection in the curve of chronic illness during the 45–55 year decade." [1] With regard to the OASI beneficiaries referred to above, the high death rate can be explained mostly by preëxisting disability rather than by the experience of retirement. The healthiest people, it is claimed, are more likely to continue in employment beyond any age limit in retirement systems such as sixty-five. Conversely, those who retire do so largely because of poor health. It may well be that many people who die soon after retirement succumb to conditions that would have induced death even if they had continued in gainful employment. The chief actuary of the Social Security Administration, United States De-

---

* *Enriching the Years,* New York State Joint Legislative Committee on Problems of the Aging (Legislative Document No. 32, 1953), pp. 10–11.

[1] Clark Tibbitts, "Retirement Problems in American Society," *The American Journal of Sociology* (Vol. 59, Jan., 1954), p. 307.

partment of Health, Education, and Welfare, recently came to virtually the same conclusion after his analysis of comparative mortality records. He said in summary:

Analyses of the mortality experience under various governmental and private pension programs indicate quite clearly that, in the absence of any special circumstances, the mortality of retired workers during the first year or two of retirement is considerably above the general level which otherwise might be expected, but thereafter merges with the general level. It seems likely that this higher mortality in the early years of retirement arises from the fact that those in poorer health are more apt to retire at or shortly after the minimum retirement age, while the healthier individuals continue at work.[2]

In short, skeptics suggest that the causal sequence does not operate in terms of retirement leading to physical and mental morbidity; rather, physical and mental morbidity are more likely to lead to retirement.

Nevertheless, the belief that retirement has a lethal influence persists. In rebuttal its proponents say it may be difficult to ascertain the effects of the sudden cessation of work, but it cannot be denied that mental and emotional conditions affect the organism. Thus it is conceivable that the shock of retirement and anxiety about finances frequently precipitate cardiovascular accidents. Another likelihood is that the reduction of income that usually follows retirement curtails the expenditure for food, housing, and medical care, and thereby has serious health implications for some retirants. Still another possibility is that the drastic social isolation frequently implied by retirement brings on severe physical and mental traumas in inflexible personalities and among those aged who are emotionally unbalanced.

To test these and other related researchable hypotheses discussed in the previous section of the book on gerontological theory, a nationwide urban survey of the chronologically aged population was undertaken at Cornell University in 1952 and completed in 1953.

Methodology of the Nationwide Urban Survey

To conduct the survey the investigators first had to determine the age limits, size, and sex distribution of the group they would interview.

[2] Robert J. Myers, "Factors in Interpreting Mortality After Retirement," *Journal of the American Statistical Association* (Vol. 49, Sept., 1954), p. 508.

As we have indicated in Chapter 2, there is little agreement concerning the chronological beginning of old age, although age sixty-five is the most frequently used point for the initiation of retirement systems. The investigators decided that a cross-sectional survey of old age in urban America should employ a sample of respondents whose chronological age at the lower level was as much as five years younger than the usual start of retirement. They decided to survey, house-to-house and door-to-door, a sample of urban people sixty years of age and over. Since the investigators saw retirement and related problems of old age as affecting mostly men, but were also interested in the impact on women, they decided to focus the survey on approximately one thousand men and, for comparative purposes, two hundred women.

With the aid of a market research organization, a sample was designed to provide a representative cross section of these men and women in 34 geographically representative cities ranging from small towns of 2,500 population to metropolitan centers of one million or more population. Interviewers used a questionnaire that had been carefully pretested and comprised 135 questions as well as factual information and observable data.

Social and Demographic Profile of the Sample

It is important, first of all, to consider what was learned about the "profile" of the sample of respondents. Who were the urban aged that were interviewed, and what were their outstanding social and demographic characteristics?

Age

Almost 30 per cent of the sample were between sixty and sixty-four years of age, and as one would expect, the proportions declined in successively higher age categories. Slightly more than 25 per cent were between sixty-five and sixty-nine years of age, almost 22 per cent were seventy to seventy-four, 15 per cent were seventy-five to seventy-nine, and slightly less than 8 per cent were eighty or over.

Sex

Even though the whole population sixty years of age and over is preponderantly female, 77 per cent of the sample were male for reasons already mentioned. Over half the people interviewed (58.6 per cent) were married and living with spouse, the others being widowed (30.7

per cent), divorced (1.2 per cent), never married (6.4 per cent), and separated (2.5 per cent).

Race, Religion, Nativity

Like the population of the United States in general, the sample consisted largely of whites (87 per cent). Negroes were the second largest racial group (10.7 per cent), followed in size by other non-whites. The majority of persons were Protestant (65.3 per cent), whereas others were Roman Catholic (24.2 per cent), Jewish (4.8 per cent), and other religious affiliations (2.4 per cent) or unaffiliated. An even larger proportion was native-born (71.8 per cent), the foreign-born making up slightly more than one fourth (27.5 per cent) of the sample.

Location

The largest proportion of the persons interviewed lived in the East North Central States (21.6 per cent), while the others lived in the Middle Atlantic region (20.9 per cent), New England (12.5 per cent), the West North Central (11 per cent), the South Atlantic (10 per cent), the Pacific (10 per cent), and the East South Central, West South Central, and Mountain regions (4.3 per cent each). The interviewees lived in small towns (16.5 per cent), large towns (4.7 per cent), small cities (25.9 per cent), large cities (28.2 per cent), and metropolitan centers (24.5 per cent).[3]

Class

In rating their own family's social class, over half the sample (59 per cent) considered themselves working class, 31 per cent middle class, and 4.3 per cent each upper and lower classes. The interviewers rated the sample somewhat differently, numbering the working class at 37.4 per cent, the lower middle class at 31.4 per cent, the "poor marginal" class at 17.3 per cent, the upper middle class at 7.6 per cent, and the "prosperous" class at 1.4 per cent.

Education

Having been born and raised in an era when formal education rarely extended beyond a person's adolescence, the sample of urban aged quite naturally showed a low level of schooling. About 5.5 per cent had no

[3] Small towns were defined as having 2,500–4,999 population, large towns 5,000–9,999, small cities 10,000–99,999, large cities 100,000–999,999, and metropolitan centers 1,000,000 or more.

education, 38.4 per cent had only one to seven grades of schooling, and 25.4 per cent graduated from grammar school. Only 12.9 per cent had some high school education, 7.7 per cent finished high school, 4.8 per cent had some college education, and 4.3 per cent graduated from college.

Occupational Status

Six occupational categories made up the sample of urban aged:

1. Those employed at what they considered their regular occupation (27.9 per cent of the entire sample).
2. Those employed at something other than their regular occupation (12.8 per cent).
3. Those unemployed but considering themselves not retired (4.9 per cent).
4. Those not employed and considering themselves retired (36.9 per cent).
5. Housewives living with their husbands (5.4 per cent).
6. Women keeping house who are single, widowed, divorced, and separated (referred to hereafter as "housekeepers") (11.8 per cent).

Occupational status and role, we should recall, were of central importance to the theory of old age developed in Section II of this book, and in analyzing the survey data we shall use occupational status as the independent (causal) variable, our purpose being to examine its economic, psychological, and social effects on the persons in the sample. But first let us look at the relationship between occupational status of the interviewees and some of the social and demographic traits summarized earlier. Looking at Table 2, we may see the age distribution of the interviewees in terms of their occupational status.

Table 2: *Occupational Status and Age Distribution by Percentages*

Occupational Categories	*1*	*2*	*3*	*4*	*5*	*6*
Under 65	54	38	30	9	42	18
65–69	27	31	33	23	29	25
70–74	13	20	20	30	18	20
75–79	5	8	14	25	8	20
80 plus	1	3	3	13	3	17

The most important feature we note in age distribution is the marked difference between the two employed categories (1 and 2) and the unemployed aged (3 and 4). The generally greater age of the unemployed may well be significant in accounting for such differences in health, morale, self-image, and other dependent (effect) variables as the survey data may reveal.[4]

As to sex distribution, most of the women were housewives and housekeepers, but some also appeared in the four other occupational categories. They constituted 7 per cent of those employed at their regular occupations, 4 per cent of those employed at something else, 13 per cent of the unemployed and not retired, and 6 per cent of the unemployed who were retired.

Table 3: *Occupational Status and Marital Distribution by Percentages*

Occupational Categories	1	2	3	4	5	6
Married	77	73	37	56	100	–
Widowed	17	19	42	29	–	93
Divorced	1	1	2	1	–	2
Separated	2	2	5	3	–	2
Never married	3	5	15	10	–	3

Looking at marital distribution in Table 3, we find a significantly high proportion of widowhood among the two groups of unemployed aged. As they are chronologically older than the other occupational categories, this is to be expected.

The racial, religious, and nativity distributions of the occupational categories suggest that Negroes, Catholics, and the foreign-born are handicapped more than whites, Protestants, and the native born in staying employed in old age. Comparing Tables 4, 5, and 6 with the statistics on race, religious, and nativity distribution given earlier in the profile of the sample, we see that the three minorities as well as Jews are over-represented among those unemployed, both retired and not retired; they are somewhat underrepresented in the two employed categories.

In their self-rating of social class, people in all occupational categories referred to themselves as "working class" more often than any-

---

[4] Therefore, a "control" (i.e., holding the age factor constant) was clearly called for in dealing with the data whenever there was suspicion that chronological age made the difference.

thing else, but highest in this regard were those unemployed but not retired (71 per cent); lowest were the housekeepers (45 per cent). A middle-class self-rating was most characteristic of the housekeepers (40

Table 4: *Occupational Status and Race Distribution by Percentages*

Occupational Categories	1	2	3	4	5	6
White	91	90	73	88	91	87
Negro	9	9	27	11	8	12
Other	–	1	–	1	1	1

per cent) and housewives (39 per cent) and least characteristic of the unemployed but not retired (14 per cent). All occupational categories had some people who called themselves upper class, ranging from 3

Table 5: *Occupational Status and Religious Distribution by Percentages*

Occupational Categories	1	2	3	4	5	6
Protestants	66	69	54	64	71	68
Catholic	23	19	27	27	24	25
Jewish	4	6	14	4	–	6
None	4	3	3	2	2	1
Other	3	3	2	3	3	–

per cent of the unemployed and retired to 7 per cent of the unemployed but not retired. Lower class self-rating was claimed by none of those employed at their regular occupation, the others claiming it in a range from 2 per cent of the housewives to 9 per cent of the housekeepers.

Table 6: *Occupational Status and Nativity Distribution by Percentages*

Occupational Categories	1	2	3	4	5	6
Native born	77	77	64	68	80	72
Foreign born	23	23	36	32	20	28

Interviewers in their social class rating of the urban aged respondents saw a larger number of the working class among those employed at something other than their regular occupation (51 per cent) than among housewives (40 per cent), the unemployed and retired (38 per cent), housekeepers (37 per cent), those employed at their regular occupation and the unemployed but not retired (36 per cent each). They gave a lower middle-class rating first to those employed at their regular occupation and housekeepers (41 per cent each), and then to housewives (40 per cent), those employed at something other than their regular occupation (29 per cent), the unemployed and retired (27 per cent), and the unemployed but not retired (24 per cent). The upper middle-class rating was given first to those employed at their regular occupation (13 per cent), while other occupational categories were so identified, ranging from 2 to 8 per cent of their total class distributions. A prosperous rating was given to only 1 or 2 per cent of the occupational categories, except housewives and the unemployed and not retired. At the other class extreme, poor marginals were found first among the unemployed and retired (27 per cent), housekeepers (14 per cent), housewives and those employed at something other than regular occupations (12 per cent each), and lastly, those employed at their regular occupation (8 per cent).

In both self-rating and interviewers' ratings of social class, we should note the concentration of all occupational categories of the urban aged in middle (or lower middle) and working classes. Even more significant is the fact more of the unemployed were working class than middle class.

Table 7: *Occupational Status and Educational Distribution by Percentages*

Occupational Categories	1	2	3	4	5	6
No education	4	3	3	8	3	8
1–7 grades	32	43	48	43	33	36
Grammar school graduate	26	28	21	24	24	27
Some high school	15	13	19	10	18	13
High school graduate	8	6	7	7	11	9
Some college	7	4	2	4	9	3
College graduate	8	3	–	4	2	2

Table 7, showing educational distribution, supports the assumption that the underprivileged older person is more likely to be unemployed than is his more privileged counterpart.

Comparing this table with the statistics on educational distribution in our earlier profile, we see those with little education overrepresented among the unemployed and underrepresented in the employed categories. On the other hand, for those whose educational level is high the tendency is the reverse, but only with regard to being employed at a regular occupation and being unemployed and retired. These facts, along with the larger proportion of widowers, ethnic minorities, the foreign born, and lower social class affiliation among the unemployed aged must be taken into account in any complete analysis of the relationship between occupational status as a causal variable and the effect variables that follow.

The Effects of Occupational Status in Old Age

We can now turn to the nationwide survey findings regarding the effects of occupational status and role on aging. First, what are the different economic, psychological, and social effects? Do these effects reveal the aged to be a group having minority-group characteristics? Do the two unemployed categories show more of these characteristics than the others? Which conduces more to a minority-group psychology in unemployed older persons: considering oneself not retired, or accepting the status of retirement?

In the examination of three criteria (standard of living, type of residence, and income and financial adequacy) measuring the economic effects of occupational status, hypotheses posing a greater advantage for the employed statuses over the unemployed statuses were verified by the survey findings. But this obviously was not surprising nor as revealing as the findings about the psychological effects of different occupational statuses in old age. In attitudes toward life, the self-image, and feelings of segregation, inferiority, and prejudice by younger people, the unemployed aged (especially those who do not consider themselves retired) were the most negative of all occupational categories. This was found to be true even when chronological age was held constant and thereby eliminated as a possible intruding factor on the findings. For example, one question concerned with the self-image of older people was: "Do you think that the people you see and care most about think of you as an old man (or woman)?" The hypothesis underlying this survey question was that the person's conception of the image of him held by his "significant others" is affected by occupational status; the employed aged, accordingly, think others look upon them as being more youthful than are other occupational categories, especially the unemployed. The findings revealed that actually less than one third of the respondents (31 per cent) thought others around them considered them to be old, and except for a slight deviation in the case of housewives, as Table 8 demonstrates, the hypothesis was substantially verified.

Table 8: *Occupational Status and Age Conception by Others by Percentages*

Occupational Categories	1	2	3	4	5	6
Yes, as old	18	22	32	44	20	37
No, not old	65	65	48	38	62	45
Don't know	17	13	20	18	18	18

But the problem of analysis is whether or not the findings have been influenced by the chronological age differences between the occupational categories. Do people who are employed think others look upon them as younger than do the unemployed simply because the former actually are chronologically younger on the average than the latter? Or is occupational status really a causal variable even when chronological age is held constant? Table 9, a threefold table, shows what happens to the above data when controls on chronological age are exercised. Table 9 is limited to (*a*) those under sixty-five, (*b*) those sixty-five to sixty-nine, and (*c*) those seventy to seventy-four, together comprising the majority of the urban sample, and ignoring the numerically insignificant aged in the sample seventy-five years of age and older.

Thus we can see that even when chronological age is held constant, the hypothesis is largely correct, for the employed aged tend to think others look upon them as more youthful than do the unemployed aged. Housewives who are sixty-five to sixty-nine and both housewives and housekeepers seventy to seventy-four also think they are regarded as youthful by "significant others."

The survey findings on the social effects of occupational status in old age for the most part were consistent with those concerning economic and psychological effects. Not only did the unemployed aged report experiencing discrimination when they sought reëmployment, but they were more isolated in their social relations than were the employed aged. Their advice was reported to have been sought less frequently by others, they had fewer close friends, and they were more passive about the future. Furthermore, the unemployed aged showed more signs of decline in activity than did their employed counterparts.

Table 9: *Occupational Status and Age Conception by Others by Percentages, with Chronological Age Held Constant*

a. Those under 65

Occupational Categories	1	2	3	4	5	6
Yes, as old	13	17	50	27	18	32
No, not old	68	67	44	59	64	44
Don't know	17	12	6	15	18	20
No answer	2	3	–	–	–	4

b. Those 65–69

Occupational Categories	1	2	3	4	5	6
Yes, as old	19	27	15	43	16	40
No, not old	63	60	50	42	74	49
Don't know	17	12	35	15	11	11
No answer	1	–	–	1	–	–

c. Those 70–74

Occupational Categories	1	2	3	4	5	6
Yes, as old	21	17	25	41	17	14
No, not old	63	73	58	38	58	69
Don't know	16	10	17	19	25	17
No answer	–	–	–	2	–	–

In short, the unemployed aged in the urban survey may be said to have revealed about themselves more "quasi-minority" traits economically, psychologically, and socially than did those who were employed. But among the unemployed aged the retirants' acceptance of their retirement status, insofar as they conceded they were no longer part of the labor force, seems to have provided them with more psychological composure and a higher degree of social adjustment than was true of the unemployed who did not consider themselves retired. The latter, unwilling to tolerate the economic idleness to which they had been relegated, had the most emphatic minority group reactions of all occupational categories of the urban aged in the survey.

Occupational Status and Health

The survey findings on the relationship between occupational status and the health of the urban aged theoretically were equally provocative.

Self-Rating of Health

Each of the respondents was asked: "How would you rate your health at present?" Implicit in this question was the hypothesis that there is a positive correlation between the more active occupational roles in old age and superior self-ratings of health; conversely, it was hypothesized that there is a positive correlation between the more passive occupational roles and inferior self-ratings of health. For the entire sample, the modal self-rating of health was between "fair" and "good," approximately one third of the aged rating their health as fair and another third rating it as good. The distribution occupationally apparently confirmed the hypothesis, even when there was a control by chronological age. The aged in the employed categories, especially those employed at what they considered to be their regular occupations, generally rated their health as poor or very poor to a lesser extent than did the people in the other occupational categories. Intermediate in the self-rating of health were the housewives and housekeepers.

Dynamics of Health

To secure data about a related matter, the dynamics of health in old age, the respondents were asked: "Was your health better then when you were fifty, or is it better now?" The hypothesis was that deterioration in old age as far as health goes is most extensive among those whose occupational roles are relatively passive, and least extensive among those whose occupational roles are relatively active. In short, the expectation was that retirants and the other unemployed aged would report significantly greater deterioration of health than those who were employed and housewives and housekeepers as well.

The majority of the sample as a whole, 56 per cent, said their health had deteriorated since age fifty. Significant differences in the distribution by occupational status were in general conformity with the hypothesis. Even though housewives and housekeepers claimed "better health now" to a greater extent than did the other urban aged, those who were employed either at their regular occupations or at something else actually reported the least deterioration of health and the greatest stability in health. At the same time, the willingly retired aged and the unemployed aged who did not consider themselves retired maintained their health had deteriorated the most. But there was no indication in these findings that the health of people had deteriorated *because* of their occupational status and roles.

Problems of Physical Health

Specifically, what are the health problems of the urban aged? To what extent are they physical problems and to what extent are they mental and emotional? The respondents were asked, first: "Do you have any physical health problems at present?" The hypothesis was that the employed aged would have proportionately fewer problems of physical health than did the less active aged.

In the entire sample, over half, 53 per cent, claimed to have no particular physical health problems. Among the 47 per cent who had, the physical problems independent of age were the most frequent, followed by those directly associated with aging. The distribution of the findings by occupational status confirmed the hypothesis, for they showed proportionately fewer of the urban aged who were employed had physical health problems than did the aged in other occupational situations, especially retirants and the reluctantly unemployed. However, it is necessary to take note of some variations when chronological age was held constant. For example, among those sixty to sixty-five years of age, the unemployed who did not consider themselves retired appeared to have been no different in this respect from the people employed at their regular occupation. But the people in this chronological subdivision who considered themselves retired surpassed all the other aged to a striking degree as far as having physical health difficulties are concerned. One can deduce from this that if people under sixty-five consider themselves retired, poor physical health is the outstanding reason in most cases for their relatively premature occupational passivity.

Problems of Mental Health

To determine the extent of their problems of mental health, the urban aged were asked: "How often are you troubled by the following difficulties: physical aches and pains, nervousness, headaches, forgetfulness, not being able to sleep, and upset stomach?" The hypothesis implicit in this question was that the aged who are engaged in the more active occupational roles are less often disturbed by psychosomatic symptoms than are those who are passive occupationally.

The over-all findings showed the majority of the urban aged were troubled at least sometimes by physical aches and pains, nervousness, and forgetfulness. Although less than half claimed to have headaches, sleeplessness, and upset stomachs at any time, it is nevertheless true that the urban aged on the whole seem to have more extensive problems of mental health than of physical health. And once again, the distribution by occupational status, even when chronological age is held constant, supported the hypothesis in most respects. The aged who were employed usually reported having fewer and less frequent psychosomatic symptoms than did the less active aged. It may be of some significance that the unemployed aged who did not consider themselves retired were relatively more disturbed in terms of physical aches and pains, headaches, and sleeplessness than were the unemployed who considered themselves retired. Possibly the inability of the former to accept the status of retirement disposed them to such disturbances to a greater extent than the latter who had accepted that status.

Summary and Conclusion

In summary, the nationwide urban survey of a cross section of the American people sixty years of age and over demonstrated that the economic, psychological, and social correlates of the different occupational statuses in old age are in turn correlated with significant differences in physical and mental health. Those aged who have the most pronounced "quasi-minority" characteristics also have the highest incidence of physical and mental morbidity. Conversely, the aged with the least pronounced traits of a "quasi-minority" are marked by the lowest incidence of poor health.

But correlations such as these are not necessarily causal relationships. There is still no adequate basis for assuming with complete assurance that poor health in old age is primarily an effect of certain occupational statuses and not others. While it may be reasonable to infer such a relationship, it can still be argued that in many cases poor health in old age is the cause, not the effect, of certain occupational statuses, such as retirement. Longitudinal studies of aging promise to shed a good deal of the necessary light on this important problem. They will permit the observation of sequential, causal relationships between the economic, psychological, and social variables of old age on the one hand, and the health variables, on the other hand, that cross-sectional surveys are intrinsically not equipped to do.

Questions and Research Exercises

1. Present the essential arguments on each side of the controversy concerning the effects of work versus retirement on health and longevity.
2. If you were to conduct an urban survey of the effects of retirement, what methodology would you use? How would it differ from the Cornell survey?
3. Into what six occupational categories do the urban aged fall?
4. Summarize the relationships between occupational statuses among the urban aged and their social and demographic traits.
5. What evidence is there that the underprivileged older person is more likely to be unemployed than is his more privileged counterpart?
6. How is the self-image influenced by occupational status in old age?
7. In what ways do the urban aged who are reluctantly retired show the most emphatic minority group reactions of all occupational categories?
8. According to research findings, what is more extensive in old age: physical or mental problems of health?

Selected Readings

Brunot, Helen M., *Old Age in New York City* (New York, Welfare and Health Council, 1944). One of the first empirical surveys of the urban aged.

Hunter, Woodrow W., and Maurice, Helen, *Older People Tell Their Story* (Ann Arbor, University of Michigan Press, 1953). A rare source of factual information about problems of aging, as told by the aged themselves.

Kutner, Bernard, *et al., Five Hundred Over Sixty: A Community Survey of Aging* (New York, Russell Sage Foundation, 1956). Results of interviews in Kips Bay-Yorkville of New York City in order to determine what stimulates older people to use or avoid community services.

Rowntree, B. Seebohm, *et al., Old People: Report of a Survey Committee on the Problems of Aging and the Care of Old People* (London, Oxford University Press, 1947). A famous English survey on the problems of aging and care of old people.

8 :

SURVEY OF THE RURAL AGED

Interviewers were once asked to report at length on cases which seemed to be representative of various types of rural problems or adjustments to aging. Here are some excerpts from their reports:

I interviewed one man who worked ten or twelve hours a day, owned three farms, had no financial troubles or unhappiness. His life seemed complete and satisfactory to him and the questionnaire seemed rather ridiculous to him.

He is just as happy now as he ever was and sees his family often. He lives by himself but gets along beautifully doing everything for himself. He has never been sick and still works a little bit if the mood strikes him. He has no cause for concern over income. He has a car and goes when and wherever he pleases and stays as long as he likes.

Several of the individuals with whom I came in contact were in their late sixties or early seventies, but still going strong. On the other hand, there were those of approximately the same age who had completely given up, retired and didn't want work, were discontented, unhappy, and looked older than they actually were. . . . When I asked one of them what he felt about death, he sneered and said everyone has to die and as you get older death gets closer. Then he said he wished he were dead now. When I asked about his relatives he quickly replied, "What good could you do if we didn't get along now—in the past or in the future?" He felt sorry for himself because he was old and no one cared for him, but still he didn't try to put himself out to be friendly toward others or to enjoy people. He was even giving up gardening which he enjoyed above everything to settle into solitude and grief.*

---

* Roland L. Warren, "Old Age in a Rural Township," in *Age Is No Barrier*, New York State Joint Legislative Committee on Problems of the Aging (Legislative Document No. 35, 1952), p. 161.

Background and Significance of Rural Retirement [1]

Studies of the economic, psychological, and social problems of aging in the United States have been concerned largely with the urban industrial population. There have been relatively few studies of the aged in rural areas.

The research emphasis on the urban segment of the aging stems from two causes. First, an explanation is to be found in American population trends that were reviewed in Chapter 2. One consequence of these trends is that about two thirds of all persons sixty-five years of age and over now live in urban communities. A second reason for the greater attention given to the urban than to the rural aged is the theoretical assumption, also developed in considerable detail in Chapter 2, that problems of aging are inclined to be an urban phenomenon and that the social and economic conditions of rural life are more favorable to the status of the aged.

But does this necessarily mean that the rural aged are so free of problems that research should turn entirely elsewhere? There are reasons for believing otherwise. Despite the shift from rural to urban communities in the distribution of the total population and of the population sixty-five years of age and over during the first half of this century, it is nonetheless true that the absolute numbers of the rural aged have approximately doubled in the past 50 years. In 1900 there were about two million persons over sixty-five years of age. By 1950, this figure had increased to almost four and a half million.

It is also true that in the past, self-sufficient agriculture and the large family with its deeply ingrained tradition of familial responsibility guaranteed the basic necessities of life and emotional security for the aging farmer and his wife. But social and economic changes—some sociologists have referred to them collectively as "rurbanization"—have brought about some economic and emotional insecurity. Family ties have weakened. Agriculture has become commercialized and mechanized, and studies have indicated that farmers themselves are beginning to feel that farming is no more secure in the modern world than other occupations in terms of preparing for retirement.

[1] The research director of the rural study and the senior author of the materials on which this chapter is based was Professor Philip Taietz, Department of Rural Sociology, Cornell University.

There are many strong hints that aging in rural areas is not as overwhelmingly idyllic as we have been led to believe. For example, Warren's survey in Almond, a rural township in upstate New York, noted that the rural aged in that community may have greater "primary group" resources than the aged in urban communities, but they have fewer organized recreational facilities, fewer commercial facilities, fewer public and private agencies, less transportation, and less opportunity to participate in retirement plans.

Meaning of Retirement

To most Americans, retirement means "administrative" retirement, a form that developed during the era of rapid industrialization early in this century and received an added impetus in 1935 with the passage of the Social Security Act. When an employed individual reaches a given age or has worked a specified number of years, or both, he is normally expected or even required to terminate his employed status. Retirement in this sense is an aspect of the personnel policy of an organization and usually includes the provision of reduced payments to the retirant in the form of a pension. Without this financial provision, retirement would hardly differ from being discharged or "laid off."

The form of retirement experienced by those who are self-employed is quite different from administrative retirement, which is generally compulsory and applies largely to employees. When the self-employed retire, it is usually a voluntary decision, for by definition the self-employed determine their own work status. The decision to retire is usually personal, although it is conditioned by such factors as health, sufficiency of financial resources, family attitudes, and the feasibility of disposing of the business or farm.

Not all the respondents in the study of the rural aged analyzed in this chapter were retirants. Therefore the term "active" is used to designate those who, at the time of the survey, continued to play occupational roles in their work, either as employees or as self-employed persons. The term "retired," on the other hand, refers to those persons whose connections with their occupational roles have been severed as a result of the company's personnel policy; or, if respondents were previously self-employed, they have drastically reduced participation in their occupations or have withdrawn from them, so that by self-definition, as well as by the definition of others, they are retired. It must be emphasized that as the terms "active" and "retired" are used in the subsequent analysis, they refer primarily to gainful occupational employment, not to functions such as formal organizational participation, informal friendship, clique participation, and hobbies. It should not be assumed that respondents referred to as "retired" are completely inactive, or that those in the "active" category are necessarily active in either formal or informal associations, or in hobbies and avocations.

One of the primary purposes of the rural study discussed here was to compare the farmers' problems of adjustment in retirement with those of the rural aged in other occupations. But the widely divergent economic statuses and social positions of farmers call for considerations of a more precise subgroup in the farm population. Therefore the analysis in this chapter is focused upon "owner-operators," since all but a few of the farmers in the study group were in that category. Elsewhere the point has been made that the farm owner-operator is financially in a more favorable position to retire than is the farm tenant or laborer, but because of the owner-operator's emotional tie to the land, he is psychologically less prepared to do so. In many respects the situations of the farm laborer and tenant are similar to those of industrial workers analyzed in the previous two chapters.

Work Situation of the Farmer

What are the distinctive characteristics in the work situation of the owner-operator of a farm? How do these special characteristics make preparation for retirement as well as adjustment to retirement different from those of rural people in nonagricultural occupations? First of all, as already observed, farming is usually a family enterprise, for the vast majority of farms in the United States are family farms. As a consequence, the farmer who is an owner-operator plays many and diverse roles. Depending upon the size of his farm and his family situation, he may act as owner, manager, employer, mechanic, laborer, consultant, entrepreneur, and teacher, to name but a few of his roles. With advancing years the farm owner-operator can drop roles that are incompatible with his physical capacity, and taper off by devoting more time to fewer roles.

This advantage is a function of self-employment. Yet the very fact of farm ownership may also involve inherent and unique complexities not confronted by persons in other occupational situations. The farm owner-operator's persistent psychological attachment to his land may be in conflict with his declining physical capacity and the necessity of reducing the scope of his work. If he has a son or son-in-law still in residence on or near the farm, perhaps an agreement between the two can be made for the joint operation of the farm. Under this type of arrangement the old farmer and his wife will probably continue to live on the farm either in a separate house or in a separate part of the family home. But the situation is quite different if the farm is sold to a non-relative, for then the farmer, in all likelihood, must change his living arrangements drastically. His retirement in such cases resembles in some respects that of an employee, for he severs his relations with his occupational locale and no longer has any prescribed occupational role.

Another qualification to the otherwise more favorable meaning of retirement for the farm owner-operator is the fact that, unlike the employee, in the past he had no pension or Old Age and Survivors Insurance benefits to ease the burden of a possible decline in income upon retirement. Farm operators, however, were finally covered by the 1954 Amendments of the Social Security Act. Finally, there may be other closely related influences at work. Drake notes, for example, that "aside from psychological unwillingness and financial inability to retire, the high cost of farming seems to be a major factor influencing the aged owner-operators or landlords to keep their property. There are more young farmers available to replace aged owners than there are farms to be released by the aged owners. However, owing to the high price of land and modern farm equipment, young farmers apparently cannot pay the price the landowners want for their farms. The aged landlords or owner-operators cannot afford to sell at less than the market value of the land because their real and personal property represents their life savings." [2]

Survey of Six Rural Counties

To check on the widely held assumption that aging in rural areas presents few, if any, of the problems of adjustment found in urban areas, a survey of 249 males sixty years of age and over, resident in the villages and open country of six predominantly rural counties in New York State, was conducted in the summer of 1952 by a staff of Cornell University sociologists.

[2] Joseph T. Drake, *The Retirement of Aged Farm Owners*, Ph.D. thesis (University of North Carolina, 1953), p. 34.

The sample consisted of men sixty years of age and over who had lived in the area for some time: in Cortland and Oswego counties for more than 3 years; in Chautauqua and Livingston counties for more than 2 years; and in Ulster and Clinton counties for more than 1 year. The six counties were selected because they were typical of central, eastern, and western nonmetropolitan New York, and they were, for the most part, similar in several agricultural, population, and social characteristics. In selecting the sample, proportionate representation was given to open country and village areas.

Characteristics of the Study Group

Of the 249 respondents, 154 (62 per cent) were found to be actively engaged in occupations either as self-employed or as employees (both are referred to as "active" in this analysis) and 95 (38 per cent) had retired, either voluntarily or as a result of the personnel policies of the companies for which they had worked (the latter 2 groups are referred to as "retired"). It has not been established that this distribution of work status is representative of all rural communities. However, the proportion of those retired appears to be considerably smaller than is true for the country as a whole.

Age

The median age of the active members in the sample was sixty-seven, whereas that of the retired respondents was seventy-three. The active farm operators were somewhat older than the active nonfarmers; similarly, the retired farm operators were distributed more heavily in the older age brackets than were those who had retired from nonfarm occupations. In short, the facts of being retired and a farm operator were much more closely associated with advanced age than were the facts of being employed and in a nonfarm occupation.

Place of Residence

There was an almost equal division between open country and village residence for the entire sample, but a considerably higher proportion of the retired than of the active respondents and of nonfarmers than of farm operators were found to live in the villages. The highest proportion of village residence was characteristic of retired nonfarmers, followed in declining proportions by active nonfarmers, retired farm operators, and lastly, active farm operators. The difference between the percentages of active and retired farm operators who reside in a village was much greater than the difference between retired and active non-farmers. Each aspect of these differences in rural residence can be explained in terms of two basic determinants: (*a*) The role of non-farmer logically is conducive to the highest rate of *initial* residence in rural villages, whereas (*b*) the role of retirant makes for the highest rate of *change* of residence to a village. Retirants presumably are attracted to village life because of more adequate health and recreational facilities there, and because life in retirement in the open country involves social disadvantages inherent in isolation.

Place of Birth and Education

The study group as a whole was predominantly native born, for immigration had not seriously affected the composition of the rural population of the six counties. But a much higher proportion of the farmers than of the nonfarmers were born in the county in which they were residing at the time of the study. In short, the farmer changes residence infrequently in the course of a lifetime. If he moves upon retirement, he is most likely to move a short distance: from farm to village within the same county, for example.

The formal education of considerably more than half of the entire group did not extend beyond the elementary level. Only a handful of the sample had any college education. This predominantly low level of education has been discovered in most studies of the aged, both rural and urban. It reflects the educational pattern of earlier years in American society as well as elsewhere. Extended education was an uncommon experience in the childhood and youth of the contemporary aged.

Living Arrangements and Marital Status

Advancing age, retirement, and widowhood increase the likelihood of living alone. The rural retired respondents (who, as we have already seen, were generally older than those who were active) more often lived alone, without spouse and children, than did the active respondents. The pattern is especially clear for the retired nonfarmers. However, the importance of family living to the rural aged as a whole is evidenced by the fact that most of those who were not living with a spouse lived with children or other relatives. Only a minority lived alone or with non-relatives.

Occupation

Contrary to the stereotype held by many persons, the gainfully employed in rural areas represent a cross section of occupations ranging from unskilled labor to professional activities. Yet of the 154 in the sample of 249 who were still occupationally active, more than half (53 per cent) were self-employed, an even higher percentage than in the nation as a whole (about 40 per cent). The reasons for this have been proposed elsewhere as follows:

> Older workers differ from younger workers, among other ways, in the relatively larger number who are self-employed. This is the product of two factors—some wage and salary workers go into business for themselves when they have accumulated sufficient capital, a process which may take years; and secondly, self-employed persons such as *farmers*, small businessmen, and members of the professions remain longer in gainful employment than wage and salary workers because they can control their own retirement.[3]

In other words, self-employment, more characteristic of the employed aged than of younger people in the labor force, is also more characteristic of the rural than of the urban employed aged or of the employed aged as a whole. The majority of the self-employed in the rural sample, as one might expect, were farm owner-operators (67 per cent); proprietors of business comprised 22 per cent, and those in the professions, 10 per cent. The principal farm operations of the active farmers were dairying and production of fruits, vegetables, and poultry. All but one of the farmer operators owned all the land they farmed.

OCCUPATIONAL STABILITY AND MODIFICATION IN OLD AGE.   Aside from retirement, there are two basic types of work modification in the later years of life in adjusting to real or alleged reduction of work capacity. The first course involves leaving one's regular occupation for work that is less demanding; the second involves reducing the number of hours of work.

An analysis of the work history of all 249 active and retired respondents combined shows the farm operators to have been more stable occupationally than the nonfarmers. Proportionately twice as many nonfarmers as farmers engaged in work different from what they considered

[3] Committee on Aging and Geriatrics, *Fact Book on Aging* (Washington, D.C., Federal Security Agency, 1952), p. 32.

to be their regular occupations after they were fifty years old. Not only did the farm operators shift to other jobs less often than did the non-farmers; when they did change it was less often, according to their own definition, to an inferior type of work. Only 13 per cent of the farmers changed to work they considered inferior, while 32 per cent of the non-farmers did so. Farm operators who were doing work different from what they had been doing at fifty years of age reported the following as typical adaptations: lighter and less work; more mechanical equipment; change from dairy and general farming to small-scale poultry operation; and change to a smaller farm.

As one might expect, an important difference in the extent of reduction of work hours as an adjustment to old age was found between the self-employed and employees. The former have much more control over their work conditions than do the latter. Only seven employees (8 per cent) reported they were working part time, in contrast to 32 farm operators (57 per cent) who had reduced their working hours since they were fifty years of age.

Nature of Income

INCOME OF THE ACTIVE. The income of the aged in this study was in line with the nationwide pattern discussed in Chapter 2, namely, lower than the population as a whole. A little more than half (55 per cent) of the nonfarm respondents reported a weekly income of less than $45 a week (or less than $2,340 annually); and approximately two thirds of the farm operators had earned less than $2,000 in net cash income during the year preceding the study. The figures for the farm operators do not include such farm-related income as the rental value of the house and the value of the food produced for home consumption. This fact, therefore, as well as the different time intervals for which the income data are reported, suggests that caution should be exercised in comparing directly the incomes of the two groups.

In addition to income derived from the operation of their farms, 40 per cent of the farm operators claimed some other sources of income, the two most important being savings and investments. On the other hand, about half (49 per cent) of the nonfarmers claimed to have supplementary income, the two most important being property and investments. Nonfarmers also reported receiving Old Age and Survivors Insurance benefits. Farm operators were not covered by the Social Security

Act at the time of the study, and accordingly did not have OASI benefits as an economic resource.

Four out of five active farm operators and nine out of ten active nonfarmers expect to have some income when they retire. The sources of expected income are, in some respects, occupationally determined. Almost seven out of ten farm operators look upon their farm equity and other property as a major source of income, while almost six out of ten nonfarmers look to Social Security benefits as an important source of income. About half of the farm operators and nonfarmers claim to have some savings.

INCOME OF THE RETIRED. All but three of the retired respondents claimed to have some retirement income, but the sources differed markedly between retired farmers and nonfarmers. For the retired farmers the major sources were property, savings, and investments; the retired nonfarmers derived their principal income from industrial and government pensions, OASI benefits, savings, and property, in the order named.

It is not known whether the independent retirement income reported by the respondents was enough to meet their maintenance needs or whether it was supplemented by Old Age Assistance grants and by contributions from members of their family. Nevertheless, a much higher proportion of the retired nonfarmers (31 per cent) claimed they received some financial help from their families than did retired farmers (15 per cent), and 16 per cent of the retired nonfarmers said they were recipients of Old Age Assistance grants, as compared with 10 per cent of the retired farmers. These findings suggest that retired farmers retain financial independence to a greater extent than do retired nonfarmers.

ADEQUACY OF INCOME. One method of assessing the adequacy of an individual's or family's income is to measure it in terms of some standard established by the Bureau of Labor Statistics or by some other professional agency. Another method, and no less useful because it is subjective, is to question the individual himself. Indeed, a useful measure of the adequacy of income is the individual's own satisfaction with it.

The respondents were asked: "Is your present income enough to meet your living expenses?" A higher proportion of those active than of those retired replied in the affirmative. This is to be expected, for a decline in income is a normal accompaniment of retirement. In this survey, 84 per cent of the respondents stated their current income was less than it had been when they were gainfully employed. Similarly, more of both the active and the retired farmers than of the active and retired non-farmers considered their present incomes adequate. This adds support to an earlier observation concerning the need for caution in comparing the stated incomes of farmers and nonfarmers. Although a higher proportion of nonfarmers than of farmers ostensibly enjoy higher incomes, they also demonstrate greater dissatisfaction with present incomes.

Almost nine out of ten active farm owner-operators considered their incomes adequate, whereas active nonfarmers and retired farm owner-operators were virtually tied for second place in self-evaluation of income adequacy. Lowest of all in evaluating their incomes were retired nonfarmers, for little more than half of them thought their present incomes were enough to meet their living expenses.

Ostensibly one of the blunt realities of life confronting many retired persons, whether rural or urban, is the necessity of adjusting to a reduced income. An important question that follows logically is: "What are the specific ways in which people reduce their living expenses in order to live within their limited income?" Although 41 per cent reported no change, 54 per cent claimed they were compelled to curtail expenses. Almost 11 per cent were doing part-time work and 3 per cent were living with relatives as a means of adjusting to a reduced income. It is significant that reductions are made in the three basic necessities: food, clothing, and shelter. Clothing economies were made by 28 per cent, food and recreation cutbacks were undertaken by 26 per cent, and 18 per cent turned to more modest housing.

Work Span of the Rural Aged

Farmers continue to be occupationally active long after rural non-farmers. In fact, almost twice the proportion of farm owner-operators as of nonfarmers among the respondents waited beyond the middle of their seventh decade of life to retire. This is a reflection of the significant difference between farming and nonagricultural occupations discussed in the introductory section of this chapter. Theoretically, farm owner-operators can persist in their work almost as long as they wish, subject only to self-defined restrictions and those that may be imposed upon them by their families. Many of the other aged, on the other hand, are subject to administrative retirement.

Sixty-two per cent of the nonfarmer respondents no longer working retired voluntarily; 21 per cent of them were compelled to retire because of employers' policies, and 17 per cent were "laid off" or stopped work for unknown reasons. On the other hand, all the farm owner-operators who were no longer working had retired voluntarily, not being subject to administrative retirement. The proportions of those who had retired because of poor health and difficulty in doing their work were similar in both occupational groups.

Another characteristic in the pattern of occupational withdrawal of farmers is that they can reduce their work load gradually. More than twice as great a proportion of the retired farmers as of nonfarmers experienced gradual retirement. Almost twice the proportion of the former as of the latter worked as long as they could. Furthermore, nonfarmers are much more likely to mention the need for money as a reason for continuing to work. Other motives for continuing to work are the desire to keep busy and the intrinsic enjoyment of work. In this study no differences were found between the retired farm operators and the retired nonfarmers in this respect.

If it is true that a higher proportion of retired farm operators than retired nonfarmers worked to an advanced age and as long as they could, one would anticipate that the work expectations of active farm operators and nonfarmers would conform to the same pattern. The active respondents were asked: "We would like to know what your prospects are for the next five years regarding your work. Do you expect to continue in your present work, stop work, or do something else?" Almost nine out of every ten active farm operators expected to continue work, in contrast to slightly more than six out of ten active nonfarmers. More than three times the proportion of nonfarmers as of farm operators expected to retire (33 per cent, as compared with 10 per cent).

Significant differences appear in the reasons given by active farm operators and active nonfarmers for their work prospects. The reason most often given by the former for expecting to continue working is enjoyment of work; the need for money is the most frequently named reason for the latter. The outstanding reason given by farm operators for not expecting to continue working is the difficulty of their work. Nonfarmers, on the other hand, refer to "wanting more leisure time" more than any other reason. Although the number of cases is limited in the analysis, it is interesting to find that a larger proportion of nonfarmers than of farmers voiced the desire for more leisure time as a reason for stopping work. This points out again that farming is more of a "way of life" than is true of nonfarming occupations.

Leisure-Time Activities

One of the problems of readjustment that many older people are said to face is the increasing availability of unscheduled time. This can be of crucial importance to those individuals whose lives heretofore revolved chiefly about their work and for whom inactivity may have a serious disintegrating impact on personality.

What are the noneconomic activities of older people in rural areas, and which of these are the most significant and satisfactory to them? Has there been any change in activities and their meaning to the individual in the course of time? Each respondent was asked to state whether he engaged in any of twelve leisure-time activities, classified as *solitary* (i.e., typically engaged in by a person alone); *spectator* (i.e., involving merely passive attendance); *interpersonal* (i.e., involving interaction with another person or persons); *hobbies;* and *other* activities.

Of the 248 respondents who indicated what their activities were, 206 reported they talked with friends more frequently than anything else. Listening to the radio ranked second, followed in order by working in the garden, reading, going to town to shop, taking rides in the country, watching television, playing cards, hunting and fishing, taking walks alone, talking with friends on the telephone, and lastly, attendance at movies. The range of activities reported by individual respondents was from none to all twelve activities.

Another area for analysis is whether participation in activities is associated with background characteristics such as the amount of education, place of residence, and occupational status, and also social psychological factors such as whether one plans or does not plan for retirement. The first step in testing hypotheses in this area is to differentiate those who participate in few from those in many activities. Respondents were classified into three categories: *low* if they reported none to three kinds of activities (65 persons); *medium* for four to six activities (128 persons); *high* for seven or more activities (55 persons). The following correlations were thereby uncovered:

1. There is a significant relationship between *extensiveness of activity and amount of formal education.* One of the consequences of education is the broadening of the individual's horizon and a stimulating of his interests and participation in a variety of activities. Not only are

educated people more aware of the opportunities about them, but they are more frequently in a position to take advantage of those opportunities. Thus it is expected that they will engage in a greater diversity of leisure-time and recreational activities than those with less education. Some of the activities in the list, such as reading, assume a certain educational level, and it is obvious that people with little education do not read as much nor as widely as do those with more education. The relationship between education and diversity of activities is operative throughout the life span and as a consequence, whether the person is old or young, it would be expected that with more education he would engage in a greater diversity of interests and activities. The significant relationship between activities and education, then, is not surprising. The proportion of those respondents in the low activity category declined steadily from those with grammar school education to those in the high school and college groups. Conversely, the proportion of those in the high activity group increased steadily from the low to the highly educated groups.

2. There is a significant relationship between *extensiveness of activity and place of residence.* A much smaller proportion of village residents than of open country residents were in the low activity category, and conversely, a greater proportion of village than of open country residents were in the high activity category.

3. There is a significant relationship between *extensiveness of activity and type of occupation.* A much greater proportion of non-farmers than of farm operators were in the high activity category, whereas a significantly greater proportion of farm operators than of nonfarmers were in the low activity category. Perhaps this can best be explained by the fact that more rural nonfarmers than farm operators live in villages. Inasmuch as extensiveness of activity and place of residence are directly correlated, it stands to reason that there would also be more extensive activity by the preponderantly village-dwelling non-farmers than by the preponderantly open-country-dwelling farmers.

4. There is no significant difference in the amount of activity between *those rural aged who are retired and those who still are occupationally active.* This tends to substantiate the point made earlier that the terms "active" and "retired" refer primarily to gainful employment, not to participation in activities such as informal friendship groups, leisure-time activities, and hobbies. Respondents classified as "retired"

are not always completely inactive, nor do those in the "active" category necessarily participate either in formal or informal associations, or in hobbies and avocations.

5. There is a significant relationship between *extensiveness of activity and socioeconomic status.* What explains the significant relationship here? Why do people of high socioeconomic status tend much more often to take part in a variety of activities than those of lower socioeconomic status? The answer may lie in the fact that high socioeconomic status implies more education, a wider range of interests, and possibly greater opportunities and resources. It is in effect a difference between a style of life in which diversity of activities is typical, and perhaps expected, and a style of life more likely to be characterized by psychological and social isolation.

LEISURE-TIME ACTIVITIES AND SATISFACTION.   In addition to their range of activities, the respondents were also asked to indicate what activities gave them the most satisfaction in life. Respondents claimed they gained the most satisfaction from activities centered in the home, for the four leading satisfaction items were clearly domestic in nature.

CHANGE IN LEISURE-TIME ACTIVITIES WITH AGE.   To determine the effects, if any, of the aging process on participation in leisure-time activities, the respondents were asked whether they had done certain things more often when they were fifty years of age or more often now. In general, the findings indicate a trend toward the curtailment of activities among the respondents after the age of fifty. Activities involving family associations (seeing children and relatives) were especially affected over the years, closely followed by such activities as club and organizational affiliation and hunting and fishing. It is interesting to note that passive activities, such as reading and listening to the radio, tend to increase with age.

Formal Social Participation

As already noted, there is a significant relationship between participation in formal organizations and taking part in a diverse number of activities. It has been revealed too that the older rural men in this study who had a high school education or more were engaged in a broader range of activities than those with less than a high school education. In view of these findings, the survey results regarding the relationship between education and formal participation in old age were to be expected. Older rural men with higher education participate more often in formal organizations than do those with less education.

OCCUPATIONAL STATUS AND PARTICIPATION IN FORMAL ORGANIZATIONS. We have already pointed out that in addition to the function of sociability and service, formal organizations serve as vehicles for social mobility and power. Some formal organizations emphasize occupational improvement, while others emphasize sociability and interpersonal satisfactions. If this analysis is substantially correct, it follows that retirement will bring about a reduction in formal participation. The retired will tend to drop out of occupationally oriented organizations and retain their membership in those organizations that provide face-to-face satisfactions. The data in this rural study indicate that 51 per cent of the active older men belong to formal organizations, as compared with 40 per cent of the retired men. The relationship is not statistically significant, but it is in the theoretically expected direction.

Preparation and Planning for Retirement

Many of the problems associated with passivity and inactivity in old age stem from the fact that older people today grew up in a period when individuals were expected to remain occupationally active indefinitely. American culture, as we noted in Chapter 4, does not at present educate adults in preparation for the retirement years with the same intensity that it devotes to the education of children and adolescents in preparation for adulthood.

Retirement, of course, has different acceptances in the various subgroups of society. Farmers, for example, are generally known to be reluctant to accept retirement as normal, for to do so would conflict with the farmers' values of usefulness and productivity during the entire life span. It is a reasonable hypothesis, then, that an occupational group that accepts retirement as a normal status in life will be more likely to prepare and plan for retirement than those unwilling to accept retirement as normal.

The data in this rural study support such a hypothesis. The majority of the respondents had not prepared and planned for retirement. However, four times as great a proportion of nonfarmers as of farmers had made plans for their retirement. Nonfarmers, it must be recalled, are predominantly employees who are subject to administrative retirement and who are aware that they will have to retire at a certain date in accordance with the personnel policy of the company. With this eventuality in mind, it is understandable that they are more likely to make plans for retirement than are persons who can decide when they will retire. Self-employed persons such as farmers, however, can more easily ignore retirement, not only as a normal probability but also as a statistical possibility for which preparations and plans are necessary insurance.

Attitudes toward Retirement

To check more precisely their attitudes toward retirement, the active respondents were asked: "Do you look forward to the time when you will stop working and retire, or do you dislike the idea?" Seven out of ten respondents disliked the idea, a finding consistent with those of some other studies of attitudes toward retirement. The study of the rural aged also showed that almost twice the proportion of nonfarmers as of farmers looked forward to retirement. This is consistent with differences in the meaning of work held by farmers and nonfarmers.

Aside from differences in the meaning of work, what else is there to explain why some respondents looked forward to retirement whereas others did not? An analysis of these attitudinal responses as they related to health, attitude toward present job, and other factors provided a large part of the answer. Those who looked forward to retirement differed from those who did not in the following respects: (1) more of them reported that their health was poor; (2) more of them indicated they disliked their present work and that continuing to work had been unsatisfactory; (3) more of them had plans for retirement; and (4) more of them believed abrupt retirement was better.

The relationships that appear suggest there is something negative in the response of "looking forward" to retirement. The attitude shows an inability and reluctance to cope with one's work rather than a positive anticipation of a satisfying experience. For example, the association of poor health with the response suggests a feeling of relief that the physical and psychological stresses of work will eventually be alleviated. This interpretation is supported by the consistent association of dislike for present work with the feeling that continuing to work has been insidious. Those who look forward to retirement are looking forward to the time when they will be released from an unpleasant and burdensome situation. The data support the expectation that the respondents who were under pressure to retire because of poor health and dissatisfaction with work would favor retiring abruptly. Finally, consistent with other relationships, "looking forward to retirement" is associated with preparation for retirement. Wanting to retire leads one to prepare for it to a greater extent than in the case of unwillingness to retire.

Adjustment to Retirement

Retired respondents were asked several questions for the purpose of assessing the satisfactions and dissatisfactions they had found in retirement. Despite the finding that active nonfarmers looked forward to retirement to a significantly greater extent than did active farmers, the retired farmers appear to have adjusted better to retirement than did the retired nonfarmers. The difference was particularly marked in the extent of agreement with the statement that "retirement is bad" and in the extent to which the respondents felt "in worse spirits" and often "didn't know how to keep occupied."

Theoretical considerations as well as additional empirical findings support the observation that farm operators actually adjust better to retirement than do the rural aged in other occupations. It has already been pointed out that the nature of farming activities provides for a gradual tapering off from work. Furthermore, farm owner-operators who retire on their farms are not physically separated from their occupation, and as a result the shock of withdrawal from work is not as great.

Another factor that probably contributes to the better adjustment of farm owner-operators in retirement is their superior economic situation. It will be recalled that twice the proportion of retired nonfarmers as of farm operators had reported insufficient income. The relatively poor economic situation of the nonfarmers must have been a factor in their dissatisfaction with retirement. More of the retired nonfarmers expressed a desire to return to work, and analysis of the reasons revealed that nonfarmers were much more likely than farmers to mention financial reasons.

TYPE OF RETIREMENT AND ADJUSTMENT. Sociopsychological theory suggests that the degree of adjustment in a new role varies with the amount of opportunity for practice or rehearsal. It has been assumed with regard to retirement that if a person moves into the role of retirant gradually he will adjust more adequately than if he is suddenly thrust into this new role. The evidence from this study, however, does not show a clear relationship between adjustment to retirement and type of retirement.

Those retiring abruptly showed a tendency toward having greater difficulties as measured by the following criteria of adjustment: (1) often do not know how to keep occupied; (2) feel in worse spirits; (3) health is worse. But those retiring gradually showed a tendency toward having greater difficulties in terms of the following criteria: (1) the feeling that retirement is bad; (2) not working turned out to be worse; (3) finding it very difficult to adjust. It should be added that the percentage differences were very small for three of the criteria, and in no instance was the difference between abrupt and gradual retirants substantial.

The Meaning of Retirement to the Older Rural Resident

The respondents answered a number of questions about their personal assessment of retirement. They differed among themselves as to whether retirement is good or bad for a person, whether workers should be encouraged to retire at sixty-five, and whether they should retire gradually.

To reach a broader understanding of retirement, the following question was asked of the active and retired respondents: "There has been a lot of talk about retirement recently. What does retirement mean to you?" Their answers showed that retirement is far from having the same meaning to everyone. To some, it means reducing one's work load, to others it means loss of physical strength, and to many others it means passivity, whereas others find it even means overtones of security and freedom. Listed below are the major themes revealed in a content analysis of the responses to this question:

1. KEEP WORKING. The resistance to retirement was evident from the following excerpts of statements by the respondents: "When you are lost, finished"; "Die in harness"; "Don't want to stop working"; "Never expect to retire."

2. REDUCTION OF WORK. Typical statements were: "Take it easier on the farm"; "Less work"; "Ease up on work"; "Work part time for someone else."

3. DISABILITY. The meaning that retirement has for people in this category was connected with some physical or social disability that forced their retirement. Illustrating this are the following statements: "Disabled so can't work"; "When a man can't work"; "Too old to work"; "Can't get used to doing nothing"; "Forced into it by heart trouble"; "Unable to work any more."

4. COMPLETE CESSATION OF WORK. For this response category,

retirement meant a complete separation from employment. Statements such as follows were typical: "Just quit work"; "Giving up a definite job"; "Giving up position occupied during most of your life"; "Just stopped work."

5. INACTIVITY. This response category differs from the others in that its orientation is away from work. Such statements as the following were typical: "Sit down and do nothing"; "Not doing much of anything"; "Take it easy"; "Relaxing around the house."

6. ACTIVITIES ORIENTED IN RETIREMENT. There is a similarity here to the immediately preceding category in that the meaning of retirement is moving away from one's employment. It differs, however, in that there is a definite activity pattern emphasizing recreation and social participation. Some typical statements were: "Working around the house and garden"; "Hunt and fish at leisure"; "Have a small place and raise chickens"; "Plenty to do fixing up the house."

7. SECURITY ORIENTATION. The responses in this category are alike in expression of concern about the income required for retirement. Such statements representing this orientation were as follows: "Having enough money to live without work"; "Draw social security"; "Reduce income."

8. FREEDOM ORIENTATION. The theme of response in this category is freedom from the responsibility of work, and freedom from the supervision and authority inherent in work. Such statements as: "Do what you want to do"; "Free from responsibility"; "Spend the rest of your life as you want to"; "Get up when you please"; "Be your own boss," are representative of the responses that comprised this category.

For all persons the meanings of freedom or security and refusal to face retirement were the most frequent responses. The evidence is rather clear that retirement means many things to rural residents. A question of related significance is whether these various outlooks on retirement are related in any way to one's occupational position. The findings reveal that the meaning of retirement does vary according to the person's occupation, as follows:

1. The active respondents mentioned the theme of "Keep working" more often than did the retired respondents.

2. Farm operators more often viewed retirement as a tapering-off process than did either the nonfarmers or those who had retired.

3. Retired persons viewed retirement more often as being related to a disability than did either of the active groups.

4. The meaning of retirement as complete cessation of work was viewed less often by farm operators than by either the nonfarmers or the retired.

In general, nonfarmers were found to think more frequently about the conditions of retirement, such as freedom or security, whereas farmers more often thought about the nature of retirement, such as reduction of work or complete inactivity. The retired respondents viewed retirement typically as either a result of disability or as something contingent upon adequate economic security. However, when the retirants were classified in terms of previous occupation, their responses were similar to those who were still active in their respective occupational groups.

Summary and Conclusions

The purpose of the study reported in this chapter was to evaluate the widely held assumption that aging in rural areas involves few of the problems of adjustment found in urban areas. Although the findings generally support the hypothesis that the problems of adjustment of farm operators in old age and retirement are less severe than those of the aged in other occupations, the situation of the aged farmers is far from carefree. The strong orientation toward work, the attachment to the land, the problems attending the sale or transfer of the farm, and a somewhat negative attitude toward leisure-time activities make the prospect of withdrawal from farming a difficult one for the farm operator.

But there are a number of compensating factors in the farm operator's situation to offset these negative factors. Farm operators are able to reduce the number of work hours and to modify the type of work in keeping with declining health and reduced work capacity. Furthermore, they are able to continue working much longer than those in other occupations. Finally, the financial situation of the retired farm operators is better than that of the nonfarmer.

Questions and Research Exercises

1. Account for the neglect of rural aging as far as research is concerned.
2. Compare rural and urban areas with regard to the importance of administrative retirement.
3. Discuss the distinctive features in the work situation of the owner-operator

of a farm. How do they make preparation and adjustment to retirement different from those of rural nonfarmers?

4. Aside from retirement, what are the two basic types of work modification for the rural aged in adjusting to real or alleged reduction of work capacity?

5. As a research project, devise and administer some projective techniques that would bring out comparisons between farmers and urban workers in the meaning of work.

6. What are the noneconomic activities of older people in rural areas, and which of these are the most significant and satisfactory to them?

Selected Readings

McKain, Walter C., Jr., and Baldwin, Elmer D., *Old Age and Retirement in Rural Connecticut* (Storrs, Agricultural Experiment Station Bulletin No. 278, 1951). A pioneering work on rural aging by two rural sociologists.

Nelson, Lowry, *Farm Retirement in Minnesota* (University of Minnesota, Agricultural Experiment Station Bulletin No. 294, 1947). Problems of retirement in the rural midwest.

Sewell, William, *et al.*, *Farmers' Conceptions and Plans for Economic Security in Old Age* (Madison, University of Wisconsin Research Bulletin No. 182, 1953). A valuable analysis made somewhat obsolete by the subsequent amendment to the Social Security Act providing coverage for farmers.

Smith, T. Lynn, "The Aged in Rural Society," in Milton Derber, ed., *The Aged and Society* (Champaign, Industrial Relations Research Association, 1950), pp. 40–53. The best general statement on old age in rural communities of American society.

Warren, Roland L., "Old Age in a Rural Township," in *Age Is No Barrier*, New York State Joint Legislative Committee on Problems of the Aging (Legislative Document No. 35, 1952), pp. 155–66. A western New York community study of all people over sixty-five, seeking information on problems and courses of action on behalf of the rural aged.

IV : Middle Age:
Theory and Research

---

*To be 70 years young is sometimes more cheerful
and hopeful than to be 40 years old.*

OLIVER WENDELL HOLMES

9 :

FROM THIRTY TO SIXTY:
PROBLEMS OF MIDDLE AGE

A married woman of 46 with no children began to suffer a gradual decline in her sense of well-being. Periods were irregular with occasional flushing and there were occasional dull headaches, fatigue, and anorexia. The latter caused her no particular discomfort but her emotional state was very troublesome. She said, "Nothing means anything to me any more. I push myself to do my work but it is hard and there is no joy in it. It is a meaningless drudgery. I get so depressed at the thought of how little I have given my husband. We have no children and while I always thought that some day we would, now I know it is impossible. I feel so guilty that I have been so uncreative. I don't want to see any-body. I don't want to go anywhere. I always thought I liked people but now I am not so sure. I guess my life has been more shallow than I ever knew."

The patient complained of waking early—sometimes around five o'clock in the morning. "I have too much time to think," she said. "That is a lonesome, frightening time of day, when you feel like I do. I get so miserable thinking of what a failure I have been. I have given so little to people. I have lived such a selfish existence. I think of the unkind things I have said. I hate myself for having been so ungenerous. I know what I ought to do but I have no enthusiasm to do it with. It seems as if love has gone out of me. Does love disappear with the hormones? I'm really drying up in every way I can think of."

This patient had been an only child of parents who had indulged her and never taught her any of the techniques of altruistic living. Her father had made a good living as an accountant and had "taken care of" her mother and herself. Little was asked of her by her mother and little was given. The patient was given to understand that when she grew up some man would marry and "take care of" her too. Her education, however, had given her enough insight into altruism and a well-rounded life that conflict was engendered, remaining on an unconscious level until the climacteric, when it resulted in acute suffering.

Such conflicts are precipitated in emotional distress and anxiety because the climacteric is a critical life period—a stock-taking period—in which one or more of the phenomena enumerated press forward for evaluation by the ego. The ego, harassed by a relentless conscience, is incapable of solving its problem because it has never been part of a resourceful personality. Adolescents who are dissatisfied with themselves in much the same way will sometimes bestir themselves to find comfort and self-approval in new ventures, new hobbies, new sports, new friends, new goals. But by 45 the personality, already unresourceful through the years, has become convinced of its inertia, lack of altruism, and inability to find compensations and new satisfactions. Such individuals have been frustrated so many times that they are overwhelmed with a feeling of self-defeat and succumb to inertia and self-criticism.*

Middle Age as the Unmet Challenge of Gerontology

The previous chapters of this book have concentrated almost exclusively on *old* age and its problems, and in this sense the book reflects what has generally been true of gerontology until now. But more and more it appears to many gerontologists that the great unmet challenge for gerontology lies in *middle* age, probably the least understood phase of the life cycle, and undoubtedly an important incubator for many of the problems that erupt in old age.

Much of the credit for stimulating interest among gerontologists in middle age belongs to Senator Thomas C. Desmond, retired chairman of the New York State Joint Legislative Committee on Problems of the Aging. Pointing out that we know very little about middle age because it is a relatively new mass phenomenon, he has noted that social scientists have done practically no probing among either the lower or upper

* O. Spurgeon English, "Climacteric Neuroses and Their Management," *Geriatrics* (Vol. 9, Apr. 1954), pp. 143–44.

income middle-agers, and very little more among the middle income group in this age category.[1]

It is not true, of course, that middle-aged people have been lacking as subjects of social science research. Along with other age groups, their attitudes, opinions, behavior patterns, and problems are constantly under scrutiny. Rarely, however, has the focus of research been on the patterns and problems these people face as a result of their age status. It is one thing to ask a 40-year-old person how he votes or what his attitude is toward his job; it is another matter to examine these and other questions in terms of middle age as an independent (causal) variable.

This is precisely what a prominent journalist and novelist also had in mind several years ago in her critical observation of the accomplishments of social science:

> For the middle years, when you come suddenly to the realization that you do not know where you are going but already you are half-way there, our social studies reveal a large and significant blank. Yet it is precisely then, in the forties, the fifties, that we begin to give at the seams. A man starts to ask of himself: Will I be able to hold my job? Will we ever have enough in the bank? Does that pain in my chest mean my heart's giving out? And women sit frozen with dread, or flit in panic to quacks, cults, and beauty salon Success Schools, hunting a defense of some sort against that hour when the kids will be married and gone, the house empty, and the reasons for living vanished.[2]

Most of the scanty, scientific knowledge about middle age is the by-product of research designed primarily for other purposes. For example, Brozek's findings about hypertensive personality differences between young and middle-aged "normal" men were determined within the framework of a research program focused on aging of the cardiovascular system, with emphasis on the development of hypertension, arteriosclerosis, and coronary artery disease.[3] The empirical data about middle age used in the Desmond article referred to above were derived

[1] Thomas C. Desmond, "America's Unknown Middle-Agers," *The New York Times Magazine* (July 29, 1956), pp. 5, 42–43.

[2] Zelda Popkin, "Widows and the Perilous Years," *Harper's Magazine* (Sept. 1949), p. 71.

[3] Josef Brozek, "Personality of Young and Middle-Aged Normal Men: Item Analysis of a Psychosomatic Inventory," *Journal of Gerontology* (Vol. 7, July 1952), pp. 410–18.

from a review of old age literature and the extraction therein of tables and findings pertaining to middle age. For example, in some of the experimental data in gerontological research, tables were found that compared the reaction time of those sixty-five years of age and over with subjects of the ages, sixteen to twenty, twenty-one to thirty-four, thirty-five to forty-six, and forty-seven to sixty-five.

One important exception to the general lack of research directly focused on middle age is the so-called Kansas City Study, the purpose of which was to determine and to describe in a systematic way how middle-aged people play the social roles of parent, spouse, homemaker, worker, friend, citizen, association member, church member, and user of leisure time; and then to discover the factors in their lives that are related to successful performance in these social roles.[4]

The Demography of Middle Age

One of the puzzling aspects of middle age is the lack of consensus about its chronological coverage. When does middle age begin? Unlike entrance into many other age-statuses, middle age has no "rite de passage." At what point does it end and give way to old age? No one can say for certain.

In part, the answers to these questions are dependent upon the age of the observer who views the subject of middle age. By the very young, middle age appears to begin at a relatively early period in life; the senescent, on the other hand, does not like to admit that he has gone past it. It has been sardonically noted that to an adolescent thirty-five years of age seems like senility and forty-five years of age is clearly dotage, but one certainty is that the adolescent observer will eventually define things differently!

Evidence in support of this came in an in-plant study of 3,515 employees, sixty-three and sixty-four years old, representing 265 industries. Sixty-eight per cent of these employees reported they thought of themselves as middle-aged or younger.[5] This finding that chronologically older people may have a younger self-image confirmed the results of an

---

[4] See Robert J. Havighurst, "Factors Related to Performance of the Common Social Roles of Middle Age in the United States," *Book of Abstracts: First Pan-American Congress of Gerontology* (Mexico City, 1956), pp. 116–18.

[5] *The Study of Occupational Retirement: First Progress Report* (Cornell University, 1953), p. 8.

earlier study of 3,000 men and women, the majority of whom up to age seventy-five thought of themselves as middle-aged.[6]

Definitions of the beginning and the end of middle age also seem to be determined by the maximal hiring and the minimum retiring specifications, varying accordingly from one occupation and vocation to another. The most frequent age coverage, however, tends to be from forty to sixty.

The maximum age designated as acceptable for hiring workers in a given occupation has been known to vary as much as 25 years in different parts of one state. According to the United States Department of Labor,[7] a worker in retail specialty sales may encounter employment difficulties at thirty-five years of age, whereas another seeking work in the field of wholesale may have no problem in finding and holding a job at fifty-five or even sixty. In New York City, a floor girl in the needles trade is old at forty years of age, but a pattern-maker at sixty-five is often preferred to a younger worker. In one city, the construction industry reportedly prefers workers under thirty-five, but in another city the same industry has hired any worker capable of performing the job, regardless of age. Similarly, in one city the food processing, tobacco, and service industries have applied almost no age restrictions, but elsewhere 82 per cent of all jobs offered in food processing and 63 per cent in service occupations carry age restrictions, often under thirty-five. Generally, hiring restrictions on the basis of age arise earlier for women than for men.

As for the end of middle age, retirement is a good index because it signifies entrance into old age, at least in the occupational sense of the term. We know that retirement varies in its starting point from the chronological thirties for most athletes to the seventies for many in business and the professions. But, as we have noted several times in this book, the most widely observed age of retirement is sixty-five.

Undoubtedly there are other, more subtle social and psychological factors at work delineating middle age. But until research identifies them with some precision, convenience dictates the use of chronological definitions. If we can think of the years from forty to sixty as a crude coverage of the period of middle age, there are about 35 million Ameri-

---

[6] *The Problem of Aging* (Chicago, The Council of State Governments, 1955), p. 5.

[7] *Workers Are Younger Longer* (Washington, D.C., U.S. Department of Labor, 1953).

cans at the present time who may be designated as middle-aged. Should one prefer to follow the path of the demographers who define middle age as the years from forty-five to sixty-four, there are close to 31 million Americans in the group. The Bureau of the Census notes that the latter figure represents an increase of 193 per cent for this age group since 1900 as compared with an increase in the total population of only 98 per cent during the same period. The projection is that by 1975 the United States will have about 42.5 million middle-aged Americans.

Even as recently as 1900, life expectancy at birth in this country was only about forty-five, and merely 10 per cent of the population was middle aged. Today, 80 per cent of the American people survive at least until age sixty, and the average adult in the labor force is forty-five. At age thirty, the remaining life expectancy is forty-three years; at age forty, it is 33.8 years; the average remaining years at fifty are 25.2, and at age sixty the remaining life expectancy is 17.7 years.[8]

In 1950 this arbitrarily defined group of middle-aged Americans, forty-five to sixty-four years of age, was fairly evenly divided according to sex distribution. Most of them were married, and most of the men were employed, many at or near their lifetime peak in earnings. Wage and salary workers were preponderant, comprising 78 per cent of the gainfully employed between forty-five and fifty-four, and 74 per cent of those between fifty-five and sixty-four years of age who had jobs. Unpaid family workers were in a very small statistical minority, making up only 2 per cent of the forty-five to fifty-four subgroup and 1 per cent of those fifty-five to sixty-four. As of January, 1952, the distribution of the gainfully employed among middle-aged people showed the greatest concentration among operatives and kindred workers; craftsmen, foremen, and kindred workers; and managers, proprietors, and officials, except farm. On the other hand, middle-aged employees were relatively scarce among farm and nonfarm laborers and foremen, private household workers, and sales workers.[9]

Problems of Middle Age

The comparatively high level of income in families headed by persons in middle age and the wide prevalence of married life in the mid-

[8] Metropolitan Life Insurance Company, *Statistical Bulletin* (Vol. 37, June 1956), p. 6.
[9] Bureau of the Census, *Current Population Reports* (Labor Force Series P-57, No. 117), and unpublished data, 1952.

dle years of life are typical of the external economic and social traits that encourage the presumption that aging is no problem yet for persons forty-five to sixty-four years. Yet beneath this seemingly benign façade, middle age is believed to involve many covert but serious economic, marital, sociopsychological, and health disturbances.

Economic Problems

In a society that is culturally geared toward upward economic as well as social mobility, the middle aged are evidently subject to severe competition from younger people who press up the age scale against them seeking advances and promotions.[10] Although the average adult in the American labor force is now near the beginning of this middle-age category, the prevailing youth cult insists there is deterioration and decline of performance in the middle as well as in the later years of life rather than continuing development. This in turn has stimulated the erection of chronological age barriers and discrimination in employment, even in a "tight" labor market, not only for those age sixty-five and over, but also for the population forty-five to sixty-four. Unemployment which is at a minimum from age thirty-five to forty-four rises gradually between forty-five to sixty-four.

The plight of the middle-aged unemployed is that he is too old to work and too young to retire: too old to get a job but too young to receive social security benefits, although he must bear the full expense and burden of maturing families. In other words, the employment problems of middle age differ in kind from those faced by the aged. The latter's problems revolve about the retention of gainful employment, whereas persons of middle age face greater difficulty in securing re-employment than in avoiding retirement.

Wide-scale prejudice exists against hiring workers over forty-five years of age—in some areas, even younger—despite the estimate that 95 per cent of middle-aged people are not disabled and can work. For example, the New York State Employment Service has found that the duration and volume of unemployment are significantly higher among persons forty-five years of age and older than among those under forty-five in New York City. The "exhaustion rate" of unemployment insurance benefits increases as the age level rises. That women are particu-

[10] See *Workers Are Younger Longer* (Washington, D.C., U.S. Department of Labor, 1953); *Older Applicants at Public Employment Offices* (Washington, D.C., U.S. Department of Labor, Bureau of Employment Security, Nov. 1954); *Labor Market Review* (April 1952).

larly vulnerable in seeking reëmployment, as early as age thirty-five, is evident in the marked increase in their unemployment period at age 35 and over as compared with younger women. About twice the proportion of men and women under 45 years of age are usually referred and placed in jobs by the employment service as are those forty-five years of age and over. This discrimination on the basis of age is said to reflect job orders received by the employment service from business and industry, at least until age discrimination in employment was banned in New York State in 1958.

Studies by the Department of Labor have revealed that ceilings on age of new employees are policies applied by the majority of employers, especially public utilities, banks, metal concerns, and large firms in general. Even where age limits have not been formally established, in practice middle-aged workers find obstacles in their way in seeking employment. That is, personnel staffs take informal cues from top management and apply restrictive age specifications. When the middle-aged applicant is eventually placed in a job, a high proportion of the placements is in temporary, marginal work, thus leaving the ultimate problem unsolved.

The reasons given by employers for not hiring middle-aged workers are virtually the same as those used in discriminating against people sixty-five years of age and over. It is argued that:

1. Workmen's compensation rates go up when older workers are employed.
2. Older workers are subject to higher accident rates and thereby endanger not only themselves but others.
3. They cannot produce as much as younger workers.
4. It is unprofitable to invest in the training of older workers because of their shorter life expectancy.
5. Absenteeism and labor turnover increase among older workers.
6. The public prefers younger workers in jobs calling for contact with the public.
7. Pension systems make it difficult to hire older workers, because the cost to employers becomes exorbitant.

Those who defend the middle-aged workers claim that not one of the above arguments against them withstands the test of facts. Either they are without factual foundation or they are based on exaggerations and distortion. Proponents of middle-age employment point to work records that indicate that the middle-aged worker is absent less, more reliable, and is actually given better ratings on the whole by supervisors than is his more youthful counterpart.

Marital and Family Problems

The statistics on marital status of the middle aged (the majority are married) suggest that in at least one respect, domestic life, the age category is free of problems. But beneath this statistical façade of marital stability lies the crisis period for husband-wife harmony that allegedly occurs in the late forties and early fifties for women and in the fifties for men. Perhaps, suggests Desmond, part of the explanation for the crisis that erupts in many middle-aged marriages is the fact that life at that time is "the period of the empty or emptying nest, when the children one has fed, dressed, scolded, advised, and cajoled fly from home." [11] Boredom develops when the children leave home and the middle-aged couple are suddenly left facing each other alone for the first time since early marriage.

Another source of middle-aged tensions in the family is in the parents' relations with their grownup children, taking the form of "moral blackmail." One frequent image in American life is that of the unmarried daughter "withering on the vine" because her mother will not be left alone, and another is that of the son who remains a bachelor because his mother will not "let go."

Problems of middle age are particularly intense in the case of widowhood.[12] In the United States, almost 7 million women are widows, and they average fifty-one years of age with nearly 6 million over thirty-five. In a society in which the sex ratio is increasingly female, for the reasons discussed in Chapter 2, remarriage is only a slim possibility for most women, particularly after forty-five years of age. Only one third of American widows are in the labor force, and the majority of these are in service occupations, factory, and sales work. Aside from the problems of self-support, widowhood in middle age is believed to encourage personality traits of self-pity and martyrdom. Furthermore, many of the widow's problems are shared by 2.5 million spinsters and half a million divorcees of the same age, and by middle-aged women whose

[11] Desmond, *op. cit.,* p. 42.
[12] Popkin, *op. cit.,* pp. 69–72.

husbands are living but whose children are adults and living independent lives.

Social Psychological Problems

There has been considerable speculation about the sociopsychological problems of middle age, more so about those in the middle classes than in others. Some of these problems have been suggested in the preceding section on marital and family problems. In addition, however, middle age has been characterized as "the period of acquisition, development of paunch, and cessation of mental growth. Our middle-aged work too feverishly, play too intensely, eat too abundantly. And tragically for the later years, our middle-aged constrict their mental exercises to the $64,000 question-type of television intellectuality. Our people, having adopted the values of adolescence, shrink from entering middle-age. We enter it begrudgingly, fearfully, sadly. For ours is a culture that worships at the temple of youth." [13]

There is the portrait of the middle-aged male as "an ulcer-coddling, tension-ridden, dollar-mad, sex-obsessed, culture-anemic individual too busy making a living to live," and the middle-aged female is often charged with being mainly concerned with such matters as "double chins, seven-day diets, her husband's waning ardor, her children's rebelliousness. . . ." [14] At most, these are caricatures of the middle classes' middle-aged, but most social stereotypes or caricatures, it should be stressed, generally have a hard kernel of truth.

The American youth cult leads to severe sociopsychological as well as economic repercussions in middle age. Wrinkles, gray hair, loss of teeth, and the changing contours of the body are viewed by many Americans in mid-life as rebukes and blows to the ego. One interesting hypothesis relates the economic problems of middle age to these sociopsychological problems by suggesting that middle-aged moodiness and irritability find expression in job dissatisfaction and job mobility.

Popkin goes so far as to assert that the largest part of the problem of middle age common to both sexes is the rising sense of defeat and frustration, of failure to reach life's unattainable goals. Accompanying this dilemma of desire versus repressions, there is in middle age a concern for the meaning of life, guilt feelings over what has and has not

[13] *New Channels for the Golden Years,* New York State Joint Legislative Committee on Problems of the Aging (Legislative Document No. 33, 1956), p. 14.
[14] Desmond, *op. cit.,* pp. 42–43.

been accomplished, and terror of growing old and dying. "It is no mere triumph of dramaturgy that men weep at 'Death of a Salesman.' Hardest to accept of all of the facts of life is that we won't be young forever and that the time to make good is running out." [15]

Health Problems

What are the health problems of middle age? Granted there is a loss of power, speed, and glamor and these may affect the middle-aged person's ego and mental health. But we also need to know how and to what extent he or she maintains equilibrium confronting the growing possibility at that period of life of affliction by degenerative diseases. Cancer ranks second only to heart disease as a cause of death in the age range forty-five to sixty-four. Annually there are more than 90,000 cancer deaths among the middle-aged population of the United States, accounting for one fourth of their total mortality, and the present estimate is that one out of every eight persons reaching age forty-five will develop cancer by age sixty-five.[16]

There is already some evidence from research that middle-aged men have more psychosomatic symptoms than do younger men. Brozek's use of a psychosomatic inventory on a sample of middle-class midwestern subjects showed the middle-aged respondents complaining more frequently of aches and pains, itching of the skin, and constipation than did younger respondents. Furthermore, the middle-aged demonstrated greater tension, were more readily hurt by criticism, and were more easily moved to tears. Finally, he found that the middle-aged were more likely to feel angry, but to keep their trouble and personal problems to themselves more often than did the younger subjects.[17]

There is reason to believe that the extent of mental illness in middle age exceeds that of all age groups except old age. Two thirds of first admissions to mental hospitals in the United States are of persons beyond thirty-five, and foremost among the diagnoses of these cases is the involutional psychosis, popularly termed "change of life melancholia." An affliction preponderantly although not entirely of women, it is said to originate in what some psychiatrists call the "narcissistic injury" associated with menopause and the other less dramatic but important traumas of middle age, such as surgery on the uterus or breasts,

[15] Popkin, *op. cit.*, p. 71.
[16] Metropolitan Life Insurance Company, *op. cit.*, pp. 1–2.
[17] Brozek, *op. cit.*, pp. 410–18.

or major dental work. A comparable type of severe mental trauma among middle-aged men may follow surgery on the prostate gland or the genitals.

How frequently these mental conditions occur is not known, but psychiatrists give higher estimates today than they did in earlier years. It is also believed that middle-aged people who retain interpersonal associations and are active in a variety of ways are less prone to such illnesses, but there has been little systematic research as yet to support this.[18] Similarly, it is a hypothesis held by some researchers in mental health that, for middle-aged individuals who have not achieved the goals they had set for themselves and who are having to realize that some of their aspirations must change, those who can accept this fact realistically and come to terms with the reality of the situation will show less mental disturbance than those who have more difficulty in adapting to the reality of their situation.[19]

Research Hypotheses on Middle Age

This chapter's picture of middle-age demography and of the problems of mid-life suggests a number of hypotheses as bases of new, intensive research in gerontology. Some "educated guesses" by which we may conclude this discussion of the still largely uncharted and unknown period of middle age are as follows:

1. A philosophy that sees life at all stages as a continuum in which one gives up some things and gains others serves as a deterrent against middle-age morbidity.

2. A philosophy that views life as a steadily declining path is conducive to middle-age morbidity.

3. The greater the versatility of activity and social relations, the lesser is the extent of morbidity in middle age.

4. The smaller the disparity between aspiration and achievement in one's life, the lesser is the extent of middle-age morbidity.

[18] Lawrence F. Greenleigh, *Changing Psychological Concepts of Aging* (Washington, D.C., U.S. Department of Health, Education, and Welfare, 1953), pp. 44–45.

[19] An interesting observation related to this idea is that "the main problem which is keeping management's psychiatrists busy at the moment is that of the middle-aged executive who hasn't gotten to the top and has come to feel that he is a failure." See *The Nation* (Oct. 6, 1956), p. 279.

5. Morbidity in middle age is a function of personality rigidity and of the ideal of a youthful self-image.

Questions and Research Exercises

1. Explain what is meant by the following: "Most of the scanty, scientific knowledge about middle-age is the by-product of research designed primarily for other purposes."
2. Design a small-scale survey which attempts to show how chronological definitions of middle age vary with the chronological age of the subjects. Administer the questions and tabulate the findings.
3. Name two of the most frequent chronological spans of middle age.
4. Why is retirement a good index of the end of middle age?
5. In your own words, explain the phrase: "Too old to work and too young to retire."
6. Discuss the importance and significance of widowhood in middle age.

Selected Readings

Crow, Lester D., and Crow, Alice, *Eighteen to Eighty: Adjustment Problems of Adults* (Boston, Christopher Publishing Co., 1949). For popular consumption, but a rare coverage of much of the life-cycle, including middle age.

Gardner, L. P., "Attitudes and Activities of the Middle-Aged and Aged," *Geriatrics* (Vol. 4, Jan.–Feb. 1949), pp. 33–50. The two age categories of gerontology compared.

Gravatt, Arthur E., "Family Relations in Middle and Old Age: A Review," *Journal of Gerontology* (Vol. 8, April 1953), pp. 197–201. Most useful for collating the literature on family and aging.

Kahn, Eugene, and Simmons, Leo W., "Problems of Middle Age," *The Yale Review* (Vol. 29, Winter 1940), pp. 349–63. A pioneering theoretical analysis and still useful.

Smithline, Jacob, "Middle Life and Old Age," *Medical Record* (Vol. 158, 1945), pp. 407–11. A medical comparison of middle and old age.

Stieglitz, Edward J., *The Second Forty Years* (Philadelphia, J. B. Lippincott Co., 1946). The medical emphasis, but rightfully begins with middle age in gerontology and geriatrics.

10:

EMPLOYMENT PRACTICES FOR
OLDER WORKERS

One of the stories of employment service success in counselling and placing older workers is the story of John Fisher. Mr. Fisher first applied to the Employment Service in July 1948. He was a graduate of a college in Texas, was married and had a teenage daughter. His previous work experience had been in teaching and in social group work in Texas. In 1948 he had been in New York for ten years. He had found it impossible to continue his professional work because New York City employers in education and social work fields were requiring graduate study which he did not have. He therefore sought and found employment as a general clerical worker with some typing.

He first came to the Employment Service in 1948, seeking employment in general clerical work. The Employment Service explored the possibilities of helping Mr. Fisher obtain employment in some professional capacity but was unsuccessful in this for the same reason Mr. Fisher himself had been unsuccessful. Therefore, at that time the Employment Service regarded Mr. Fisher's problem as a straight placement problem. He knew what kind of work he wanted; he had experience in the occupation in which he was seeking work and a job was found for him. It was a temporary job.

During the next eighteen months, Mr. Fisher had a series of jobs—some of which the Employment Service helped him get—some of which he got on his own. He did very well on all of these jobs, but they were only temporary. Later on, Mr. Fisher undertook free-lance commercial art work and continued to report to the Employment Service for part-time work to supplement his earnings from his business.

This went on for some time until September 18, 1950, when an employment service counsellor, reviewing the record, questioned if it was the best plan for Mr. Fisher to continue as he had for the past two years or whether some more permanent and stable job solution was not possible. The counsellor decided to talk to Mr. Fisher about this when he next came to the office.

Later the chief counsellor reported: "Four days after the interview, we were able to call Mr. Fisher. It was a full-time, permanent opening with a banking organization to work in a mailroom. The job called for intelligence and dependability, clerical experience and a knowledge of typing. We referred Mr. Fisher. Two days later, the counsellor called to learn if Mr. Fisher had been hired. At first the personnel man didn't recollect his name. Then he said 'Oh yes, Mr. Fisher—we had not intended to take him.' At this instance the counsellor couldn't resist a final effort: 'You know he had excellent references from his former employers and he is also a thoroughly likeable person to have around. Won't you reconsider the decision?' Well he would—and Mr. Fisher was hired!

He has worked in the mail-room now for more than 14 months. He is well liked by his employers and he is enthusiastic about his job; he has been given increased responsibilities and a substantial increase in pay.*

What Is Now Being Done to Meet the Problem of Older Workers

This chapter is concerned with the workers who usually, after the age of forty-five, begin to encounter employment difficulties either in obtaining new jobs or retaining old ones because of chronological age. Confining ourselves to middle age and not to the problems of retirement after sixty-five, the "older worker" here is within the age range from forty-five to sixty-four.

A growing realization of the extent and seriousness of the problem of the older worker has led in recent years to many constructive efforts by management, trade union organizations, and private welfare groups.

* Jean Wallace Carey, "A New Way to Tell an Age-Old Story of Old Age," in *Age Is No Barrier*, New York State Joint Legislative Committee on Problems of the Aging (Legislative Document No. 35, 1952), pp. 112–14.

While these efforts are far from adequate either in substance or in coverage, they are important as marking the path of progress in this basic area of industrial and social relations. It is impossible, of course, to describe here the policies, procedures and practices now in operation in all their functional variety and human effectiveness. All that can be done is to give a brief and general summary in order to convey the character of the present trend and to serve as a point of departure for future action. We present the main facts separately for the several industrial and social groups.

Management Policies

From the management point of view, the retention of the older worker presents a problem when he becomes unable to perform effectively in the particular job he has been doing, though continuing to be potentially productive. When this happens, management is faced with two broad alternatives: it can retain the worker and either change his job content or transfer him to another job which better fits his capacities; or failing this, it can assist him in finding suitable employment elsewhere.

Many firms follow the practice of retaining older workers. To do so in a manner that maintains efficiency of operations and desired costs of production, firms make use of the following procedures:

1. Assignment of older workers to lighter or less demanding work.

2. Transfers of employees to new jobs on the basis of medical and psychological examination.

3. Job analysis to determine which jobs can best be performed by older workers.

4. Establishment of objective criteria for determining retention in the same job or reassignment to a new job.

5. Adjustment of compensation in the same job in accordance with reduced productivity of the worker owing to age.

6. Change in the amount of compensation of the worker dependent on reassignment.

7. Arrangement with labor unions, when negotiating contracts, for provisions in the contract that would allow the employing firm to adopt and apply the above practices.

8. Establishment of in-service training programs that prepare workers for new jobs.

The policies and procedures enumerated above have created many problems for management. The practice of reassignment, for instance, requires more objective knowledge than is now available about the physical and psychological demands of each job and about the corresponding abilities of the older workers. There seems to be no practical set of criteria that can be used in individual companies to determine at what point each worker in each job should either be transferred to more suitable work or have his present job redesigned, and at what point he should be retired. Currently, many individual employers are grappling with this vital problem.

For any employer whose employees are unionized, a program aimed at adjusting work assignments of older workers depends heavily upon a cooperative attitude by the union leadership. The labor unions are far from eager to approve generally the practice of reassignment, especially if it involves a lowering of compensation, since they tend to regard it as a "down-grading" of the worker not only in earnings but also in social status. However, where good will between management and unions prevails and sincere efforts are made to overcome obstacles, e.g., with regard to union rules or transfer, seniority, etc., the results have been positive. In fact, the very attempts to deal with these difficulties, to refine medical and psychological tests, to establish objective standards for measurements of output, attendance, promptness, morale, errors, and spoilage, and to analyze the relation of the age factor to the realization of these standards, are proving to be the most practical and promising way of developing more definite methods and techniques for dealing with the problem of the retention of the older worker.

Insofar as the hiring of older job seekers is concerned, the growing shortage in recent years of skilled workers in many occupations and in many geographic areas has tended to stimulate an increasing number of employers to turn their attention to the feasibility of removing (or at least liberalizing) existing age barriers in their hiring policies. In New York City, a survey conducted in 1956 by the Commerce and Industry Association showed that of 318 employers, 124 (or 39 per cent) are easing their previous age requirements in hiring office personnel. In January 1957, this Association received requests from over 200 New York City employers for opportunities to interview "plus-40" job seekers for a large variety of occupations. It should also be noted that the liberalization of rules concerning both retention and hiring of older workers is encouraged by employers through their collective agreements with trade unions as is shown in the section of the chapter that follows.

Employers who have begun hiring older workers have generally reported a very satisfactory experience. It may be expected that as more facts emerge establishing the essential soundness of hiring older workers, and as management-union agreements devise practical ways of achieving them, arrangements for lowering existing barriers to their employment will become more general.

Trade Union Rules and Practices

In general, trade unions lay great stress on job security for their members and on the application of reasonable rules in hiring and firing employees.

While they have developed few policies explicitly concerned with the older worker, their general drive to increase job security and to improve working conditions has also benefited the older worker. In practice, the unions have shown the greatest interest in the retention of older workers in existing jobs, though they are aware of and interested in all aspects of the problem of employing older persons.

Trade union policies are reflected in their collective agreements with employers and in the administration of their own rules. An examination of current provisions of collective bargaining contracts and union rules with regard to the employment of older workers shows that they may be classified into three categories:

1. Provisions and rules that affect the employment of older workers *indirectly*.
2. Provisions and rules for the *retention* of older workers in employment.
3. Provisions and rules encouraging the *hiring* of older workers.

The equitable application of these provisions is a major objective of the grievance and arbitration machinery that unions and managements have set up in most industries and in business. While the living experience of such grievance adjustments is more interesting, it is too complex and varied to be dealt with in this chapter. All that can be done here is to summarize the three sets of rules referred to above.

1. INDIRECT RULES. The important rules affecting indirectly the employment of older workers are those relating to hours of work and

to fringe benefits. The adoption of the five-day work week with the two-day week end, paid vacations and paid holidays, work breaks, and the deterrent effects of premium pay requirements for overtime and holiday work, all help to reduce fatigue and otherwise to extend the working years for older workers. The fringe benefit programs, especially those providing for health service, promote indirectly the capacity of older workers to perform satisfactorily on their jobs for a longer period of time.

2. PROVISIONS FOR THE RETENTION OF OLDER WORKERS. According to research conducted by the United States Department of Labor, it is a common practice in collective bargaining agreements to provide greater job security and more liberal benefits to workers of longer service. Insofar as there is a relationship between age and length of service, this means that the older worker can benefit by seniority provisions giving him greater privileges in the matter of layoffs and rehiring, and also in such matters as transfers, promotions, choice of work shifts, and length of paid vacations. Some of the specific provisions are as follows:

1. The age alone of an experienced employee shall have no bearing on his qualifications as to continued employment. The company shall not discharge, transfer, or demote any employee on account of age.

2. Employees who have given long and faithful service and who become unable to handle the work at which they have been regularly employed shall be given preference on lighter work that they are able to perform.

3. Preference should be given to workers on the basis of length of service in the choice of work shift. This favors the retention of older workers because the shift selected may be more in keeping with the capacities or more conducive to maintaining the health of older workers.

4. Unions and managements may work out on an individual basis special arrangements for older workers which include adjustments in rates of pay as well as in seniority status. Such arrangements facilitate their transfer to jobs more suited to their capacities.

3. PROVISIONS RELATING TO THE HIRING OF OLDER WORKERS. Some union-management collective agreements, according to research findings, contain clauses that encourage or require hiring of older work-

ers. These clauses take many different forms. The more important of these are:

1. A general statement banning hiring age limits or discrimination because of age. The company agrees that there shall be no established maximum age limit in the hiring of employees.

2. Permission to hire older job seekers at special wage rates under certain circumstances.

3. Requirements to employ one older worker for a specified number of journeymen employed. Such rules are common in the building trades. For example, in three agreements covering electricians, carpenters, and painters, respectively, the requirements are that: (*a*) On all jobs employing five or more journeymen, if available, every fifth journeyman shall be fifty years of age or older; (*b*) Where there is a job employing 15 members of the organizations, there must be one member over the age of sixty years; (*c*) An employer employing ten or more journeymen shall take in his employ at least one journeyman of sixty years of age for every ten men in his employ, who shall receive the prevailing rate of wages set forth in the agreement.

4. Under some agreements, managements give preference in the selection of employees to applicants referred by the union. To that extent, unions, especially those which maintain employment offices, can influence the hiring of workers, including older workers.

It should be noted that the degree varies to which the above rules and provisions are applied in practice. On the other hand, the absence of such provisions in collective agreements does not mean that there may not be satisfactory informal arrangements in the plant, which aim to give job protection to the older worker.

On the whole, it is clear from available data that provisions for the retention and hiring of older workers have not as yet gained a prominent place in collective bargaining. A study by the United States Bureau of Labor Statistics [1] analyzed 1,687 major wage agreements covering seven and a half million workers. Of these collective bargaining contracts, only 212 contained provisions about older workers' retention rights, and only 76 included clauses encouraging or requiring the hiring of older workers. As the older workers increase in numbers and as their employment problems become more insistent, the limitations of existing

[1] See Bureau of Labor Statistics Bulletin 1199, Part I, Aug. 1956.

provisions both in content and in coverage will become an increasingly serious issue for both unions and management in collective bargaining proceedings.

Federal Government Activities

The increasing concern of the federal government with problems of the older worker is evidenced in its many studies on the subject. The central aim of these studies is to bring facts to bear on the discussion of the reasons given against the employment of older workers. Thus, pilot studies have been made by the federal government on productivity, absenteeism, accident rates, and labor turnover by age groups; collective bargaining agreements covering seven and a half million workers have been analyzed to ascertain the effect of provisions in these agreements on the hiring and retention of older workers; employer practices and policies affecting the utilization of older workers in seven major metropolitan areas have been studied; demonstration projects have been carried out on methods, time, and cost of counseling and placement of older workers in the same seven metropolitan areas and in New York. In addition to these and other studies, the federal government has provided funds, on a limited scale, to state employment services for counseling and placement service to job applicants over forty-five years of age. In August 1956, Secretary of Labor James P. Mitchell announced that he was making $449,500 available for that purpose to state employment security agencies.

New York State Government Activities

1. JOINT LEGISLATIVE COMMITTEE ON PROBLEMS OF THE AGING. For more than ten years, New York State has had a Joint Legislative Committee on Problems of the Aging, Senator Thomas C. Desmond, Chairman, which has been holding annual public hearings and publishing the reports of these hearings. The Committee has also published many studies on employment, unemployment, and productivity of older workers. Among its other activities, the Committee has sponsored legislation to provide funds to the public Employment Service for personnel to serve unemployed older workers. In the 1956 Legislature, the Committee sponsored legislation to provide funds to private nonprofit agencies for special service to older workers.

2. THE GOVERNOR'S OFFICE.   Shortly after he took office, Governor Harriman appointed Philip M. Kaiser, formerly Assistant Secretary of

Labor, as a Special Assistant on Problems of the Aging to work with the Governor's Interdepartmental Committee. In October 1955, the Committee convened a three-day conference on problems of the aging, at which one special work group devoted itself exclusively to employment questions. The major recommendations of this group were: (*a*) to collate all available data on employment practices affecting older workers; (*b*) to stimulate the interest of employers and communities throughout the state in hiring older workers; (*c*) to promote the establishment of proper training and retraining facilities for workers.

3. STATE LABOR DEPARTMENT. The New York State Department of Labor has long been concerned with the problem of the older worker. Its Division of Research and Statistics has made and published a large number of studies on the subject. Its Division of Employment was the first public employment service in the country to establish special counseling and placement service for unemployed older workers.

The New York State Employment Service now has a total of 38 older worker counselors assigned to and working with those older workers who need special help in finding reëmployment. These 38 counselors are assigned to 25 offices in the state, and they work with an average of 4,000 individuals a month, averaging 400 to 500 placements a month.

In New York City, the offices of the State Department of Labor make a monthly average of 15,000 placements of persons over forty-five years of age, and the distribution by occupational and skill level runs about the same. For example, in the month of October 1956, which can be considered typical, the New York City offices of the State Labor Department made 18,072 placements of persons over forty-five. Of these placements, 823 were in professional and managerial jobs; 1,415 in clerical and sales jobs; 7,713 in service jobs; 1,871 in skilled jobs; 5,755 in semiskilled jobs, and 495 in unskilled jobs.

New York City Public and Voluntary Organizations

1. COMMUNITY COUNCIL OF GREATER NEW YORK. For more than 30 years the Community Council of Greater New York (formerly the Welfare and Health Council of New York City) has spearheaded activities to alert the community to the growing needs of the rapidly increasing number of older persons in New York City and in urging the establishment of services designed to maintain their health, dignity, and productivity. It made numerous studies and reports identifying specific problems and recommended action for their solution, pioneered recrea-

HA 1066 . 05 46

9750.9950566

EDISON
Phonograph

EXACT REPRODUCTION
By
Wendell Moore

First Edition
July 1979

MISSION OAK FINISH (CLOSED)

tional programs for the aged, sparked the organization of Day Centers, was instrumental in the creation of Goldwater Hospital, and established the Elder Craftsmen Shop and the Hobby Show for Older Persons.

2. MAYOR'S ADVISORY COMMITTEE FOR THE AGED. In New York City, the Mayor's Advisory Committee for the Aged has concerned itself with employment as well as other problems of the aged. In 1953 this Committee published a comprehensive report on New York's Senior Citizens, which included much valuable material on the problems of the unemployed older workers. Each year the Committee also sponsors New York City's participation in Senior Citizens Month held under the general auspices of the New York State Joint Legislative Committee on Problems of the Aging.

3. FEDERATION EMPLOYMENT AND GUIDANCE SERVICE. An affiliate of the Federation of Jewish Philanthropies of New York, the Federation Employment and Guidance Service has been for many years interested in the job-finding problems of older workers. Its activities in this area include the establishment of Job-Finding Clubs for Older Workers, a program of vocational counseling and testing of mature women long absent from the labor market, and a study of the job performance of a group of older workers it had placed. Currently it is conducting an operation study financed by a state grant to determine the problems and skills required to place older workers.

4. COMMERCE AND INDUSTRY ASSOCIATION OF NEW YORK, INC. This organization has been active in clarifying the employment problems of older workers. Through its circular letter, it has alerted its members to the availability, desirability, and feasibility of employing older workers; it has presented statements on this subject at public hearings of the State Joint Legislative Committee on Problems of the Aging; it has supported legislation for expanding job counseling service for older workers, and for establishing pilot projects in counseling and placement of older workers to be undertaken by nonprofit placement agencies.

While the work done by various agencies, both public and private, has been important and helpful, further action could profitably be taken by them. There is need to expand research on worker productivity, on the effects of aging on job performance, and on the effects of certain personnel policies and practices on the hiring of older workers. Public and private agencies are also in need of funds for counseling, special placement service, training and retraining of older workers. It is estimated, for example, that at the present time in New York City the pub-

lic and private agencies combined can give counseling and special placement service to less than half of the unemployed workers over forty-five
who need such service. Yet repeated studies have indicated that such
a worker's chance of securing employment is doubled if he can receive
such special service.

Guiding Principles for Further Action

The lines along which further action is needed take form from
what has been said above. Purposeful action should be more effective,
however, when guided not only by empirical understanding of the problem but by general principles that express the moral and social value of
the action contemplated. The starting point for a statement of principles is the general idea that age discrimination in employment is
destructive of the dignity of the individual, a drain on our socioeconomic system, and a waste of human material. In *A Bill of Objectives
for Older People,* which it proposed, the Council of State Governments
formulated the general idea as "equal opportunity to work." According
to this statement, our society recognizes the value of work to the person and to the community. The older person should have equal opportunity, if physically and mentally able, to be gainfully employed.

The general idea stated above may be translated into the following
guiding principles for action:

1. Each person has the responsibility, as a right and a duty, to make
whatever contribution he is able toward his own support and that of his
family during his effective working life, including the later years, and
should have the appropriate opportunity to do so.

2. All persons able to meet job requirements and willing to work
steadily should not be deprived of the opportunity to work because of
age, either by employer or union restrictions.

3. Each person should be considered as an individual with respect
to employment, to be hired or fired in accordance with his or her skill,
experience, knowledge, and physical capacity. We must not create
classes based on age.

4. All employers should make the greatest possible effort to provide job adjustments (through transfer or otherwise) and job changes
to enable them to retain and hire older workers.

5. Labor and management should formulate and interpret their

collective agreements so as to facilitate the hiring and retention of older workers.

Operative Recommendations

The principles presented above can become a vital force in our industrial life only if they are embodied in operative policies and procedures. To develop appropriate methods of implementing these principles is primarily the task of those concerned with the problem of the older worker in a direct and practical way, namely, employers, organized labor, government, and social welfare agencies.

No attempt can be made here to spell out in detail how the task of implementation should be carried out. But some specific recommendations are in order here as a means of indicating the scope and direction of the task. With such purpose in view, we can suggest the following lines of action:

1. More job counseling facilities, specifically directed at the employment problems of older workers, should be established in business, industry, labor unions, voluntary counseling agencies, and government.

2. Job analysis and classification as well as in-service training procedures should be developed to fit older workers into jobs appropriate to their capabilities.

3. Relaxing age restrictions is not enough. Office and plant managements and personnel directors should review the job descriptions and requirements to determine whether improved methods or equipment have changed requirements to the extent that older workers can qualify.

4. Every device now available should be used by employers to the extent possible to distinguish between functional and chronological age.

5. To convince themselves of the validity of hiring older workers, employers should compare their older and younger workers with regard to production, spoilage, absenteeism, and turnover, as well as investigate comparative costs of insurance, workmen's compensation, and other fringe benefits.

6. Systematic research into specific problems connected with the employment of older workers should be made by qualified and objective agencies, based on grants from public and private sources.

7. Broad educational campaigns should be organized to bring home to management, labor, and the public the latest scientific data on

what older workers can and cannot do, as well as how and to what extent the economy as a whole is weakened by arbitrary age limits.

In the last analysis, the problem of the older worker can best be solved by the two groups directly concerned: management and labor. But government and the community have an important role to play in creating the climate of opinion and the social attitudes favorable to rational and constructive action.

Questions and Research Exercises

1. Discuss the procedures used by management in retaining an older worker who is no longer able to perform his particular job effectively.
2. What are the "indirect" rules and provisions appearing in collective bargaining contracts and union agreements that affect the employment of older workers?
3. Discuss the more important provisions in union-management collective agreements that encourage or require the hiring of older workers.
4. What is the role of an employment counselor in dealing with the problems of older workers? Interview one within your district in order to determine the answer.
5. Spell out in detail what is involved in the general principle of "equal opportunity to work."
6. If you were an employer, what devices would you be able to use in order to distinguish between functional and chronological age among your older employees?

Selected Readings

Abrams, Albert J., "Barriers to the Employment of Older Workers," *The Annals of the American Academy of Political and Social Science* (Vol. 279, January 1952), pp. 62–71. An authoritative analysis of obstacles to employment by the director of the New York State Joint Legislative Committee on Problems of the Aging.

Bancroft, Gertrude, "Older Persons in the Labor Force," *The Annals of the American Academy of Political and Social Science* (Vol. 279, January 1952), pp. 52–61. Statistical changes by a government expert on labor force demography.

Barkin, Solomon, "Jobs for Older Workers," *Journal of Gerontology* (Vol. 7, July 1952), pp. 426–30. A penetrating analysis of obstacles and opportunities in employment for older workers by the director of research, Textile Workers Union of America.

Breckinridge, Elizabeth, *Effective Use of Older Workers* (Chicago, Wilcox & Follett Co., 1953). Survey findings of practices in the employment of older workers in American business and industry.

Clague, Ewan, "Labor Force Trends in the United States," *Journal of Gerontology* (Vol. 7, January 1952), pp. 92–99. A statistical analysis of labor force dynamics, including the older worker, by a statistical specialist in the Bureau of Labor Statistics.

Donahue, Wilma T., ed., *Earning Opportunities for Older Workers* (Ann Arbor, University of Michigan Press, 1955). A valuable symposium in the University of Michigan's annual series of gerontological studies.

I I :

RELIGION AND AGING ADJUSTMENT

For eleven years, and including all of World War II, I was in general practice. Since then, my practice has been limited entirely to the special field of physical medicine and rehabilitation. The general practice period represents an over-all approach to illness; the specialty offers experience in devastating, often sudden and catastrophic physical handicapping, and often affecting older persons. A very large percentage of my experience in this specialty has been with older people.

The general practice was done in my home town of Muncie, Indiana, a town of 50,000 and with less than one per cent foreign-born population, which had been chosen by the Lynds in 1925 for their sociological study of the typical American city. Their first report, *Middletown,* was followed by a second study in 1935, *Middletown in Transition.*

My parents and I had a wide acquaintance and mine broadened in active practice. Today, I still have a very wide acquaintanceship there, and a pretty general idea of the activities of my parents' friends who are still living, as well as of the community leaders of my generation. I make these introductory remarks, not to report a factual study but only to offer one basis of continuity in expressing my own opinions.

The remark has often been made that "people turn to religion as they get older." In my own personal experience, I have not been aware of this fact. Neither have I known people to "turn to religion" when they are seriously ill, the victims of catastrophic illness, or severely, even permanently, physically handicapped. I am inclined to think that the statement is an empirical one which should be evaluated with a true statistical study and with numerous samplings.*

* Nila Kirkpatrick Covalt, M.D., "The Meaning of Religion to Older People —The Medical Perspective," in Delton L. Scudder, ed., *Organized Religion and the Older Person* (Gainesville, University of Florida Press, 1958), pp. 78–79.

Man, the saying goes, does not live by bread alone. Adapting the idea implicit in this saying to our concern here with problems of aging suggests that employment is not the salvation of the middle and later years of life. It poses the possibility that religion too facilitates adjustment to aging.

The purpose of this chapter is to explore the relationship between religion and aging. It will be our task, first, to consider the *theory of religion and aging*. What are the alleged and ideal functions of religion in the lives of older people? What spiritual and secular needs in later life can religion meet? Second, we shall survey *religious programs and services* for the aged. How extensive are they and what do they seek to accomplish? Third, we shall look into research findings on *religiosity* in the attitudes and behavior patterns of aging people, including those in middle age. What religious ideas and feelings do they have, and to what extent do they participate in religious institutional life? Fourth, we shall utilize research findings in an attempt to measure the impact of religion in the *adjustment of aging people* to their personal and social situations. Last, the *shortcomings of organized religion* in the lives of older people will be examined and the *need for further research* into the question of religion and aging will be evaluated.

The Theory of Religion and Aging

In recent years many social scientists have vigorously developed an interest in the theoretical as well as the empirical aspects of religion in general. It is noteworthy, however, that religion's role in old age, with few exceptions, has escaped their attention. One sociologist has registered his surprise at this deficiency, for, as he put it, "phenomena associated with old age always have aroused the anxiety of man and thus created a special need for comfort and reassurance, which throughout the ages have come from the sources of religion." [1]

The reasons for this neglect of the relationship between religion and aging are not entirely clear, but it is likely that part of the answer is to be found in the youth-centered focus of social science. Yet anthropology suggests a striking rationale for the study of religion in association with the study of aging. In his cross-cultural survey of the aged

[1] Otto Pollak, *Social Adjustment in Old Age: A Research Planning Report* (New York, Social Science Research Council, Bulletin No. 59, 1948), p. 161.

in "primitive" societies, Simmons observed that it is more than mere coincidence that the attributes of old age have been ascribed to the deities as well as glorified in primitive mythology. Primitive gods are frequently described as old, wise, and powerful, never senile. One may say, then, claims Simmons, that the aged in primitive societies created gods in their own image. Indeed, even in Western societies, one may go so far as to say that the image of the deity is usually not only anthropomorphic, but, in fact, "gerontomorphic"! [2]

The alleged or ideal functions of religion in the lives of older people are suggested by the scriptural reference: "Cast me not off in the time of old age; when my strength faileth, forsake me not." [3] Religion's gerontological task is essentially fourfold:

1. To help face impending death.
2. To help find and maintain a sense of meaningfulness and significance in life.
3. To help accept the inevitable losses of old age.
4. To help discover and utilize the compensatory values that are potential in old age.

1. TO FACE IMPENDING DEATH.   "We might say," Pollak explains, "that every aged person is in a fox hole, and we might expect that older people would show increased needs for religious experience. The anxiety caused by the thought of approaching death seems to be related to various motives. First of all, the desire to live and to continue living is apparent in most individuals regardless of age. Furthermore, religious teaching concerning punishment and rewards after death may have created a considerable amount of anxiety in the minds of many regarding the afterlife. Finally, there may be concern over the fate of dependents who would be left without support." [4]

2. TO FIND MEANINGFULNESS IN LIFE.   "No matter how well the older person's physical needs are met," claims Frakes, "unless he senses a reason for existing, unless he calls on a source of strength to help him see his life as a whole and his relationships to those about him in an

---

[2] Leo W. Simmons, *The Role of the Aged in Primitive Society* (New Haven, Yale University Press, 1945), *passim*.

[3] Psalm 71:9.

[4] Pollak, *op. cit.*, pp. 161–63.

unselfish light, his evening is likely to be a time of unhappiness and fear rather than of fulfillment." [5]

3. TO ACCEPT THE INEVITABLE LOSSES OF OLD AGE. Frakes also points out that "many old people, plagued by fears of rejection or beset by infirmities, withdraw from the church just when they need its ministrations most. Others who have had little contact with the church in their active years need to find their way again to its doors, yet hesitate to do so. Still others, unchurched, wait outside lacking access to the spiritual solace it has to offer." [6]

4. TO DISCOVER COMPENSATORY VALUES. Cicero recognized this when he wrote in *De Senectute:* "Those who have no resource within themselves to live a good and happy life find every period of life burdensome, but those who seek their blessings within themselves regard nothing as evil that the necessity of nature brings." And in answer to the question: "But are there not old men who are churlish and fearful and irascible and hard to get along with?" Cicero replied, "Of course, but these are defects of character, not of old age."

That there are special spiritual needs in the case of older people has long been the conviction of religious educators.[7] For instance, the belief among some Protestant sects in the supreme worth of human beings created in the image of God, and the belief in God as the Creator, Preserver, Redeemer and Sanctifier of life have provided the basis for the following formulation of spiritual needs in old age: (*a*) assurance of God's continuing love; (*b*) the certainty that life is protected; (*c*) relief from heightened emotions (especially guilt, grief, fear); (*d*) relief from the pangs of loneliness; (*e*) a perspective for life that embraces time and eternity; (*f*) continuing spiritual growth through new experience; (*g*) a satisfying status in life as a person; and (*h*) a feeling of continuing usefulness.

There are, in addition, secular needs that religion can help meet, stress some theorists. Alongside its unique responsibility to give its older members "spiritual undergirding," organized religion can help

[5] Margaret Frakes, "Older People Confront the Churches," *The Christian Century* (Fall 1955), p. 5. Reprint of the series of eight articles.

[6] *Ibid.,* p. 6.

[7] See, for example, Federal Security Agency, *Man and His Years* (Raleigh, N.C., Health Publications Institute, Inc., 1951), pp. 207–10; also *The Fulfillment Years in Christian Education* (Chicago, National Council of the Churches of Christ, 1953), p. 5.

modify the negative attitudes in the community toward the aged, inspire secular efforts in their behalf, and help determine the means and goals of those efforts.[8] It can provide companionship, give a sense of usefulness that may have been lost elsewhere, and help the individual retain a feeling of self-respect. Indeed, assistance to the aged through housing and economic support has been a traditional secular function of all the major branches of organized religion in the Western world.[9]

It would be a mistake to assume, however, that all theoretical signs point to a natural relationship between religion and aging, thereby minimizing the role of religion in relationship to other age groups. Orbach, for example, taking serious exception to the proposition that religion goes along with the aging process, argues as follows:

> Sociologically there are good grounds for casting doubt on such a view. In the first place, religion as one of the dominant institutional forms of historical society has performed diverse functions in the organization of societies ranging from almost complete dominance of all aspects of social, cultural, and economic life to rather subsidiary functions. It would seem that its appeal and attachment to different age groups would consequently depend upon the nature of these functions. Secondly, the organization of religious bodies historically has involved a rather complete set of social roles and relationships for all age groups. Within the organizational structure it would appear that a central concern of all religions has been upon the proper socialization of the young and maturing members of a given society since the future of any institution lies with the young.

> The history of the world's great religions reveals that their charismatic founders have been almost without exception young, and that the control of religions has passed into the hands of the elderly through the processes of routinization and bureaucratization as institutions arose to replace the loose associations of leader and followers. Perhaps one source of the conception of the aged as religiously inclined also derives from an easy identification of an entire age stratum with the prominence of some of its members in positions of institutional authority.

> Furthermore, systematic study of the phenomena of religious conversion has shown that the most intense periods of religious feeling and concern culminating in intense preoccupation with religious belief and religious conversion are associated with youth and adolescence. This is consistent with other experimental studies showing the period of the teens as the time of most rapid religious development and change.[10]

[8] Frakes, *op. cit.*, p. 7.
[9] Pollak, *op. cit.*, p. 162.
[10] Harold L. Orbach, "Aging and Religion: Church Attendance in the Detroit

Religious Programs and Services for the Aged

Typical of so many other phases of American life, historically there has been a marked disparity between the aforementioned religious norms and precepts regarding older people and the actual programs and services geared to meet their needs. That is, theory and practice have seldom been contiguous. In the nineteenth century many American churches and synagogues narrowly confined their geriatric responsibilities to providing "homes" or sheltered care for those older members who had become isolated socially or indigent economically. However, by 1950 only a fraction more than 3 per cent of Americans over sixty-five years of age were living in institutions of all types, religious and otherwise. With the increase in pensions and public assistance funds, and the development of a variety of community services for older people, sheltered care has become obsolete except for the indigent and the physically infirm. The new concept is that the denominational home for the aged is merely one modest part of a battery of services, each specializing in function.

Today geriatric programs and services offered by organized religion include participation in rites and sacrament of worship, chaplaincy service for those too ill or infirm to attend public worship, pastoral counseling, social service, foster homes, friendly visiting, golden age clubs and social centers, and use of the pulpit as an educational medium.[11]

Some denominations have developed programs that are especially noteworthy. The Methodists have trained special directors for work with older adults. Their Church has arranged for regional workshops to demonstrate effective methods of leading older people in crafts and music, and it has also organized courses designed to help in planning local programs. In 1954 the Methodists began publication of the first journal in the field of religion and gerontology, *Mature Years,* a quarterly that has offered a variety of articles on aging and its problems. The Lu-

---

Metropolitan Area," a paper presented at the annual meeting of the Gerontological Society, Philadelphia, November 1958.

[11] See Geneva Mathiasen, *Role of Religion in the Lives of Older People* (New York, The National Committee on the Aging, 1955), pp. 3–8 (mimeographed); see also The Committee on Services to the Aging, *How to Serve Your Older Members* (Portland, Oregon, Community Council, June 1956), 6 pp.

therans have established centers for older people in some communities, offering opportunities for daily fellowship, craft activities, and a camping program. They have also prepared literature on church responsibility to the aged, set up visitation committees, organized casework agencies that provide counseling services, and initiated their own golden age clubs and foster homes. In some localities, Protestant churches are beginning to function interdenominationally, and through its Department of Welfare, the National Council of Churches offers a meeting ground where denominational leaders may consider cooperatively the problems of aging.[12]

Among Roman Catholics and Jews, the impact of growing numbers of aged people requiring services has not been ignored either, for even before the turn of the century, as Entman has recorded, there were homes for the aged in large urban centers populated by both religious groups.[13] The first Jewish home for the aged was founded in St. Louis in 1855. Before 1900 there were only 9 Jewish homes, but now there are 84 homes in the United States with over 11,000 beds available. And like the Protestants, Catholic and Jewish family agencies have created "aged" departments including foster home care supervised by trained personnel; hospitals have developed home medical services; recreation centers have established golden age clubs; and in the communities each denomination has developed resident clubs in housing for the aged.

Ostensibly vitalizing and professionalizing these religious programs and services are numerous conferences and publications. In 1950, the National Conference on the Aging convened for the first time representatives of all the approaches to the problems of aging, and for the first time at any gerontological conference a special section was devoted to religion's concern, alongside study and practice in such other fields as population, income, employment, health, education, housing, and recreation.

It suffices to observe that, no matter how extensive are religious programs, services, conferences, and publications, they are obviously no guarantee that the needs of older people will be met. Mathiasen wisely cautions that what programs the churches have for, with, and

[12] Frakes, *op. cit.,* pp. 7–10.
[13] Sidney Entman, "The Ministry of Organized Religion to the Jewish Aged— Its Philosophy and Practice," in Delton L. Scudder, ed., *Organized Religion and the Older Person* (Gainesville, University of Florida Press, 1958), pp. 34–42.

by older people seem less important than the understanding, first by the minister and then by his congregation, of both problems and potentialities of older years, and the dialectical relationship between them. When such understanding exists, a good program is likely to follow, and when it is absent, no program is likely to be very meaningful.[14] Others have gone as far as to acknowledge that of all community institutions, religious ones have the best record of service to older people. Yet there is much more that the church and synagogue might usefully do.[15]

Religiosity of Older People

One of the two crucial tests of the effectiveness of organized religion in meeting the needs of older people is their religiosity in attitude and behavior.[16] We need to know how much the inner and the overt lives of the aged are religiously oriented. Fortunately, we are able to go beyond conjecture to various research findings in order to answer many of the questions about religiosity and aging.

The over-all picture that research provides is that religion actually plays a smaller part in the lives of older people than theory leads one to assume. It will be recalled, for instance, that the nationwide survey of the urban aged discussed in Chapter 7 had a sample of 1,206 respondents, of whom almost two thirds were Protestant, one fourth Roman Catholic, and almost 5 per cent Jewish. This distribution was about the same as that of recent estimates of the religious affiliation of the American population as a whole. The survey revealed, among other things, that the Bible is a relatively insignificant part of the reading material of these older urban Americans. "What is it that you usually read?" the respondents were asked, and 1,021 replied they read newspapers, 601 read magazines, 299 read books other than the Bible, and 206 read the Bible. The Bible, we may conclude, is not only in last place among the various types of literature read by city-dwelling older Americans, but percentage-wise only 17 per cent admitted usually reading the Holy Scriptures.

[14] Mathiasen, *op. cit.*, pp. 2–3.
[15] Robert J. Havighurst and Ruth Albrecht, *Older People* (New York, Longmans, Green & Co., 1953), p. 205.
[16] The second test is the extent to which religiosity facilitates life adjustment to a degree significantly higher than does irreligiosity.

"Do you belong to any clubs or organizations in town, such as lodges, unions, church clubs, or card clubs?" they were also asked. The nationwide sample replied as follows:

636 No
1 No answer
569 Yes. What are they?
   a. 222 Lodge, fraternal
   b. 196 Church club
   c. 118 Union
   d. 93 Social (not fraternal)
   e. 55 Patriotic
   f. 35 Civic or service
   g. 30 Professional
   h. 21 No answer

Whereas these statistics show that a church club was the second most popular type of association among the urban aged, percentage-wise this actually involved only 16 per cent of the total sample. Probably more sensitive than either reading or associational membership as a measure of overt religiosity in old age is attendance at religious services. In fact here the nationwide study revealed a decidedly more active involvement by people sixty years of age and over. When asked: "How often during the past year did you attend religious services?" the answer was "every Sunday or Sabbath" in the case of 306; "most Sundays or Sabbaths" by 221; "occasionally" by 399; and "not at all" or no answer in the case of 280. In summary, at least occasional church or synagogue attendance is the experience of slightly more than three fourths of the urban aged throughout the country, judging from the nationwide survey. Attendance is apparently higher in the smaller communities than in the urban communities as a whole. The Prairie City Study found about the same proportion of those sixty-five years of age and over attend church at least occasionally as in the case of the nationwide study, but 61 per cent of the former were found to attend frequently as compared with only 43 per cent of the latter.[17]

As we have already indicated in the section on theory, it is widely assumed that, with increasing chronological age, religiosity increases. Yet one gerontologist claims that his research evidence is to the con-

[17] Havighurst and Albrecht, *op. cit.,* pp. 201–2.

trary: older people are actually no more religiously inclined than younger people.[18] There are considerable research-derived data elsewhere to support his findings. The nationwide survey, for example, learned that the modal or typical response to the question: "Do you attend services more or less often than when you were fifty?" was "The same." While 568 of the 1,206 respondents thus indicated no change in attendance at religious services, 356 replied "less often" and only 276 said "more often," with 11 failing to respond. The greater change in attendance, then, was in the direction of less rather than more attendance since age fifty. A more recent study of religion and aging in a Roman Catholic parish in St. Louis showed the same attendance pattern, even with respondents predominantly female rather than male as in the case of the nationwide study.[19] Still another confirmation in research that people do not necessarily "get religion" as they age came in Orbach's survey of about 7,000 adults in the Detroit metropolitan area. The number of persons in the survey who attended church once a week ranged from 43 to 49 per cent, according to Orbach, but showed no steady increase with age. Women in all age groups attended church more frequently than men. Among Protestants, only Negro men showed a persistent increase in church attendance with advancing age. Among Roman Catholics, church attendance among men declined with age, whereas among women it showed a steady level of attendance. The only group showing a trend toward increased religious attendance with advancing age for both men and women were the Jews.[20]

Undoubtedly the most extensive survey on religious behavior in the United States so far has been the study sponsored by the *Catholic Digest*. A national sample was taken by an independent polling organization, and religious observance was cross-tabulated with age in tenyear intervals from ages eighteen to twenty-four to sixty-five and over. The results showed no significant difference by age in the rates of regular weekly attendance.[21] Pertinent too is the fact that the study of religion by the Bureau of the Census in 1957 showed those over sixty-five years of age reporting 3.0 per cent with no religious affiliation com-

[18] H. Lee Jacobs, *Churches and Their Senior Citizens* (Iowa City, State University of Iowa Press, 1957), p. 2.

[19] *Older People in the Family, the Parish and the Neighborhood* (St. Louis, Catholic Charities of St. Louis, 1955), p. 35.

[20] Orbach, *op. cit.*, pp. 7–14.

[21] "Do Americans Go to Church?" *Catholic Digest* (Vol. 17, Dec. 1952), pp. 7–12.

pared to an average of 2.7 per cent for all ages. The lowest percentage reporting no religion was 2.1 for the fourteen to nineteen-year-old group, while those twenty to twenty-four years of age and those sixty-five and over reported the highest percentages. Although these differences were not statistically significant, they indicated a trend opposite to what is commonly assumed.[22]

The Social Research Laboratory of The City College of New York, in a survey of problems of middle age, secured data of a different order on this question of the alleged correlation of chronological age and religious attendance. With respondents who ranged in age from thirty to sixty-five and who were stratified by five-year intervals, it was possible to obtain cross-sectional data on religious attendance.

Table 10: *The Relation of Chronological Age
to Church and Synagogue Attendance*

(496 Cases, New York City, Spring 1957)
(Social Research Laboratory, The City College)

How often do you attend church or synagogue?

		30–35 *(133 cases)*		40–45 *(125 cases)*		50–55 *(122 cases)*		60–65 *(116 cases)*	
Total	*Answer*	*No.*	*%*	*No.*	*%*	*No.*	*%*	*No.*	*%*
130	Often	34	25.6	29	23.2	32	26.2	35	30.1
199	Sometimes	55	41.4	55	44.0	44	36.1	45	38.7
167	Hardly ever or never	44	33.0	41	32.8	46	37.7	36	31.2

Table 10, which relates chronological age to church or synagogue attendance, brings forth no significant differences in the distribution of attendance levels at religious services between the various age strata in New York City. The modal or typical pattern of attendance for all (except those fifty to fifty-five years of age) was occasional, with attendance avoidance ranking second, and frequent attendance the least popular pattern.

Nor were there any significant differences between the early and

[22] Bureau of the Census, "Religion Reported by the Civilian Population of the United States: March 1957," *Current Population Reports* (Series P-20, No. 79, Feb. 2, 1958).

later chronological age strata in the religiosity of their adjustment to trouble. According to Table 11, which relates chronological age to type of trouble adjustment, only 20 per cent of New York City respondents typically prayed to God for help when they were troubled, and hardly

Table 11: *The Relation of Chronological Age to Religious Adjustment to Trouble*

(496 Cases, New York City, Spring 1957)
(Social Research Laboratory, The City College)

When you are troubled about life and its meanings, what do you most often do?

Total	Answer	30–35 (*133 cases*)		40–45 (*125 cases*)		50–55 (*122 cases*)		60–65 (*116 cases*)	
		No.	%	No.	%	No.	%	No.	%
98	Pray to God for help	28	21.0	22	17.6	23	18.8	25	21.5
7	Talk it over with minister, priest, or rabbi	2	1.5	1	0.8	2	1.6	2	1.7

Table 12: *The Relation of Chronological Age to Religious Self-Image*

(496 Cases, New York City, Spring 1957)
(Social Research Laboratory, The City College)

Would you say you are a religious person, or doesn't religion mean very much to you?

Total	Answer	30–35 (*133 cases*)		40–45 (*125 cases*)		50–55 (*122 cases*)		60–65 (*116 cases*)	
		No.	%	No.	%	No.	%	No.	%
222	I'd say I am a religious person	50	37.5	52	41.5	56	45.9	64	55.1
125	Religion doesn't mean very much to me	31	23.3	37	29.7	34	27.8	23	19.9
149	Undecided	52	39.2	36	28.8	32	26.3	29	25.0

anyone talked his or her trouble over with his or her clergyman. In fact, the chronologically youngest (thirty to thirty-five years of age) had virtually identical trouble responses to God and their clergymen as did the chronologically oldest (sixty to sixty-five).

Table 13: *The Relation of Chronological Age
to Belief in Life after Death*

(496 Cases, New York City, Spring 1957)
(Social Research Laboratory, The City College)

Do you believe in a life after death (heaven)?

		30–35 (133 cases)		40–45 (125 cases)		50–55 (122 cases)		60–65 (116 cases)	
Total	*Answer*	*No.*	*%*	*No.*	*%*	*No.*	*%*	*No.*	*%*
167	No	48	36.09	46	36.8	44	36.06	29	25.09
153	Not sure	45	33.8	37	29.6	32	26.22	40	34.4
176	Yes, I'm sure of it	40	30.11	42	33.6	46	37.72	47	40.51

However, as demonstrated by Tables 12 and 13, the City College Study did shed signs of a positive correlation between chronological age and religiosity in two highly subjective respects, the religious self-image and belief in an afterlife.[23] The modal answer of all New York City respondents to the question: "Would you say you are a religious person, or doesn't religion mean very much to you?" was in the affirmative (44.7 per cent), as compared with those who were undecided (30.1 per cent) and those who expressed an irreligious self-image (25.2 per cent). The most significant aspect of the chronological age distribution in answer to this question was the steadily increasing proportions of the religious self-image and the steadily declining proportions of indecision regarding the self-image in the ascension of chronological age.

Beliefs concerning the afterlife among the respondents of the

[23] Cf. Charles T. O'Reilly and Margaret M. Pembroke, *Older People in a Chicago Community* (Chicago, Loyola University, 1957), pp. 1, 30–31. This study of a predominantly Roman Catholic sample in the Chicago area known as "Back of the Yards" also showed a disparity between religious attitudes and behavior among the aged. Although church attendance did not generally rise after sixty-five, the majority of the respondents said that religion had become more helpful to them in the past ten years.

City College Study were almost evenly distributed between the three possibilities: affirmative belief (35.6 per cent), negative belief (33.6 per cent), and uncertainty (30.8 per cent). Yet there was a clear pattern of increase in the proportion of affirmative belief in afterlife as one ascended the chronological ladder. Denials of an afterlife remained proportionately the same from thirty to thirty-five through fifty to fifty-five years of age, and then declined significantly, as one would theoretically expect, in the age-group sixty to sixty-five. Uncertainty regarding the afterlife was the response that showed no clearcut relationship to chronological aging.

Research data on belief in the afterlife culled from other studies on the religiosity of older people substantiate, as in the case of attendance at services, the importance of the conditional influence of type of community. More than 90 per cent of the Prairie City elders were reported to have expressed confidence in an afterlife, and only one per cent of these small-town Midwesterners definitely expressed disbelief. This was a slightly higher score of belief than that reported for a sample of older people in Louisville, 87 per cent of whom were believers and two per cent definite disbelievers; and significantly higher than a representative group from larger cities, reported by Cavan, of whom 76 per cent were certain of an afterlife. Lastly, Mack's findings in her study of a group of native-born people in Chicago were that only 58 per cent were certain of an afterlife, whereas 18 per cent definitely did not believe this. The smaller the community, then, the higher is the proportion of belief in an afterlife.[24]

Research also substantiates that it is not only the smaller community that shows the greater religiosity in old age, but sex also makes a difference, with the older women remaining more active in religion than do older men. This is especially evident in the matter of leadership positions in organized religion, conclude Havighurst and Albrecht:

It is customary for older people to drop out of leadership positions in the churches gradually after they reach the age of 60. . . . Older men drop out of church activity more rapidly than women do, probably because their activities are more involved with administrative and teaching positions, in which there is a considerable turnover, with new officers being elected annually. Women, on the other hand, have the women's organizations to keep them occupied, and even though they may drop out of leadership roles, they

[24] Havighurst and Albrecht, *op. cit.,* pp. 201–2.

have many meetings to attend during the week. Furthermore, older women often find themselves in demand for service at church dinners, as well as for sewing, quilting, and other church projects. Older women are generally of more use in a church than older men, and, for this reason, they get more out of church life.[25]

In summary, we have observed that religiosity among older people is a surprisingly modest part of their overt lives, and that there appears to be no significant increase chronologically in such matters as Bible reading, associational membership, and attendance at services in accordance with what theory leads us to anticipate. But in the inner or subjective lives of older people, religion, such as in the self-image and belief in an afterlife, does play a larger role and does tend to intensify as people grow older. Important conditional variables in these relationships between religion and aging are size of community and sex of respondent.

Religion and Adjustment in Old Age

The second crucial test of the effectiveness of organized religion in meeting the needs of the older population is to determine whether or not there is a significant difference in personal and social adjustment in old age between those who are highly religious and those who are, relatively speaking, irreligious in their attitudes and behavior patterns. The hypothesis derived from the general theory of religion and aging is that church-going and positive religious attitudes are related to adjustment in old age.

Available research data on this relationship, however, have not been consistent. On the one hand, the Landis study of older rural people in Iowa found that on all scores those who attend church regularly are not only better adjusted but enjoy better health than those who do not attend. But precisely what there is in church participation that leads to salutary results was not determined.[26] On the other hand, the Prairie City Study concluded that the professed attitude of the respondents toward religion had very little relationship to personal adjustment.[27]

We know there is a very high incidence of personal and social

[25] *Ibid.,* p. 203.
[26] Jacobs, *op. cit.,* p. 2.
[27] Havighurst and Albrecht, *op. cit.,* pp. 203–4.

maladjustment among the urban aged. In the nationwide survey of these people, between one third and one half of the respondents admitted to having such symptoms as daydreaming about the past, absent-mindedness, "blue" feelings, and thoughts about death at least occasionally. One third of them claimed that at least sometimes they had feelings that their lives were not very useful. Physical aches and pains troubled almost two thirds of the urban aged, and such psychosomatic symptoms as nervousness, headaches, forgetfulness, sleeplessness, and upset stomachs afflicted from 30 to 50 per cent of the respondents.

Nor are the lives of the urban aged very well organized, for in answer to the question: "How much do you plan ahead the things that you will be doing next week or the weeks after?" more than half (57.6 per cent) indicated they did no planning at all. Furthermore, the urban aged live, in a sense, in social isolation. They were asked: "About how many really close friends do you have here in town with whom you occasionally talk over confidential matters?" The modal response was "none" (36.5 per cent). In answer to the question: "Would you say that you go around with a certain group of close friends who visit back and forth in each other's homes?" the overwhelming response (76.7 per cent) was negative.

Religion and the church are stated by only 39 per cent of the urban aged as giving them the most satisfaction and comfort in their lives today. Surpassing these were "just being with my family at home," "having relatives visit me," and "spending time with close friends." In addition, religion and the church are by far the least dynamic of all these things as a source of comfort and satisfaction, for in answer to the question: "May I ask you whether certain things gave you more comfort and satisfaction when you were fifty, or more comfort and satisfaction now?" 61.6 per cent replied "neither" or "the same," with 16 per cent actually claiming more comfort and satisfaction at fifty years of age and only 19 per cent more comfort and satisfaction now.

The crucial question still remains. Do the religiously oriented achieve greater adjustment in old age than do those who have no religious orientation? In an effort to help resolve this question, the City College Study investigated the relationship of comfort and satisfaction from religion to feelings about aging. It sought to determine whether those who receive the most satisfaction and comfort from religion worry less about getting older than do those who do not derive maximum comfort and satisfaction.

Table 14: *The Relation of Comfort and Satisfaction from Religion to Feelings about Aging, Controlled by Chronological Age*

(496 Cases, New York City, Spring 1957)   (Social Research Laboratory, The City College)

Are religion and church work the things that give you the most satisfaction and comfort in life today?

| | | *Yes (132 cases)* | | | | | | | | *No (364 cases)* | | | | | | | |
| | | *30–35* | | *40–45* | | *50–55* | | *60–65* | | *30–35* | | *40–45* | | *50–55* | | *60–65* | |
How do you feel about getting older?	Total	No.	%	No.	%	No.	%	No.	%	No.	%	No.	%	No.	%	No.	%
Worry	197	12	29.2	4	16	15	42.8	18	58	28	30.4	37	37	34	39	49	57.6
Don't mind at all	279	27	65.8	17	68	19	55.2	12	38.7	57	61.9	62	62	51	58	34	40.0
Like the idea and no answer	20	2	4.8	4	16	1	2.0	1	3.3	7	7.7	1	1	2	3	2	2.4

As Table 14 demonstrates, only an insignificantly smaller percentage (37 per cent) of those who derive comfort from religion worry about aging than do those who do not find religion comforting (40.6 per cent). Controlling chronological age in the analysis, however, does show a significant difference in the forty to forty-five-year-old group, for only 16 per cent of the religiously oriented among them worried as compared with 37 per cent of their irreligious counterpart. In short, the answer to the question of the impact of religion on adjustment to old age remains somewhat inconclusive.

Shortcomings of Religion as a Geriatric Factor

Without doubt research exposes the shortcomings of religion as an effective geriatric force. Although, as we have seen, there are some indications of inner religiosity intensifying in later years, there is little change of interest in the church and synagogue with advancing age and very little indication that organized religion has succeeded in helping most of the aged adjust to their personal and social situations. Instead of a large-scale "turning to religion" as people grow older, most people simply persist in the religious pattern of their earlier age levels.

What are the reasons for these shortcomings? Some students of the problem assert that people tend to crave satisfying religious experiences as they age, but simultaneously hesitate to take the steps necessary to gain them.[28] Obstacles in the path of these steps toward more active religious participation and greater success by religion in helping the aged adjust are said to include the youth-centeredness and family-centeredness of organized religion, physical infirmity, the feeling of no longer being needed or welcome, and far distance from their places of worship.[29] Maves and Cedarleaf suggest that the limited incomes of many older people preclude their involvement in organized religion, for "vast numbers of the aged are frozen in a continual economic depression, regardless of the degree of prosperity among other groups."[30]

Conclusion

This chapter has revealed the sharp diversity between the prevailing theory about the positive relationship of religion to aging on the

[28] Frakes, *op. cit.,* p. 6.
[29] See Mathiasen, *op. cit.,* p. 2; Frakes, *op. cit.,* p. 6.
[30] Paul B. Maves and J. Lennart Cedarleaf, *Older People and the Church* (New York, Abingdon-Cokesbury Press, 1949), pp. 27, 41–42.

one hand, and the actual accomplishments of religion in bringing meaningful and helpful attitudes and experiences into the lives of middle-aged and older people. Research has answered many questions and at the same time has left many other important ones unanswered.

Do the physical immobility, distance, and financial straits of older people necessarily discourage them from more religious participation, satisfaction, and comfort? How can organized religion live up more efficiently to its precept that "in the economy of God there are no useless persons"? Greater emphasis will have to be placed in research on the special needs of older persons that only organized religion can meet, as compared with those needs it can meet better, and those which it can meet at least as well as other social institutions.[31] More research is needed on the effects of age changes in capacities and predispositions upon the participation of older people in religious activities. We still do not know very much about the influence of such conditional variables as social class, denomination, education, and ethnic group on the relationship between religion and aging. Finally, we need to know more about the opportunities that churches and synagogues actually offer the middle-aged and aged for meeting their needs, and the ways in which these opportunities could be increased and improved.

Questions and Research Exercises

1. Sociologically, explain why the image of the deity in western culture is usually both anthropomorphic and gerontomorphic.
2. Discuss the alleged or ideal functions of religion in the lives of older people.
3. Explore historically the secular functions of organized religion in the western world in meeting the aged's needs for housing and subsistence.
4. Theoretically, what is the exception to the view that religion is naturally enhanced in the course of the aging process?
5. List fully the instances in which there have been disparities between the religious norms and precepts regarding older people and the actual effects of religion in their lives.
6. Discuss the two crucial tests of the effectiveness of organized religion in meeting the needs of older people.

Selected Readings

Biller, N. M., "The Role of the Synagogue in Work with Old People," *Jewish Social Service Quarterly* (Vol. 28, 1952), pp. 284–89. A brief but

[31] See Pollak, *op. cit.*, p. 163.

adequate summary of the organized Jewish religion's traditional role in aging.

Jacobs, H. Lee, *Churches and Their Senior Citizens* (Iowa City, State University of Iowa Press, 1957). One of the few good monographs on the church and aging, though limited to midwestern data.

McCabe, F. H., *Catholic Institutional Care of the Aged* (Washington, D.C., National Conference of Catholic Charities, 1945). An authoritative account of Catholic principles and practices.

Maves, Paul B., and Cedarleaf, J. Lennart, *Older People and the Church* (Nashville, Abingdon-Cokesbury Press, 1949). Generally acknowledged as the best monograph of its kind, even though Protestant in point of view.

Scudder, Delton L., ed., *Organized Religion and the Older Person* (Gainesville, University of Florida Press, 1958). The proceedings of the annual Southern Conference on Gerontology.

V : Social Geriatrics

We do not look at the aged people as a class apart,
but seek to ensure that they live full lives within
the ordinary stream of the community.

RT. HON. IAIN MACLEOD, M.P.

12 :

THE RANGE OF AMERICAN
SOCIAL SERVICES FOR THE AGED

When scientific inventions and discoveries which have social implications and consequences are not followed by the required adjustments which they suggest to society, we sometimes find ourselves with a new problem on our hands created by the solution of an old problem. This dilemma is clearly seen in the geriatric task that is before us. It is one thing to have greater longevity conferred on us by the genius of scientific effort and quite another to make full social use of the added years. If the newer concepts of environmental medicine (which is the essence of social medicine) are to have any meaning for geriatric service, we must take into consideration the milieu in which the elderly pass their declining years, as well as with the elderly themselves, in the same way, for example, as we deal integrally with the psychic and somatic problems which they present so frequently. This requirement at once brings into prominence the social worker, the psychologist and the psychiatrist and the part which they must play in helping to rearrange the pattern of living for older persons wherever this becomes necessary.

As matters now stand, we are at a point in geriatric history and practice when a little soul-searching should be helpful. There are tendencies in the care of the elderly (like overinstitutionalization) which must be controlled and reconsidered, just as there are tendencies (such as continued and subsidized home care) to be applauded and emulated. The science of Geriatrics was not created for the purpose of transferring the burden of the aged from the family to the institution, producing a growing estrangement between youth and age in a period when the life-span is increasing. My plea is for coexistence as opposed to severe separation of the generations. We need no "cities of refuge" for the normal aged. There is no substitute for individualization of planning and care in dealing with the problems of the aged. Entrance into a collective institution for the aged should never be a matter of choice; it should be a matter of necessity. The integrity of the home and the family should be preserved as long as possible, and by subsidy if necessary. The pathology of old age is the pathology of prolonged illness and should be treated that way.*

The purpose of this chapter is to examine social geriatrics in American society, with a view toward delineating the range of different social services that seek to correct, control, and prevent problems of aging rather than engaging in detailed analysis of any single program or service.

Some aspects of American social geriatrics have already been covered in previous chapters as integral parts of the problems under consideration. In Chapter 2, for example, old age and survivors insurance was taken up in connection with the economic problems of old age, and in Chapter 3 antidiscrimination legislation was discussed as a measure for combating the quasi-minority status of the aged. In Chapter 10, social geriatrics was represented by the detailed analysis of employment practices to help older or middle-aged workers. Finally, part of Chapter 11 was devoted to religious programs and services that are meant to facilitate adjustment to aging.

Important as these are, they represent only small segments of the total range of social services available to the aging American, but the problems of aging and the aged thus far have not yielded easily to any of them. Like any other age group, older people are individuals with problems as well as interests and circumstances that are almost infinite in variety of combination. Years ago, our society did not recognize this fact, and to a large extent our principal approach was to treat the problem-ridden aged as a homogeneous class of public charges requiring one kind of care.

Institutional Care

An outstanding form of this traditional treatment of the indigenous aged was the almshouse or poorhouse, an institution transplanted from

* E. M. Bluestone, "The Conflict of the Ages in an Era of Increased Longevity," *Gerontologia Clinica* (Vol. 1, 1959), pp. 230–42.

England to colonial America. Ever since then the fear of ending one's days in the almshouse has been ever-present to many older persons. "Over the hill to the poorhouse" represented the lowest type of economic and social degradation. The early poorhouse sheltered an aggregation of aged paupers, mentally disordered individuals, the feeble-minded, alcoholics, chronically ill persons, and the unemployables of all ages. It became an institution limited almost entirely to custodial care.

During the past century, however, one group after another has been salvaged from the poorhouse for care in specialized institutions or even in noninstitutional settings, leaving behind a remnant that could not be cared for elsewhere. Recently many poorhouses, almshouses and so-called county farms have been abolished or else converted into infirmaries. Among those that remain, few have prospects for more than a few lingering years before they are put out of existence.

Replacing these traditional almshouses are private homes for the aged, nursing homes, boarding homes, chronic disease hospitals, and mental hospitals that provide facilities for older persons that are free from many of the degrading features of the county poor farm or almshouse. Very important for the self-respect of the aged is the removal of the stigma attached to residence in the poorhouse.

Yet many of these newer facilities for the institutional care of older persons still possess some of the less fortunate characteristics of the traditional institutions. First of all, many of them often follow the older pattern of custodial care rather than the newer one of rehabilitation. Second, they seem to expect passivity in the patients or residents rather than physical and mental activity. Third, they tend to regiment the residents and to require conformity to rules and regulations rather than to allow latitude for individual preferences and self-expression. Fourth, their staffs often become impersonal and overprofessional, ceasing to give personal attention and individualized service to which their residents are ideally entitled. A fifth characteristic that carries over from the past is that in order to reduce per capita cost, institutions for the aged often expand in size beyond the optimum number for the welfare and happiness of their residents.

A criticism often made is that the paid personnel of institutions for older people appear frequently to forget that the residents do not exist for the sake of the institution but that the institution is organized for service to its residents. The problem is to make institutions more home-like, and to accomplish this aim the superintendent and staff need understanding of the attitudes and potentialities of older people, training in the concepts and practices of rehabilitation, and sensitivity and skill in interpersonal relations.

"Institutional" features can probably never be eliminated from institutions for the aged. For this reason, institutional placement of older persons is rapidly becoming a measure of last resort. More and more, opportunities for residence in one's own home or with relatives or in a foster family are being explored and presented as an alternative to institutional living for the aging person in American society.

Approximately 500,000 older people now have to live in homes for the aged, nursing homes, and other institutional establishments. Waiting lists for these facilities, despite their often paralyzing dread, are long and the institutions themselves are usually overcrowded and only recently have they begun to introduce programs of rehabilitation, recreation, occupational therapy, work maintenance, and a community-centered approach.

The fact that nursing home care tends to be terminal is a psychological nightmare to older, infirm persons and their families. But low levels of institutional care generally are not due as much to lack of standards for nursing and old age homes as to insufficient appropriations for an adequate, trained staff for inspection, enforcement, and other services. They are also related directly to the low grants for medical care under old age assistance in many states.[1]

Mental hospitals as institutions providing care for the aged are even more open to criticism. Thirty per cent of all patients in American mental hospitals are more than sixty-five years of age, yet it is becoming increasingly clear that many older persons do not belong in such institutions and are admitted only because they have no families or for the convenience of their families. They could be cared for better in nursing homes, foster homes, day care hospitals, or homes for the aged, undesirable as the latter often are. Psychiatrists generally agree that early counseling, employment services for the aged, and better medical services could also cut down considerably on their admissions to state hospitals.

Moosehaven

One of the few progressive types of institutional care for the aged in the United States is Moosehaven, maintained in Florida by the Loyal

---

[1] Committee on Labor and Public Welfare, U.S. Senate, *Studies of the Aged and Aging: Surveys of State and Local Projects* (Washington, D.C., U.S. Government Printing Office, Jan. 1957), p. 6.

Order of the Moose, a fraternal association, for its aged and dependent members. Over 200 of its 350 residents take part in a work program that deviates drastically from the usual passivity one finds in old age institutions. The work program has the following features:

1. Participation of residents is voluntary.
2. It is a maintenance program comprising about 50 activities essential for the operation of the institution.
3. The work period for each person varies, but it averages about three hours a day.
4. Those who work receive a small monthly allowance.

Cold Spring Institute

Another variant among institutions for the aged is the Cold Spring Institute, located on the Hudson River 60 miles north of New York City. Its purpose has been twofold:

1. To develop a program of living suited to the needs and interests of older men and women, mostly college graduates.
2. To discover possible evidence of change and growth in the men and women over fifty-five who have participated in the development of such programs.

In the first year of its operation, from October 1951 to June 1952, three groups participated: men and women over fifty-five, totaling 32 in number. The program enabled each individual to work out a creative plan for living, learning, and doing based on his or her own unique capacities, experience, and interests.

Change and growth were studied by means of a variety of psychological, medical, and physical tests, both at the beginning and the end of the term of residence. In addition to these objective tests and examinations, continuous records were kept by the staff, and tape recordings were made of all group discussions. The analysis of these data gave evidence of change as follows:

1. Depression was lessened.
2. Self-esteem and sense of identity were increased.
3. Relating to others became easier and freer.
4. Attention was better directed and sustained; speed of performance increased; intellectual performance improved.

5. Acceptance, understanding, and expression of differences increased with concomitant decrease in prejudice.
6. Fears were lessened.
7. Enjoyment in the use of the body increased.
8. Heightened blood pressure was reduced.
9. Vital capacity increased.
10. Hemoglobin increased up to 2.5 grams.
11. Height increased.
12. Blood chemistry outside the normal range returned to well within normal limits.
13. Instances of distressing, chronic low back pain upon entrance entirely disappeared.
14. Cases of anemia were alleviated.
15. Neuromuscular coordination improved markedly.
16. Greater physical energy was available and used.[2]

Housing the Aged

In general, older persons want to remain in their own homes as long as they are physically able and mentally competent. Gerontologists and geriatricians tend more and more to support the wisdom of this preference. Social geriatrics has much evidence of a shift in recent years from institutional care to living in a private home, such as follows:

1. Extension of the work of homes for the aged to provide assistance in the community for older people who otherwise would be placed in an institution.

2. Provision of part-time housekeeping and homemaking services to disabled and infirm aged persons. However, homemaker service has been slower to develop in the United States than in other countries. In Sweden, for example, there is one "home helper" for each 4,000 people in urban areas, and one for each 2,000 persons in rural areas. Homemaker service is household help given the elderly to enable them to stay in their own homes rather than move into institutions because they can no longer cope with household problems. It is distinguished from "home care" service, which is technically what a medical-nursing-social work team does to keep the aged person who is ill in his own apartment or

[2] Ruth Andrus and Richard Benjamin, "The Cold Spring Idea: Adventure in Living," a paper presented at the First Pan-American Congress of Gerontology, Mexico City, 1956.

home by providing the necessary services. Homemaker service has not yet developed rapidly in the United States because American culture stresses autonomy and independence. Furthermore, American communities are still unaware of how useful such service can be, and work involved in home service does not have the status it has in other countries. In New York state, local welfare departments can receive state reimbursement for providing such service to old age recipients. It is provided not only to aged and incapacitated individuals but also to children who would otherwise have to be removed from their homes. Such service is paid out of public welfare funds when the recipient is receiving public assistance or is in need of such service and unable to pay for it.[3]

3. Provision of "meals on wheels" (one hot meal a day or every other day) at a low cost to housebound aged couples and individuals.

4. Development by welfare agencies of programs to place aged, homeless individuals in foster homes under mutually satisfactory financial and personal arrangements.[4]

Housing Needs

We observed in Chapter 2 that in many respects the aged are the worst-housed segment of our population. They tend to occupy rela-

[3] *Good News for Later Life,* New York State Joint Legislative Committee on Problems of the Aging (Legislative Document No. 8, 1958), pp. 41–42.

[4] Consistent with this is the trend to make institutional care of the aged as homelike as possible. Some ways in which this is being done are the following:

1. The central, large building of the home for the aged also provides one-room efficiency apartments for single occupancy, where residents can prepare their meals.

2. On the same grounds as the home for the aged are small, single dwellings for couples, detached or in a row, and small multiapartment units of 3, 4, or 5 apartments for them, with provision for cooking their own meals.

3. Permission to couples and individuals, upon admission, to keep some of their possessions, such as chairs, table, and clock, so that they may retain continuity with the past.

4. Reduction of the institution's red tape on matters such as visiting hours, freedom of coming and going, taking vacations, and trips to visit children, friends, and others.

5. Encouragement of participation by the aged residents in activities and events in the outside community.

6. An activities program in the institution, planned and operated by the residents, to develop their sense of participation and stimulate their sense of independence.

7. A work-maintenance program, participated in voluntarily by residents for small compensation, which gives them a sense of activity, usefulness, and independence.

tively more very low rent dwelling units and houses of low value, and their housing is more dilapidated and deficient in plumbing facilities.

A housing program for the aging obviously has to consider the wide variety of attitudes toward housing of older people, the level of their income, their frequent physical disabilities, their relatively short life expectancy, the large number of unattached individuals among them, the general need for small apartments or dwellings rather than large ones, and the desirability of special community facilities to meet their physical and social needs. After making a study of the problem in 1955 and 1956, Congress concluded that these needs could best be met by private industry with the help of the government.

United States Housing Act of 1956

To accomplish this, the President in 1956 proposed a three-pronged program designed to make available new housing opportunities for the aged. His recommendations were incorporated in the Housing Act of 1956, involving the following provisions:

1. Friends, relatives, or even a corporation can make a down payment on a house being purchased by a person over 60 years of age. Where the latter would not otherwise qualify as an acceptable credit risk because of his age, he now becomes eligible by obtaining a cosigner on the insured mortgage.

2. The rental housing program of the Federal Housing Administration will, when a nonprofit agency such as a church, fraternal group, or union sponsors a project for the aged, allow a maximum mortgage of $8,100 per dwelling unit.

3. The legal bar is removed that kept single elderly widows and widowers out of federally aided public housing projects.

4. The Public Housing Administration has the authority to assist in the construction or remodeling of existing projects to accommodate the aged.

5. Local public housing authorities are required to give first preference to the admission of the aged to low-rent units.

6. Federal Housing Administration insurance is made available for cooperative housing and nonprofit housing for the aged, and for retirement homes.

7. A special trade-in feature on old homes is provided, so that the elderly with large equities in an old house can finance a more suitable

new home using a mortgage backed by the Federal Housing Administration up to 85 per cent of the amount an owner-occupant can borrow on the same property.[5]

State-Aided Projects

To secure at least a minimum availability of housing for the aged, the New York State Housing Commissioner in 1951 announced that thereafter in all state-aided public housing projects it would be required that approximately 5 per cent of the dwelling units be set aside for the aged, and that upon application from local authorities this could be increased as the need was demonstrated. The New York State legislature in 1956 reënforced this policy by amending the public housing law to authorize the housing commissioner to provide an "adequate number" of necessary dwelling units for the aged. This was the first official acceptance in the United States of the "set-aside" principle as a basic step toward providing adequate housing for the aged, a principle that had already been adopted in Peru, Sweden, Denmark, and Holland.

Since its inception in New York State, public housing for the aged has provided real low-rent apartments of two types:

1. Type A. Designated for aging couples, this type has a double bedroom, separate full-size living and combination dining room, kitchen facilities, and separate bathroom.

2. Type B. Designated for couples seventy years old and over, and single persons sixty-five years old doing light housekeeping, this type has a combination living and sleeping room, with separate combination dining and kitchen space smaller than in Type A, and a separate bathroom.

Apartments for the aged in New York State are often located together in separate wings of the housing project in order to encourage mutual help and to reduce the noise from children, although there is now growing sentiment against this kind of segregation because it allegedly enhances the already broad gap between the young and the old in our society. Some apartments are provided in sheltered areas on the ground floor for the feeble aged. In large public housing projects there are special

---

[5] Henry O. Talle, "Housing Needs of the Elderly," *Modern Maturity* (Vol. 2, Oct.–Nov. 1959), p. 35; *Brightening the Senior Years,* New York State Joint Legislative Committee on Problems of the Aging (Legislative Document No. 81, 1957), pp. 31–32.

visiting and modified recreational rooms for them in addition to the community facilities provided in state-aided projects for tenants and residents of the neighborhood.

In what have now become standard features in designing apartments for the aged, New York State's projects seek to serve the special needs of the aged in the following ways:

1. Bathrooms have nonslip floors.
2. Square bathtubs with seats and hand grips in the walls are provided to facilitate getting in and out of tubs.
3. In some cases, showers with seats and hand grips are provided for older couples who feel insecure in getting into and out of bathtubs.
4. Thresholds are eliminated to lessen the danger of tripping.
5. Electric instead of gas stoves are provided to prevent asphyxiation from smothering of the flame by the boiling over of liquids.
6. To simplify housekeeping, shelves and cabinets are placed at low, easy-to-reach levels, and windows have mechanical operators for easy and safe opening and closing of casements.
7. Apartments wherever possible face the sunny side and more heat is provided in these apartments than in those of younger people.[6]

Other states have also developed a real interest in housing for the aged. For example, Colorado established a state building authority to investigate the housing needs of the aged and to examine the ability of local organizations to provide such housing and to facilitate their work. The authority has power to acquire land by condemnation, purchase, or lease. Connecticut now has legislation establishing a state commission to study and integrate services for the elderly, including housing. Its first state-sponsored housing for the aged consisted of 30 single story units at a cost of $500,000. Indiana allows a person over sixty-five whose annual income is not more than $2,250 to deduct $1,000 from the assessed value of his property. Massachusetts has provided a total of $30 million for the erection of model-type housing for the aged. Under this program the State provides annual contributions as subsidies equal to 2.5 per cent of the development cost for projects by local housing authorities for older persons of low income. Standards are

---

[6] *Age Is No Barrier,* New York State Joint Legislative Committee on Problems of the Aging (Legislative Document No. 35, 1952), pp. 12–13.

established by the state housing board to meet the special needs of older persons, including a preponderance of apartments for one-person occupancy. An average proportion of three single dwellings to one dwelling for couples is the suggested pattern. The Board also insists that housing for the aged should be designed to rent for an average of $40 per month.[7]

Some states are also creating loan funds to be made available to nonprofit agencies for the construction of housing for the aged, such as low-rental apartments with special facilities, motel-type cottages, hotel-type facilities, and modern boarding and foster homes. States are encouraging and aiding local housing authorities that develop housing projects for older persons or reserve special facilities for them in more general community housing programs. One technique used is to guarantee the notes or bonds of local authorities that undertake such housing. In fact many local housing authorities have gone ahead on their own to design and provide housing for the aged without direct state help.[8]

An Adequate Income for the Aged

For those aged who cannot secure employment or who for various reasons no longer wish to work, an adequate income is essential in order to secure housing, proper nutrition, medical care, recreation, and mental health. Apparently there is no geriatric service as therapeutic for the normal aged as an adequate income. To meet this fundamental problem, many states are adopting the following programs.

1. Individual Financial Planning for Retirement

Through interdepartmental committees on aging, large-scale educational programs have been developed stressing that all individuals *who can* should provide during their working lives a systematic program for their financial security. This is being accomplished through savings, purchase of life insurance and securities, and investment in a home early in life. The emphasis here is on the responsibility of the individual to provide a large part of his security in old age. This educational effort is being combined with a wide campaign whereby industry is stimulated to establish pension and profit-sharing plans to meet in part, at least, the

[7] Committee on Labor and Public Welfare, United States Senate, *op. cit.*, pp. 12–13.
[8] *Ibid.*, p. 13.

special needs of their own employees, supplementary to the minimum income they will eventually receive under Federal old age and survivors insurance.

2. *Increasing Old Age Assistance Grants, Especially for Medical Care*

Grants under old age assistance are being increased to bring them into closer line with actual costs of living. This trend has also tended to emphasize the vital medical costs of older persons through legislation designed to eliminate maximums as far as medical needs are concerned. Many states are taking advantage of the federal legislation providing additional matching funds for expanded medical care programs.

Other measures for the maintenance of an adequate income in various states are the liberalization of eligibility requirements for unemployment compensation and extension of the payments for older persons, as well as additional credit to employers who provide employment for older workers; tax relief for older persons with respect to state or local property and income taxes; and more adequate pension and retirement programs for state and local employees.

There are many indications of new federal programs to provide an adequate income for the aged. For example, after conducting hearings in cities throughout the country in 1959, the Senate Subcommittee on Problems of the Aged recommended a substantial increase in social security benefits, and utilization of the social security system to pay for high-standard medical care and hospital expenses of older persons.

Health Care for the Aged

Neither income, housing, or any other geriatric measure makes much difference to an older person who is acutely or chronically ill. A secure old age calls for adequate health and medical care, the major objective being to prevent as far as possible the onset of disabling physical or mental illness. Medical and hospital care are, however, especially burdensome for the aged. A large part of the difficulty stems from the fact that the majority of the aged have annual incomes under $1,000 so that they cannot afford the care they need. The average stay in general hospitals of men and women over sixty-five years of age is estimated at 22.5 days, compared with an average of 10.1 days for all hospital admissions. It is, accordingly, safe to assume that the health costs of the aged are considerably higher than for the population as a whole.

Because health and medical care of the aged is clearly one of the most crucial aspects of geriatrics, there are many programs and services that have been developed in recent years. Some of the developments include:

1. Drugs at Reduced Prices

In 1959 the American Association of Retired Persons, a private organization on a nationwide scale, established a drug service providing drugs for ill older people at greatly reduced prices. The establishment of this drug service came at a time when the high costs of drugs were receiving Congressional attention.

2. Health Insurance

The growth of voluntary health insurance (prepayment) plans in the United States has been dramatic, but a far higher percentage of those under sixty-five in the population hold such insurance than do those over sixty-five years of age. Those aged who are covered by health or hospital insurance attribute their coverage to group policies issued to the company for which they are working; group policies issued to the company for which they formerly worked but from which they are now retired; and individual policies sold on a city-wide basis regardless of age, or to individuals within a maximum age limit.

One serious difficulty the aged have in obtaining health or hospital insurance is that most of them are not in the labor force where most group policies are made available. Furthermore, insurance companies themselves frequently exclude older persons from the opportunity to buy individual policies, or charge such high premiums that the aged usually cannot afford to take them. A frequent provision calls for a decrease in benefits with age. Many older patients with chronic health conditions who must seek nursing homes rather than general hospitals find that their contract does not meet fully the special problems they have.

3. Bureau of Chronic Diseases and Geriatrics

To intensify an emphasis on diseases of the aging in public health programs, many states are creating bureaus or divisions of degenerative diseases in their health departments. For example, in 1956 the legislature in New York passed an act establishing such a bureau, its purpose being to develop a program designed to improve and protect the health of middle-aged and aged persons in the state. Among the specific duties of the bureau are the development of a plan for periodic health inventories of the middle-aged and aged; programs for integrating community agencies in a comprehensive plan of prevention, rehabilitation, and control of degenerative disease; the education of trained professional personnel; and demonstration projects of "day hospitals" and "meals on wheels."

4. Mental Health Consultants on Aging

A number of states are convinced that many older persons now in mental institutions could be cared for and treated more appropriately in special geriatric facilities or in well-equipped and staffed homes for the aged and chronically ill. Some of them are authorizing special mental-health personnel responsible for insuring that older persons who do not require psychiatric attention in a mental hospital will not be committed merely because no other resource is available. These special personnel are being made responsible for developing plans to care for aged persons who are nonpsychotic but who need some psychiatric attention in facilities such as psychiatric nursing homes, cottage-type facilities, and old-age homes. Other efforts are being made, through voluntary admission procedures and family payment plans, to utilize outpatient services, to develop day-hospital care, and to undertake research and demonstration projects to prevent or improve the mental illnesses of older persons.[9]

Education and Recreation for the Aged

Many states are assuming an increasing part of the responsibility of providing opportunities for older persons to contribute their energies, wisdom, and skills outside of their regular employment. In general, two kinds of opportunities are being recognized:

1. Activities which, in retirement, become substantial substitutes for the regular jobs and family responsibilities recently given up.

2. Activities that are primarily recreational and educational, giving older persons the opportunity to make and keep friends, to stimulate social interests, and to develop creative and intellectual talents.

Some of the considerations in undertaking recreational and educational programs for the aging include the following:

[9] *Ibid.,* pp. 13–15.

1. The activity must be so meaningful to the older individual as to avoid any possibility of its being considered mere "busy" work.

2. The activity that results in real contributions to the community has the best chance of sustaining the status, self-respect, and energy of the older person.

3. The activity must be attuned to the individual, helping him to find one or more continuing interest to which he can give himself and succeed sufficiently to win the approval of those whose opinion he values.

With these principles in mind, we can examine two outstanding ways of meeting the educational and recreational needs of older persons.

1. A Bureau or Division of Adult Education

Many states have already established a division within their departments of education, with full-time workers, to stimulate and aid localities, school districts, industries, and labor organizations in planning and carrying out education programs of special interest to older persons. These divisions of adult education are administering state aid to schools or other agencies that undertake approved adult education activities. They are also developing programs of leadership training at schools or on an in-service basis, and they are acting as an educational center for the collection and dissemination of materials on problems of aging.[10]

2. Day Centers for the Aged

But far more publicized have been the golden age clubs and day centers for the aged that have been organized all over the country. The claim for them is that they meet an urgent need of an important segment of the aged, providing a way of life to substitute for the work-life of the individual when he ages. It is also claimed that they relieve the heavy loneliness that weighs on the aged and help combat the regressive characteristics of the aging process that tend to isolate the individual socially.

There are many examples of such centers, the most notable being Hodson Center in New York City. Nevertheless, they apparently have met the needs of only a small proportion of the aged, for many are not attracted to the golden age clubs and centers. Some are reluctant to join because of the "welfare" sponsorship of some of the clubs; others are too independent to want to be organized into clubs; and still others think

[10] *Ibid.*, pp. 15–17.

the activities are too childish and otherwise meaningless for older people like themselves. And lastly, despite all the publicity about these clubs and centers, there are many aged who do not know about them and who have not been properly motivated to take advantage of them.[11]

Day centers for the aged have been the objects of both lavish praise and blame. They have been praised for the extremely low incidence of mental breakdown among those who take advantage of their facilities. On the other hand, they have been criticized for being irrelevant to the interests of the aged. When younger people see an older person sitting and doing nothing they become impatient with his or her passivity, the reason being that younger people are always judging their elders by their own values and standards. Day centers may, in some instances, merely be the projection of younger people's values and standards onto the reluctant shoulders of their elders.

Casework Services for the Aged

In recent years in many social work agencies some exploratory work has been done to test the possibility of the helpfulness of casework services for older people. The basic concepts of social work include respect for the individual, acceptance of the client, respect for the client's right to self-determination, the confidentialness of the client's contact with the agency, the involvement of the client in the planning so as to develop and strengthen his self-dependence, and the importance of the social worker's self-awareness in his relationship with the client so that he does not impose his own moral standards, ideals, and feelings on the client.

The casework process is the same for older persons for the most part, except that the problems are apt to be more intensified because they are of longer duration. Furthermore, the length of time necessary for growth and change is likely to be longer for a person who is older. All this makes the casework process slower and requires more patience on the part of the social worker.[12]

Because the face-to-face interview is the modus operandi of all

---

[11] *New Channels for the Golden Years,* New York State Joint Legislative Committee on Problems of the Aging (Legislative Document No. 33, 1956), pp. 34–35.

[12] Alice Smout, "Casework Services to Older Clients," a paper presented at the First Pan-American Congress of Gerontology, Mexico City, 1956.

casework with the aged, it is imperative that those who implement programs learn to overcome stereotyped and condescending attitudes toward the aged. Good interviewing must be geared to the slow pace of the aged, close listening to and careful assessment of anecdotal material, even of "senile productions." There is a need for careful individualization and objectivity. In subtle fashion the aged feel depreciated by not inter-. viewing them alone, first-naming them, interpretation to their adult children rather than to the aged person himself. Social workers often forget they are seen and heard and that their language is directed at persons of another generation and perhaps another culture when they interview an aged client. It takes conscious skill to focus the interview when the aged client wanders without conveying the impression that his remarks are unworthy or trivial. The good interviewer must accept the wide range of "normalcy" in aging and must overidentify neither with the aged person nor with his troubled children. He or she must be conscious of the anxiety-provoking identifications the aged have for social workers and the usual identifications he has for the aged person.[13]

Conclusion: Principles Underlying Service to the Aged

This review of social geriatric services in the United States has been far from exhaustive and has presented only a few examples of the available alternatives. But enough has been discussed here to enable us in conclusion to develop inductively the following principles underlying service to the aged in American society:

1. PURPOSEFUL ACTIVITY.   There are sound physiological and psychological reasons for utilizing purposeful activity to decelerate senescence. But to be effective, activity must be purposeful rather than something for its own sake.

2. UTILITY.   By spurring older people to continue useful lives, geriatrics can help them meet a fundamental need. Usefulness in American culture in turn is related to social acceptance.

3. SOCIAL ACCEPTANCE.   All people, regardless of age, need to be socially accepted, but in the case of the aged who are often actively rejected by the community and the family, the need is especially intense.

4. GROWTH.   All people, even the aged, need to grow by learning

[13] Esther M. Golber, "The Art of Interviewing Older People," a paper presented at the First Pan-American Congress of Gerontology, Mexico City, 1956.

new skills, new hobbies, engaging in new tasks, meeting new people, and accepting new ideas.

5. OPPORTUNITY. A democratic society can do no less than give each human being, regardless of age, an opportunity to realize his economic and social opportunities. We cannot at a given chronological age suddenly withdraw them without violating our cultural values.

6. FREEDOM OF CHOICE. Those aged who wish to retire should have the opportunity to do so, whereas those who wish to continue working should, if able, be free to do that.

7. NONSEGREGATION. Specialized service for older persons should be carefully appraised to make certain that it does not involve the unnecessary segregation of people on the basis of age.

8. INDIVIDUALIZATION AND DIVERSITY. The aged must be treated as individuals as much as possible. No one service, no one approach, no one type of institution will meet all their needs at any given time. Furthermore, the needs of older persons vary not only in kind but also in degree.

9. SELF-RELIANCE. The aged must assume a part of the responsibility for aiding themselves. To give service where none is needed is to encourage a dependent attitude and a feeling of inadequacy.

10. LOCAL RESPONSIBILITY. In the administration of services for the aged, major responsibility rests upon local communities. National and state action are taken to stimulate, guide, lead, and provide a residual of services that cannot be performed effectively at local levels.

11. EARLY PREPARATION. Applying remedial measures to problems of aging only when old age has arrived is shortsighted. The earlier the planning and preparations for old age, the less likely there are to be problems to be faced.[14]

Questions and Research Exercises

1. Research the beginnings of the almshouse in England, and trace its transplantation to and development in America.
2. Visit a home for the aged and arrange to make a study of its admissions policy, program, and social structure.
3. Is the type of program found at Cold Spring Institute feasible on a large scale? Why or why not?

[14] *No Time to Grow Old*, New York State Joint Legislative Committee on Problems of the Aging (Legislative Document No. 12, 1951), pp. 12–14.

4. Discuss the trend to make institutional care of the aged resemble domestic life.
5. What are the standard features today in the architectural designs of apartments for the aged?
6. Investigate three different voluntary health insurance plans, and explore the extent to which the aged may participate and under what conditions they may do so.
7. Discuss the "pros" and "cons" of day centers for the aged.
8. Relate each principle underlying service to the aged to a specific geriatric program.

Selected Readings

Donahue, Wilma, Rae, James, Jr., and Berry, Roger B., eds., *Rehabilitation of the Older Worker* (Ann Arbor, University of Michigan Press, 1953). The proceedings of the University of Michigan's fourth annual conference, with emphasis on the handicapped worker over forty.

Kaplan, Jerome, *A Social Program for Older People* (Minneapolis, University of Minnesota Press, 1953). Techniques for the development of group work with the aged based on observation of experiences of existing groups.

Kubie, Susan H., and Landau, Gertrude, *Group Work with the Aged* (New York, International Universities Press, 1953). An account of the authors' experience of working nine years in the establishment of Hodson Center.

Welfare and Health Council of New York City, *Creative Activities: A Manual for Organizing Activities for Older People* (New York, Welfare and Health Council, 1955). A nontechnical manual in organizing recreational activities for older people.

Welfare and Health Council of New York City, *Homes for the Aged: A Study of Developments* (New York, Welfare and Health Council, 1955). A study of thirty homes for the aged in terms of trends over a decade.

Williams, Arthur, *Recreation for the Aging* (New York, Association Press, 1953). An activity handbook for leaders in clubs, centers, camps, churches, industry, and labor.

13 :

GERONTOLOGY AND GERIATRICS
IN WESTERN EUROPE

In a careful survey of 71 different peoples, distributed world-wide and over a long lapse of time, the recurring interests of aging persons can be summed up pretty well in a five-fold way:

1. To live as long as possible: or at least until life's satisfactions no longer compensate for its privations, or until the advantages of death seem to outweigh the burdens of life. Life is, indeed, precious to the old.

2. To get more rest: or release from the necessity of wearisome exertion at humdrum tasks and to get protection from too great exposure to physical hazards. Opportunities, in other words, to safeguard and preserve waning physical energies. Old people have to learn to hoard their energies.

3. To remain active participants in group affairs in either operational or supervisory roles, any participation being preferable to idleness and indifference. "Something to do, and nothing to be done," is perhaps the main idea.

4. To safeguard or even strengthen any prerogatives acquired; i.e., skills, possessions, rights, authority, prestige, etc. The aged want to hold on to whatever they have. Seniority rights are zealously guarded.

5. Finally, to withdraw from life, when necessity requires it, as honorably and comfortably as possible and with maximal prospects for an attractive hereafter.

These five interests—longer life, rest, participation, prerogatives, an easy and honorable release—probably can be subsumed under the two words "influence" and "security" if they are used with broad connotations. We have observed impressive uniformity in these interests regardless of time and place.*

In order to provide some cross-cultural perspective on the aging American, this chapter turns to a descriptive account and a critical evaluation of western European *gerontological research* pertinent to sociomedical problems of retirement and health, and also to *geriatric services* (i.e., day centers, institutional homes, housing, geriatric clinics, and hospitals) that the author visited and observed.

For the most part my learning experience with regard to gerontological research in western Europe took place in a preconference seminar at the University of Sheffield, England, and at the Third International Gerontological Congress in London during the summer of 1954.[1] Although there were several worthwhile visits to observe geriatric services in Sheffield and London, most of the latter observations were made in a post-Congress tour of Norway, Sweden, Denmark, Holland, and Belgium.

Gerontology in Western Europe

Social research in Europe on occupational retirement and related problems of aging is, for the most part, just beginning. For example, in Holland, according to the coordinator for gerontology in the Dutch National Health Research Council, sociologists have initiated studies on the attitudes and behavior patterns of the aged. Under the sponsorship of the Institute for Social Research of the Dutch People, a private organization, they are doing surveys of old age in each province of the country, the findings in Groningen and Utrecht already having been published.

Until now one of the obstacles in the way of such research has been the lack of field-oriented social scientists in European universities. Another serious handicap has been the belief that physicians, not social scientists, are best equipped to survey sociomedical problems of old age.

---

* Leo W. Simmons, "An Anthropologist Views Old Age," in *Brightening the Senior Years,* New York State Joint Legislative Committee on Problems of the Aging (Legislative Document No. 81, 1957), pp. 47–48.

[1] For the complete coverage of the Congress proceedings, see *Old Age in the Modern World: Report of the Third Congress of the International Association of Gerontology* (Edinburgh, E. and S. Livingstone Ltd., 1955), 647 pp.

This bias against social science is still vigorous in Europe. At the Sheffield seminar, for instance, one of the English delegates maintained that medical experts should conduct research of this type because, as he put it, "they have health entry into the home." The delegate from Holland, himself a physician, was of the emphatic opinion that physicians alone are equipped to interpret sociomedical data. Nevertheless, social scientists such as Shelsky, Kleber, Adorno, and Koenig in Germany, Abrams in England, and Friedmann in France have undertaken survey research on problems of aging and retirement.

There is some dissatisfaction in western Europe with American leadership in defining the researchable problems of aging. The prevailing point of view is that American social scientists, utilizing middle-class norms in defining these problems, have failed to keep in mind that the problems of old age may be subject to other norms elsewhere. For example, in France and to a lesser extent in Switzerland and Holland there are more positive attitudes toward old age than there are in the United States. Similarly, the meaning of work and its implications for the psychological effects of retirement are not necessarily the same in all European societies as they are in American society. According to the Danish delegate at Sheffield: "We Danes do not fear retirement as much as you Americans do. We are not as compulsive about work." France is especially different in this respect, for the philosophy of life there affects attitudes toward work and retirement to the degree that retirement as early as age fifty carries prestige, even if the standard of living is thereby lowered.

Yet to a large extent, European gerontologists resemble their American counterparts in their theoretical approach to retirement. While they agree that retirement for many Europeans has economic, psychological, and social consequences that make problems just as they do in America, they are skeptical about the alleged deleterious influence of retirement on health. Most English gerontologists, for instance, feel that people in good health are likely to continue working, whereas those in poor health are inclined to retire. This may produce an apparent rather than true substantiation of the hypothesis that retirement has a negative impact on health. European gerontologists also agree with American gerontologists in their recognition that stereotyping the aged is a crucial social problem.

The European delegates at Sheffield and London granted that while they were not entirely satisfied with American leadership in defining the problems of aging, they recognized the superiority of gerontological research in the United States. One of the more persistent points of concurrence among European and American delegates was the expressed need for systematic cross-cultural information on the various aspects of aging.

It is appropriate at this point to discuss at length the avid interest in and important contributions to gerontology and geriatrics of the Nuffield Foundation in England. Established by Lord Nuffield in 1943, one of the objects enjoined upon the Foundation by its trust deed was "the care and comfort of the aged poor." The first step that it took to implement this aspect of its trust was to appoint a committee under the chairmanship of B. Seebohm Rowntree to prepare a report, *Old People,* that was published in 1947, thereafter a classic in gerontological literature. The Nuffield Foundation has acknowledged that the Rowntree Report has accomplished the following:

It has served not only to inform and advise the Foundation but also, in a remarkable way for a private report, to create and guide public opinion and action in the days when some of the legislation for the welfare state was being drafted. As an independent, sympathetic, and sensible assessment of the problems facing old people and the community, the report (which cost the Foundation eight thousand pounds) has led, on the Foundation's side, to the private expenditure of nearly one million pounds; but the wider effect on provision for old people, both by voluntary bodies and by the public authorities, has been much larger. The Foundation's contribution, made mostly through the National Corporation for the Care of Old People which the Foundation established in 1947 on the Rowntree Committee's recommendation, has been to encourage and assist the provision of many more voluntary homes and welfare services for old people; and, by experiment and demonstration, to influence the growing amount of official provision. The efforts of local authorities in establishing small residential homes under the National Assistance Act (instead of the old large institutions under the Poor Law) have already equalled, and will soon surpass, these activities of the voluntary agencies which pioneered in showing the way. The National Corporation, having made many grants to other voluntary bodies towards the cost of setting up homes, turned gradually to other needs —first those of the infirm and semi-sick, who need special homes that are not only more costly than those for the comparatively able-bodied but also more complicated to arrange because two Acts and two sets of authorities are involved when old people are not ill enough for hospital nor well enough for ordinary "welfare" homes. Here the National Corporation has itself undertaken the whole task of establishing some rest homes, three of them (in Scotland, Northern Ireland, and England) financed from the South Africa gift to Britain, part of which was entrusted to the National Corporation to spend on experiments to help old people. Now that an increasing number of homes for the more able-bodied, and a few for the more infirm, are being set up, the National Corporation is beginning to think in terms of total provision for old people, and is starting to try out its ideas in two areas, to see how completely the various kinds of services can be arranged to give adequate help as and when it is needed.

While continuing itself to contribute to the National Corporation, and through it to discharge one part of its obligation to old people, the Foundation has also sought other ways of helping in the problems created by an ageing population. Not only is a large part of the Foundation's grants for biological research relevant to the general study of the process of ageing; some scientific work has also been specially financed to throw light on the disabilities and diseases of old age. As has already been stressed, continued and normal activity by the elderly is an important contribution both to their self-reliance (and so, self-respect) and to the general body of workers who have to produce the community's means of living. For this reason the Foundation has been, and is still, financing research by experimental psychologists at Cambridge into the way and rate at which skill declines with age— and ultimately into ways in which the middle-aged and elderly can be helped to continue or change to tasks better designed to take account of any failing or compensating skill. Starting in the laboratory, so as to establish the fundamental aspects of the problem of skill, the investigation is now moving into industry and agriculture to see the problems in practice and to suggest practical ways in which the demands of this machine age can be better adapted to human faculties and functions. The benefits of such research, if it succeeds, will not be confined to the elderly but should have lessons for the improvement of all conditions of work in modern industry. For the findings so far show that there is no definite stage at which old age can be said to begin; some kinds of skill start declining in the twenties and thirties. So scientifically as well as socially, it is improper to regard and treat old people as something apart. Like the rest of the community they are entitled to their share of what the community can provide, of happiness and congenial work, and of help in sickness or need.[2]

Geriatric Services in Western Europe

To provide order and clarity, my observations of western European geriatric services are discussed in terms of the following classification:

[2] *Ten-Year Review, 1943–53* (Oxford: Nuffield Foundation, 1953), pp. 39–41.

1. Day centers for the aged.
2. Institutional homes for the aged.
3. Housing the aged.
4. Geriatric hospitals.

A general, preliminary observation is that western European countries, unlike the United States, have given virtually no thought to and have provided very little service in the realm of "preventive geriatrics." For example, programs of preparation for retirement such as are increasingly found today in American industry are almost unknown in Europe. Clubs for the aged do exist, but they are not as extensive as they are in the United States. On the other hand, in "the care and comfort of the aged poor," to quote a key phrase from the Nuffield Report, especially with regard to institutional homes and housing for the aged, western European countries appear to have gone far beyond the United States.

Day Centers for the Aged

My first visit to a club or day center for the aged was in Sheffield, England. In many respects this club resembled many of the day centers organized in America. Established on a neighborhood basis by middle-aged housewives for people sixty years of age and over, the club meets once a week in the afternoon in a neighborhood schoolhouse. More than 200 members gather to play cards, entertain each other, and have tea, the traditional afternoon meal. On the afternoon of my visit, the club members were being entertained at the piano by one of their oldest, a man ninety years of age. I was informed that the club meeting is the most important social activity of an otherwise generally drab week for its members.

Somewhat different was the Troy Club, which I visited the following week in London. It is an outgrowth and adjunct of the Troy Town housing project for old people that will be described in the subsequent section on housing. Membership in the club, although primarily for residents of the housing project, is also open to other old people (sixty years and over for women; sixty-five and over for men) in the neighborhood. It meets daily in the recreation room of the project, and midday meals as well as social amenities are provided.

Denmark was the only other country that I visited beside the United Kingdom where one could find day centers for the aged on a significant scale. In Copenhagen I learned that the Confederation of Parish Societies arranges for regular gatherings among the aged during the winter season. In the summer excursions and summer camps are arranged for them. Another organization in Copenhagen, "Ensomme gamles vaern" ("Care of Lonely Old People") has eight places of refuge where every week throughout the winter season the aged gather for entertainment; during the summer many of them have vacations in a house in the north of Sealand. Similar activities have been taken up by other organizations and associations in Copenhagen, such as the Saxogaard Settlement and the Christian Students' Settlement.

Copenhagen also has an autonomous "Old People's Club," which not only creates and provides club life for the aged but also arranges for visits to the movies, theater, and concerts during the winter season, and excursions during the summer. A unique aspect of this organization is its service in arranging for the acceptance of the aged as guests in private homes on Christmas Eve and with private families in the country during the summer season.

Outside Copenhagen there is an "Old People's Club" at Arhus, which makes use of the premises of a juvenile club during the daytime when the latter's members are in school. The aged are charged a nominal fee for the use of newspapers, card playing, billiards, or needle work.

Institutional Homes for the Aged

These are the earliest and still the most numerous of all types of geriatric services in western Europe. It was appropriate, therefore, that my visits and observations were more frequent here than in any other single type of service. The following homes were visited in the course of my geriatric tour:

London, England, District of Camberwell
    1. Holmhurst, Home for the Aged Sick
    2. Ripon Lodge (under the auspices of the Salvation Army)
Stavanger, Norway
    3. Handelsstandens Aldershjem
    4. Old Age Home of Stavanger Parish
    5. Home for the Chronically Ill and Convalescent
Oslo, Norway
    6. Municipal Old People's Home
Stockholm, Sweden
    7. Sabbatsberg Old Age Home

8. Gustavsberg Home for the Aged
Copenhagen, Denmark
    9. Alderdomshjemmet Engskraenten (The Old People's Home)
    10. De Gammles By (Old People's Town)
Amsterdam, Holland
    11. Haarlem's Old People's Home
Brussels, Belgium
    12. Le Home Jean Van AA

While it is true that homes for the aged in western Europe, like those in the United States, usually deal with terminal cases of the aged, they are not entirely reflections of the early institutions that provided custodial care of the aged exclusively. Many of the homes are modern and progressive in philosophy and program as well as in design and construction.

Holmhurst, the first home, is one of ten experimental institutions established in London by King Edward's Hospital Fund. At the present time the Home cares for 23 women and 7 men, and it is closely linked with the geriatric unit of a hospital from which all the "patients" come. These patients stay in the home on the average from two to six months, and they are expected while they are in residence to engage in some sort of creative work, ostensibly for psychological therapy, until such time as they are well enough to return to their own homes. The maintenance cost for all residents is met by the National Health Service of the United Kingdom. They come to Holmhurst and to the nine other homes for a variety of reasons. Originally many of them came because they had been in the hospital for so many years that they had almost forgotten what an ordinary home was like. Such details as moving up and down stairs, even walking over mats or in and out of the garden and having meals in a dining room, were strange and tiring experiences that might well precipitate a relapse.

The use of Holmhurst and the other homes now depends on the methods of the doctors who supervise them. But I learned that all agree with the basic principle that the home facilitates the discharge of the patients from the hospital and curtails, or may even obviate, their stay there without putting an undue strain on the patients and their relatives. It is not the policy of the Fund to encourage long-stay patients in these homes. This view is supported by the doctors in charge, for if they consider any one patient as likely to stay disproportionately long in the home, they may take that patient back to the hospital for a short period to break the continuity of his or her stay. This in turn influences newcomers to accept without question the fact that their stay cannot be permanent.

At the other end of the scale is the patient who comes for a short stay, less than a month, merely a convalescent period. The home is then doing the work of a convalescent home, for there can be no question of rehabilitation or continuation of treatment in so short a time. But there are believed to be good reasons for using the home this way in some cases. It is not easy to find convalescent homes in England willing to take elderly patients. Even if one could be found, the patient must be strong enough to face the relatively long and arduous trip there before being discharged from the hospital. The Fund's homes such as Holmhurst are near the hospital and the trip there is far less formidable and can be undertaken at a much earlier stage, thus reducing to a minimum the stay in a hospital bed.

The Fund has apparently gained much experience by trial and error in the planning and designing of their homes. The ideal has been to build a specially designed house, but in recent years this has been found to be impractical. The conversion of large private homes has proved to be the next best alternative. This has had advantages as well as disadvantages: their gardens are mature, the rooms have a dignity and character that might well be lacking in a new building, and they are all from a period and style of architecture familiar to the aged residents.

The standard to be reached by each home has not been easy to fix. At an early stage the Fund had to decide whether to plan for single rooms or cubicles for each patient, or whether to put as many patients together as the rooms would allow with comfort. The latter course was taken for several reasons. First of all, the patients are not intended to remain indefinitely in these homes. Even though their stay may be a matter of months rather than weeks, the home is to be regarded as temporary rather than permanent or terminal. The patients still are in need of some medical and nursing care and they are able to do relatively little for themselves. To provide nursing care and supervision for many of these patients in single rooms necessitates a staff uneconomically large. Furthermore, many of the patients have come from hospitals where they have been confined a number of years. It is felt that the change from a bed in a large ward to one in a room with at most five or six beds brings much satisfaction to them. Few of them, it is claimed, would be able to appreciate fully the benefits of a single room, and many of them might even fear and dislike its loneliness. Another point against the single room is that the division of a big room into smaller ones or even into cubicles would, however well planned, waste space and reduce to an uneconomic figure the number of beds that the house could take.

Some of the adaptations necessary in the homes were obvious from the very beginning: ramps to replace steps, handrails of a comfortable girth on either side of the stairs and passages, baths low enough to be used by patients with a minimum of help, and room everywhere to allow for wheelchairs or crutches. But there have been other adaptations that came to light only with experience: awkward corners that needed a protective rail, shelves of an inconvenient height, and rounded door-handles that were difficult to grasp. Special attention has been given to the heating systems in the homes in order to secure a comfortable temperature for the aged residents.

In equipment, preference has been given to what the patients find easiest to manage for themselves rather than what is easiest for the nurses or attendants. Low beds are favored over the high hospital type, and there is also a preference for chairs that are not easily overturned.

A homelike atmosphere is sought in all ten of the Fund's homes. The furnishings at Holmhurst are varied from room to room and the decorations resemble those found in a private English middle-class household. The homes in general have cost an average of 890 pounds per bed, including all the incidental expenses in the purchase and alteration of the property and its furnishings.

Ripon Lodge, the second institutional home for the aged that I visited in London, is decidedly more traditional in several respects, especially in its predominantly custodial function and the fact that it is terminal or permanent in its care of 32 older men. The Salvation Army operates this home along with many similar ones elsewhere in the United Kingdom and the United States. This is part of the organization's so-called "evening-tide" program. Referred from any source, the residents must be in need but ambulatory. They must be able to wash and dress themselves and climb stairs. Unlike Holmhurst, there is no creative, dynamic, and goal-oriented program for the residents. Rather, they watch television, play billiards, smoke their pipes, and presumably wait to die. Although they are accepted regardless of creed, the residents are expected to attend religious services. The atmosphere is more depressing and the physical structure and furnishings are decidedly inferior to those of Holmhurst, although cleanliness and order do prevail.

I found no such variation in the quality of the homes for the aged that I visited and observed in Norway. Virtually all of them were modern, cheerful, and conspicuously lacking in such telltale symptoms as the "institutional odor." Three of the homes were situated in Stavanger, a west coast community of 65,000 population in which fishing and canning industries are the core of the economy. Handelsstandens Aldershjem, The Old Age Home for Businessmen, has 36 residents, one person to a room. The mean average age of the residents is about seventy, and their eligibility for residence is based on prepaid fees at a nominal rate during their younger, more active years. The present cost of maintenance for each resident is approximately 15 dollars a month. For those residents who become chronically ill, hospitalization is provided which costs them nothing if they have been members of Norway's National Health Act, in effect since 1911. Membership is compulsory if the person earns less than 15,000 kroner a year; it is voluntary if he earns more than this amount.

The Old Age Home of Stavanger Parish is another private type of institutional home for the aged in Norway. The cost of maintenance per resident is only 200 kroner per month.[3] This is paid for by the contribution of the old person's entire pension, 175 kroner per month; the remaining 25 kroner are contributed by the local government, which also gives each resident a small amount for pocket money.

The third home I visited in Stavanger is the Home for the Chronically Ill and Convalescent, a modern dwelling built in 1928 and operated by the city. One unusual feature common to all three homes in Stavanger is that they are situated in clear view of the magnificent fjords for which the west coast of Norway is noted.

In Oslo, the capital of Norway, the only home for the aged that I visited was one of the four Municipal Old People's Homes. Like the homes in Stavanger, this is a modern dwelling, marked by an atmosphere of considerable dignity that is enhanced by such unusual features as murals. An infirmary is annexed for those residents who become ill and require medical care. Privacy in this home is attained to a degree most unusual for homes for the aged. The residents' individual rooms may be

---

[3] One Norwegian kroner at that time was worth about 14 cents.

said to constitute quasi-apartments, for they have their own furniture brought in from their former private residences.

At present Oslo has 32 homes for old people. Besides the four homes owned by the Municipal Town Council, there are homes founded and operated by voluntary organizations, religious, humanitarian, and philanthropic. In the establishment of these homes for the aged, the Council has given grants-in-aid in the form of building sites, loans, guarantees, and tax reductions. The homes are inspected by municipal authorities, both elected officers and functionaries. The Health Board supervises the sanitary arrangement, and to each home is attached a medical officer who, as a rule, attends weekly. Most of the larger homes have special wards for people who need regular nursing and who are not up to the routine of the ordinary departments. This kind of specialization within the institution precludes the necessity of transfers to other institutions. The rate of cost in old people's homes is at present 175 kroner a month for ordinary residence and 225 kroner for places in the special wards. In all, there are about 2,000 places in homes for old people in Oslo.

An interesting feature of homes for the aged in Oslo is the Central Office for Old People's Homes. This office has been established in co-operation between the municipal authorities and the voluntary organizations that run most of the homes. Its aim is to secure the most effective utilization of facilities that are available. It keeps records of all applicants and of free places. The office, accordingly, is in a position to advise on the allocation of places.

Sweden differs from many other countries with regard to the usual chronological definition of old age. It is more common there to define the minimum level of old age at sixty-seven years of age than at sixty-five. Local governments in Sweden maintain homes for the aged primarily for relief applicants who are not ill but who need supervision and assistance that they cannot get in their homes. But old people who are physically ill may be housed temporarily in these homes for the aged while they await a hospital bed. More and more old people in Sweden who do not need relief are being permitted to enter these homes as paying boarders. In fact, the Swedish Social Welfare Committee now recommends that homes for the aged should be set apart from the public assistance program and be converted into locally administered and inexpensive homes for all old people who require the kind of care they provide. The goal in Sweden today is that every municipality, rural and urban, shall have its own home for the aged, preferably small in size. Financial assistance will be given by the government for the construction of such homes.

Sabbatsberg's Home for the Aged was the first of the two homes for the aged that I visited and observed in Sweden. It is the oldest in Stockholm, its first building having been erected in 1752. Accommodating 700 people who are for the most part old age or invalid pensioners, the home is under the jurisdiction of the Social Welfare Board and it is supported by the public assistance authority of the city. The first building still stands unchanged in external appearance to the left of the main entrance. The other buildings, with one exception, were added successively until 1872. In 1950 a new building was erected in the form of a seven-story point house in which each pensioner has his own "flat" (one room, a small hall, wardrobe, water closet, cold and hot water, and a small electric cooking apparatus). On the second floor there is a refectory where the pensioners take their meals. On each floor there is a community room, a telephone booth, and a refrigerator.

Until 1937 the institution functioned solely as a home for the aged. Now it has essentially three functions. It continues to serve as a home for the aged in that it has pensioners who are well enough to look after themselves, but who for social reasons must be taken care of in homes of this type. It also functions as a nursing home and geriatric unit for the chronically ill. A third, intermediate function is to take care of a group of old people who are not in need of the medical resources that a hospital has to offer, but whose health and strength are so impaired that the resources of a traditional type of home for the aged are inadequate to meet their needs. These persons need greater personal care and attention than the healthier aged residents. For example, they need help in making their beds, in dressing themselves, and in taking food.

Inasmuch as most of the residents at Sabbatsberg are pensioners, it should be pointed out that the national pension they secure is sufficient to pay the fees fixed for care in the nursing department, and for board and lodging in the case of those requiring no special health care. The balance of their national pension provides pocket money. In short, the residents are not penniless dependents; they are boarders living at their own expense even though they are not gainfully employed.

A much smaller home for the aged was found in the village of Gustavsberg, Sweden. The Gustavsberg Home for the Aged is equipped to care for only 20 old people no longer able to take care of themselves. It caters to individuals only, not couples. Actually, the need for a home of this kind is relatively slight in a face-to-face community like Gustavsberg. The population there is just over 4,000 and the economy revolves about the internationally famous chinaware factory that employs 1,500, having become a coöperative enterprise during the depression when private enterprise sold out. Retirement in this factory may take place at sixty-seven for men and sixty-two for women, but this is not compulsory. Many of the employees prefer and actually do continue working beyond these ages. Housing in the community is constructed and subsidized by the factory.

In Denmark welfare programs such as institutional homes for the aged were among the earliest reforms undertaken in the period of modern Danish social welfare legislation beginning about 1890. Since that time the various provisions for the welfare of the aged have occupied a place of primary importance in the field of social legislation. Measures for the aged in Denmark now rank first in the Danish social welfare budget, accounting for one third of local expenditures. As early as 1891, when the old age assistance scheme was enacted, it was realized that some of the country's old people were not able to shift for themselves. On the other hand, it was felt that such people should not be placed in poor houses. Consequently, homes for the aged were established. Today one third of all municipalities in the country have homes for the aged intended solely for old age pensioners. In accordance with the National Insurance Act of 1933, individuals who are insured against illness and disability through a government-approved sick club are entitled to an old age pension at sixty-five (single women are eligible at the age of sixty) provided they are Danish citizens. The pension is given either in cash payments or in the form of maintenance in the homes for the aged. There they receive free room and board, clothing, and medical assistance.

The Danish municipalities that have no homes for the aged have agreements with municipalities that do, and in this manner there is practically universal coverage of the aged in need of the service. The general rule is for each single person and each married couple to have their own room. To many of the homes for the aged is attached an infirmary, thus relieving the pressure on the general hospitals of Denmark.

As long as they do not draw public benefit other than an old age pension, the old people of Denmark are free to decide whether or not they want to be accommodated in a home for the aged. As a rule they bring their own furniture into the home. Each resident of a home receives a small amount of pocket money for minor necessities, which amounts to 336 kroner a year in Copenhagen, 312 kroner in other cities, and 264 kroner in rural areas. The amount of pocket money is reduced if the residents have other income, those having large incomes paying a fixed amount to the local government.

The over-all scheme summarized above is based on joint contributions from the local and central governments. In addition there are homes for the aged in Denmark established and operated by charitable organizations, religious groups, handicraft associations, trade unions, and employers' associations, all with restricted admission policies.

The newest municipal home for the aged that I visited and observed in western Europe is Alderdomshjemmet Engskraenten (The Old People's Home) located in Rodovre, a suburb of Copenhagen. Construction of this modern, garden-type structure was completed in 1952 and occupation began late that year. The total cost of the home was about 3,000,000 kroner. There is room here for 65 residents, 43 in the nursing wing and 22 in the infirmary. Residents pay a nominal fee of 25 kroner a month for a single room and 35 kroner for a double room. The nursing wing consists of 37 single rooms and three double rooms for married couples, whereas the infirmary has 12 single rooms and five rooms with twin beds. All rooms face south or east, and each has hot and cold water and is connected with a ventilation system. Above each door there is a calling lamp to show when and where help is wanted. Beds and bedding are furnished by the institution, and if the residents do not have any of their own furniture the home provides that too.

The infirmary is set up like a hospital, fulfilling all the requirements of the Board of Health. There is a room for medical examination, a laboratory, and a covered balcony in an open-air shelter. The kitchen is electrically equipped entirely and it is designed for a capacity of 175 people because old age pensioners in the surrounding area are allowed to have their dinner at the home, paying 1.50 kroner for a two-course meal. The home also has a large hall with a seating capacity of 150 for festive occasions. There is a laundry, room for a library, billiards, a lift for stretchers, two other lifts, and a funeral chapel situated in the infirmary wing. In each part of the home there is a tea kitchen operated by the old people themselves, and there are three lounges, one on each floor. The following staff members are employed: a lady principal, a physician, a head nurse, four other nurses, a housekeeper and her assistant, a stretcher bearer, a laundry manager, and ten maids.

The visit to De Gamles By (The Old People's Town) in Copenhagen was in one respect most interesting and significant of all. This is a "home" for the aged that has expanded in the course of many years into a segregated subcommunity, supporting the hypothesis that most contemporary social policies in urban industrial societies are inadvertently making a quasi-minority group of their older people. "The Old People's Town" occupies an area of almost 26 acres. It is the home for old age pensioners of the municipality of Copenhagen, and it has been in use in its present form since 1919, with the exception of some newly constructed buildings comprising single rooms. Designed on a quadrangle plan, there are two main sections: a general section for the physically able pensioners and a hospital for those who are ill. The home can accommodate 1,560 people, 735 in the general section and 825 in the hospital section.

The hospital was built in 1901 and has wards with from two to ten beds, the six-bed ward being the most common type. On each floor there are sitting rooms and smoking rooms for the comfort and use of ambulatory patients. In the older part of the general section each room is occupied by four pensioners. Every floor has its own common sitting room as well as a dining room. Married couples occupy their own room and have their meals served there. In 1946 the City Council decided to modernize the general section, having in mind to provide each pensioner with his own room. By now modernization has resulted in three new buildings with a total of 314 single rooms, and six other buildings will be reconstructed and modernized to the same end.

The new buildings have four floors and are equipped with lifts or elevators. The rooms incorporate small anterooms with accommodations for washing as well as a wardrobe. The home either provides all the furniture or part of it if the pensioner prefers his own. The furniture provided consists of a bed with a spring mattress, a small chest of drawers, a table, an easy chair, a chair, and a standard lamp. A reading lamp is installed by the bed and there are facilities for the installation of a radio. In case of emergency, a nurse can be called by means of an electrical signal system directly from each room. An annex to each of the new houses contains a section kitchen with modern electrical equipment. On each floor there is a small kitchen for the use of the pensioners if they want to prepare an extra cup of coffee or tea. Each floor also has a comfortable sitting-room where a radio is installed and papers and periodicals are provided. When the planned modernization has been completed, The Old People's Town will accommodate about 1,650 people, or 3.5 per cent of Copenhagen's 47,000 old age pensioners.

The average age of the pensioners in The Old People's Town is about seventy-six years for men and seventy-eight for women. No work is expected of these pensioners, and having given up their own homes, life for them has become terminal. But some of the more able pensioners are voluntarily engaged in some sort of light labor in the gardens and kitchen for which they receive a small reward. There is also occupational therapy on a small scale for hospitalized pensioners as well as for those who are ambulatory and want to continue their old skills in woodwork, weaving, basketwork, and knitting. Products of this activity are sold to visitors, reminding the observer from America of the practice of selling curios and craftwork produced by Indians on their reservations.

For recreation and entertainment there is a library with about 8,000 volumes and a movie projector for films. Concerts and theatrical performances are often held in the entertainment hall. As a personal allowance, all pensioners without private incomes are entitled to a monthly sum of 26 kroner, but a private income reduces this personal allowance. The pensioners are at liberty to come and go as they please, and they may stay away on a visit with relatives for a period up to one month.

In Holland the one home for the aged that I visited was Tehuis voor Ouiden van Dagen (The Old People's Home) in Haarlem. The most distinctive feature of this institution is its evolution over six centuries from a leprosarium, an asylum for the mentally infirm and the indigenous poor, to a home for the aged exclusively in 1932. As one might expect, this is an archaic structure in appearance, dark and bare, with an obvious "institutional" façade. Nevertheless it has a reputation for high morale among its residents because of its unusually dynamic and competent personnel.

The last home for the aged I was able to visit was Le Home Jean Van AA in Ixelles, a suburb of Brussels, Belgium. First opened in the 1860's, it was completely renovated and reopened in 1952, thus transformed from a dingy asylum to a modern institution resembling a small hotel. Bedrooms have twin beds and there are nameplates on the doors to enhance the feeling of individuality and privacy. Married couples are not separated, for each has its own bedroom. Nursing care is available to all, and for the more seriously disabled there is an infirmary. The Commission of Public Assistance that operates this home is also responsible for the care of all other types of needy people in the community. Hence on the same "campus" with the home for the aged are facilities for orphans and widows as well.

Housing the Aged

In western Europe as well as in the United States, ecological segregation seems to be an inadvertent consequence of providing special housing for the aged. Many countries are now worried about this kind of segregated housing and are trying to offset it in their plans for the future. However, there is already an impressive array of services being rendered for the aged to enable them to maintain their own homes. For example, various countries have:

1. A district nurse who is on call to visit the aged who are ill and who may need to be bathed or given occasional injections.

2. A night attendant who performs service for the aged somewhat like that rendered for babies by baby-sitters; their chief function is to relieve the family of the aged so they can have a good night's sleep.

3. A meal-on-wheels program to enable the aged to obtain in their own flats at least three hot, nourishing, inexpensive meals a week.

4. A home visitor who renders from one to three hours' service a day, cooking a meal, making beds, or sweeping up the flat of the aged person.

5. A recuperative holiday home for old people suffering from debility following an acute illness.

6. Transportation service to clinics enabling the aged to return from the hospital to their own homes and receive outpatient service.

7. Domiciliary consultant service so that a patient removed from the hospital to his home may have the benefit of a visit by a hospital specialist.

8. Vacation homes for the aged, which enable families to get needed rest from continuous care of the aged.

Some countries correlate their pension systems with housing. In Denmark, for example, pensions are reduced about 3 per cent for those living in state-subsidized pensioners' flats. However, the rents in these flats are low, 29 kroner a month for single persons, 34 kroner for married couples, or between 11 and 14 per cent of the monthly pension. This compares favorably with data indicating that recipients of old age assistance in New York City have paid more than half of their subsistence allotment for rent, and with New York State regulations that limit rent to one sixth of income in state-aided housing.

Three types of housing subsidies aid the aged abroad. One, like that in New York State, provides for subsidies and loans to localities building public housing projects for the aged. The second and more recent provides a subsidy toward the rent of those living in approved housing for the aged. The third gives a subsidy to private builders who erect and rent approved and inexpensive rental apartments for the aged.[4]

Contemporary programs in housing the aged in western Europe seem to have done much to offset the deterioration in standard of living and self-respect that withdrawal from the labor force frequently brings. In Sheffield, England, for example, the Housing Committee of the City Council has established on its several estates, embracing 42,000 houses, interspersed groups totaling nearly 1,500 modern, one-bedroom dwellings for aged couples and widows unable to manage financially a home of their own. The qualifying age is sixty-five years.

These dwellings are mainly of the "flat" type, made up of a living room, bedroom, water closet, bathroom, kitchen, and pantry. A hot-water circulating system is generated from the back boiler of the coal range in the living room. The rent at present, including water charge, averages eight shillings (equivalent to $1.12) per week.

Where there is a large concentration of these dwellings, there is a resident nurse-attendant in cases of emergency. Generally on the Estates there are also health visitors who come under the jurisdiction of the Health Department and whose duties include a watch over the aged.

Besides these flats for the aged in Sheffield there are two groups of bungalows for the aged. All gardens on the grounds of these flats and bungalows are cultivated for the aged tenants by the public authorities.

For those Americans who assume that all social services in western

---

[4] *Making the Years Count*, New York State Joint Legislative Committee on Problems of the Aging (Legislative Document No. 32, 1955), pp. 13–14.

Europe, such as housing for the aged, are provided by the taxpayer in the welfare state, and that the American brand of private enterprise is lacking, Troy Town housing in the Camberwell section of London is an adequate antidote. After World War II, a group of public-minded citizens in Camberwell decided to establish a Housing Society, an entirely voluntary organization. They rented a piece of land from the Local Authority and raised money, mostly by loans, in order to build a specially designed block of modern flats for old people. Completed in 1952 in their own neighborhood, Troy Town now provides accommodations for 80 people in single and double flats. The age qualifications are a minimum of sixty for women and sixty-five for men. The residents pay a rent of 21 shillings a week for a single flat and 27 shillings for a double flat. The total rent income is sufficient not only to meet the expenses of upkeep and land rent, but also to repay the building loans.

In Stavanger, Norway, I found another expression of private enterprise in housing the aged: the Seamen's Institute. Operated by shipowners, the "institute" comprises a modern development of 24 apartments for retired seamen and their wives sixty years of age and over. There is no charge to the residents except that they provide their own food and their own furniture and furnishings. When the husband-wife unit is broken by death, the surviving individual is moved to an old people's home.

Public housing for the aged is also a prominent feature of social services in Norway. For example, in Oslo I visited several old age flats in a modern six-floor building constructed with public funds. This represents a new venture in investment undertaken by the city after the liberation from the Nazis. The building has 400 flats for old people. Each of these flats is small and is designed for old people who can manage their own household but who have had difficulties in finding suitable housing. Most of the flats consist of one room, a kitchen, and balcony. Some consist of two rooms and a kitchen, and they are intended for married couples. The rent in any case is fixed so as to be within the resources of the pensioners: 30 kroner a month for single persons and 40 kroner for couples, including heating. Any deficit that is incurred is paid by the City Council.

In Stockholm, Sweden, I visited another modern public housing development for the aged, the Nockebyhof Dwellings for Pensioners. This is in double-decker design, providing for 207 people in 180 apartments (there are provisions for 27 couples). The development is centrally heated and it includes a "sammlingshaal" or social hall for the residents.

As in the other Scandinavian countries, consideration of the problems of housing the aged in Denmark must be viewed in terms of the fact that the vast majority of old people live in their own homes or as lodgers in the homes of their relatives. Public intervention is for the benefit of the small proportion of the aged, 5 to 10 per cent, who, because of limited financial means, are confined to substandard flats lacking modern conveniences and unsuited to their needs. In 1937 special legislation was introduced in Denmark authorizing the government to give subsidies to local authorities for the construction of special housing projects for old age pensioners. The general aim was to establish appropriate accommodations at reasonable cost to old people still in good health so as to facilitate their maintenance of independent home life as long as possible. The construction of these "pensioners' dwellings" by local authorities has assumed vast proportions. Since 1937 more than 10,500 flats have been built by the local authorities, taking care of a total of 13,500 people, or about 6 per cent of all old-age pensioners. The rent is 29 kroner a month for a single person and 34 kroner for a married couple in Copenhagen, corresponding to 14 and 11 per cent, respectively, of the pension. The net deficit in operating apartments of this type is borne by the local and central governments at about an even ratio. Besides Copenhagen, most of Denmark's provincial towns, and many suburban municipalities now have dwellings of this type.

Pensioners' dwellings are in great demand in Denmark for there are usually long waiting lists for admittance. Nevertheless there is a growing feeling of doubt regarding the desirability of segregating numbers of old people in large blocks where they have almost no direct contact with younger people. In 1951, therefore, an Act was passed to rent flats to old-age pensioners in general public housing units, the rents for pensioners being fixed at the same low level as in the old age pensioners' blocks. The difference between the actual rent that is charged to other tenants and the one fixed for the pensioners is refunded by public authorities.

In Holland I visited three alternative types of housing for the aged. Haarlem, a suburban district of Amsterdam, boasts of the so-called Modern Flats, constructed for the aged in 1953 with government subsidization and operated today by the Roman Catholic Church. The flats provide for single people for the most part, but there are also facilities for 50 couples as well. Although Catholic nuns are the staff in this housing unit, not all of the aged who live here are Catholics. There is a central building for the aged who become ill, and there is a chapel, which also serves as an entertainment room. Somewhat different is Haarlem's Broveniere. About 400 years old, it was at one time an almshouse founded by wealthy citizens. Today it is an apartment house for the needy aged subsidized by the municipal government. Part of the tenants' expenses is met by their own state pension. A third variation in housing the aged in Holland is represented by Huize Wildhoef in Blumendaal. These are private luxury apartments exclusively for wealthy, retired men.

Geriatric Hospitals

As in the United States, most western European countries are establishing geriatric units in hospitals and clinics to rehabilitate the chronic sick among the aged. The old premise that debility and illness among the aged are terminal is giving way to the newer assumption that it is possible and desirable to return as many of these cases to their homes as is possible, preferably with a high degree of independence and renewed economic productivity.

The first geriatric unit I visited and observed is the world-famous Fir Vale Infirmary in Sheffield, England, a unit that comprises 792 beds. There are, to begin with, three male and three female sections. Each male section contains 112 beds, and each female section has 107 beds. Each section in turn is subdivided into seven small wards and serves as a complete unit in itself. One small ward is reserved for acute admissions, in which diagnosis and investigation are carried out, after which the patients are transferred to the other wards in appropriate classifications.

Besides the six sections already mentioned, there are two long-term geriatric wards for permanent cases, many of which are the "halfway" type: not ill enough for the sick wards, and not well enough to be cared for by the local Welfare Department.

Three consultant physicians cover all the admissions to the geriatric unit. Psychiatric cases are seen in consultation with a psychiatrist. The consultant physicians are assisted in their work by one senior medical registrar, two registrars, and four house physicians. Cases are admitted every day, throughout the 24 hours, according to the availability of beds. The consultant physicians can call into consultation the entire consultant medical staff attached to the adjacent City General Hospital, which is a large "acute" hospital. Nursing of the patients is under the direction of the matron, assisted by a deputy matron and two administrative matrons. The wards are in charge of state registered sisters or male charge nurses.

Ancillary departments are the following: (1) *Social Services,* or medicosocial work under the direction of the almoner. The latter is the link between the physicians and social services available to the patient in the outside world; (2) *Welfare,* which involves general matters of welfare and recreation such as the library, shop, motor coach excursions, and clubs; (3) *Physiotherapy,* which is under the care of a head physiotherapist and one assistant; (4) *Occupational Therapy and Rehabilitation,* which is in the hands of three trained occupational therapists and one handicraft teacher; (5) *Health Aftercare,* which on discharge of the patients is under the care of their own National Health medical practitioner to whom a full clinical report is sent. Aftercare services are provided by the Local Health Authority and they include such services as visiting by health visitors, nursing by home nurses, and domestic help by "home helps."

In Oslo, Norway, I visited the geriatric department in the Ulleval Sykehus, the general hospital of the city. More than one fifth of the hospital's beds are in its geriatric unit. One measure of the success of this unit in physical and psychiatric rehabilitation was to be found in the outcome of the 739 geriatric patients admitted in 1953. One fourth of these people were eventually discharged to their homes, a most encouraging performance in what used to be considered a hopeless field of medicine. Like Fir Vale Infirmary in England, this geriatric unit uses occupational and physical therapy extensively. It also employs "situational" therapy, the reintroduction of gadgets that the patients are likely to face in the external world, such as keys, locks, and faucets.

In Stockholm, Sweden, my visit was to the geriatric unit and nursing home associated with Sabbatsberg's Home for the Aged. This unit affords geriatric care for 370 patients suffering from chronic diseases, among which circulatory disturbances are the highest in incidence. Then come impairments of the nervous system when the aftereffects of cerebral hemorrhage are included. Next in order are diseases of the muscles and joints, foremost of which is chronic rheumatoid arthritis. The unit has an outstanding bath department where different forms of medical baths are administered and where trained medical gymnasts provide massage and movement treatment. This service is consistent with the theory that older patients should not be allowed to remain in bed continuously, but rather they should be up and about at least part of every day.

Occupational therapy is an important feature of this unit's program, facilitating the work of the medical gymnasts and tending to shorten the long, monotonous day for the patients. The unit claims that 25 per cent of its patients are discharged in an improved state of health and that the institution has thereby eliminated the character of a "death hospital."

Conclusions

The description and analysis of geriatric services presented in this chapter did not cover all the ways and means by which the needs of the aged are met in the various countries of western Europe, but only those services personally visited and observed by the author. Comprehensive coverage would have required giving consideration to other vital programs such as old age pensions and public assistance, the training of personnel for homes for the aged, health insurance, and income tax relief.

On the basis of my observations and conferences, it seems to me that one of the obvious "next steps" as far as problems of old age are concerned in western Europe is to bridge the gap between gerontological research and geriatric services. I have already pointed out that social research in gerontology is not as highly developed in Europe as it is in the United States. On the other hand, geriatric services, especially in the terminal sense, have reached a high point of development in the welfare states on the continent. It is logical to deduce that action research is the most practical research potential facing western European countries concerned with finding the most effective methods of caring for their aged.

It would also be interesting and fruitful to determine the relationship between the attitudes of western Europeans toward the aging process and its accompaniments, such as occupational retirement, and the social services on behalf of the aged. It is conceivable that Europeans are not as anxiety-ridden about aging as are Americans because they provide more security through their social services at that stage of life. By the same token it may be wise to examine the extent to which there is a relationship between present American attitudes toward aging and retirement and our relative paucity of social services on behalf of the aged. If the hypothesis implicit here is correct, American problem-mindedness with regard to retirement should recede as we increase and broaden our concept of social security in the last period of life.

Questions and Research Exercises

1. Compare the geriatric services of western Europe with those of the United States, and show how the fivefold recurring interests of aging persons are served in each case.
2. Discuss western European dissatisfaction with American leadership in defining the researchable problems of aging.
3. Show how western European countries differ from the United States in "the care and comfort of the aged poor."
4. What are the earliest and still the most numerous of all types of geriatric services in western Europe? Describe some representative forms.
5. What are the services being rendered in western Europe to enable the aged to maintain their own homes? Compare them with the services in the United States that have the same goal.
6. Compare the legislative action in Denmark with that in New York State to avoid the segregation of the aged in public housing.

Selected Readings

Hohmann, Helen F., *Old Age in Sweden* (Washington, D.C., Federal Security Agency, 1940). An early but still useful analysis of Swedish policies in dealing with problems of aging.

Old Age in the Modern World: Report of the Third Congress of the International Association of Gerontology (Edinburgh, E. and S. Livingstone Ltd., 1955). Proceedings of the London Congress in 1954, with excellent papers on gerontology and geriatric services in various countries.

Rowntree, B. Seebohm, *et al., Old People: Report of a Survey Committee on the Problems of Aging and the Care of Old People* (London, Oxford University Press, 1947). A classic in British gerontological literature that led to many geriatric programs in the United Kingdom.

Sheldon, Joseph H., *The Social Medicine of Old Age* (London, Oxford University Press, 1948). A penetrating analysis by one of England's leading medical geriatricians.

Shenfield, B. E., *Social Policies for Old Age* (New York, Humanities Press, 1957). A review of social provisions for old age in Great Britain.

VI : Retrospect and Prospects

Growing old is no more than a bad habit which a busy man has no time to form.

ANDRÉ MAUROIS

14:

OCCUPATIONAL ROLES AND HEALTH IN OLD AGE

Any problem, whether it be the problem of an aging population or divorce or war or marriage or any other catastrophe needs to be viewed from at least three perspectives, namely, the naked eye—viewing the individual as a unit, mind and body; two, viewing the individual with a microscope, where we take the individual apart and study him; and, lastly, with the telescope, standing far enough back so that we can view the individual in relation to his environment.

On the one side, man is composed of millions of cells and complex tissue reactions and chemical changes. Analysis of these elements is the science of senescence, or the biology of senescence. On the other hand, society is composed of millions of men. En masse we have the sociological aspects of this whole problem. The individual man stands in the middle. These are theoretical relationships between these three factors but they are also extremely pragmatic relationships in the sense that the more we know about the biology of senescence, the more intelligently we can apply the principles of geriatric medicine, the more geriatric medicine can tell what the limitations of aging men and women are, the more intelligently we can plan and act on the sociological problems. And then finally the circle is closed by the fact that the more society as a whole is aware of the importance of these problems the more funds will be available for research in the biology of senescence. So that we have a circle which I hope, ultimately, will not be a vicious one but a constructive one.*

---

* Edward J. Stieglitz, "Aging, Today and Tomorrow," in *Birthdays Don't Count*, New York State Joint Legislative Committee on Problems of the Aging (Legislative Document No. 61, 1948), p. 195.

In this, the final chapter of the book, it is appropriate that we take stock of the key points made in the previous chapters and attempt to clarify some of the tasks that remain in gerontology and geriatrics. Looking backward will in turn help us to look forward to new research on aging and to new services that can better the situation of the aged in American society.

We have seen that the dynamics and interrelationships of occupational roles, health, and aging comprise one of the crucial problems of gerontological research. Some of the relationships between these three variables are now clearly measured and understood; others still call for intensive thought and investigation.

For example, gerontologists in general now would accept as reasonable the hypothesis that occupational roles and health are significant causal factors in relation to the social psychology of aging. In the chronologically advanced years of life, especially for men, aging as perceived by oneself and by others is largely a function of withdrawal from "making a living" and decline in the state of health. This is to be expected in a culture which has established as normal the consistency between an active occupational role, good health, and youthfulness. Research, as we have seen, in fact does show that people sixty years of age and over who are occupationally active and in good health by self-evaluation are younger in their own eyes and in the eyes of others than are those who have withdrawn from the labor force and are in poor health.

The Interrelationship of Occupational Roles and Health

Somewhat less success has been derived from efforts either to establish or to interpret the relationship between occupational roles and health in old age. Most, but not all, research findings in this area show a positive correlation between the two variables.

But even if our findings were consistent, we would still be confronted by the problem of the meaning of the correlations. Which of the two variables is independent (causal) and which one is dependent (the effect)? On the one hand there are those who claim that occupational roles are causal and health is the effect. Increasingly vociferous and armed at the moment with the more convincing data are those who argue the opposite is true, namely that health is a predisposing factor rather than a consequence of occupational roles.

The following type of compromise has come to be widely accepted as a tentative resolution of this gerontological controversy:

> It would appear in the light of these figures that the persons who die soon after retirement are in all likelihood succumbing to physiological conditions which would have caused death whether they had retired or not. This of course does not rule out the possibility that in some cases retirement itself may be the cause of death—that "retirement shock" may precipitate an occasional fatal cardiovascular accident. Certainly it cannot be denied that mental and emotional states affect bodily conditions. In the absence of any techniques for measuring quantitatively the effects of emotional disturbance on health, however, or for separating precisely the psychosomatic disorders from organic disease, it is difficult to estimate the effect of the sudden cessation of work on health.[1]

There is, of course, the perennial promise of the ultimate resolution of this controversy in longitudinal research. Many gerontologists are optimistic that this kind of research approach will permit the observation of sequential and etiological relationships between the occupational role variables and the health variables, a feat cross-sectional surveys are intrinsically not equipped to do. But we may invite continuing frustration if we persist in taking an "either-or" theoretical position, even in the modified, compromise form presented by Mathiasen. For there is an inherent limitation in assuming that occupational roles and health are related to each other exclusively as independent and dependent variables in a yet unknown pattern. It may be more rewarding in the long run to consider them, among other things, as interactive partners in a reciprocal relationship. Each probably acts and is acted upon by the other, although not with equal influence or weight.

Problems of Dynamic Occupational Roles

This book has also revealed that emphasis in research on the dynamics of occupational roles in old age seems to be misplaced. Most gerontologists working on this problem seem to assume that the transition from employment to retirement is the crux of the difficulties associated with occupational roles. Yet research findings indicate that the unemployed aged who *do not* consider themselves to be retired have

---

[1] Geneva Mathiasen, ed., *Criteria for Retirement* (New York, G. P. Putnam's Sons, 1953), p. 109.

more acute economic, psychological, and social problems than do the unemployed aged who do consider themselves to be retired.

The retirants' acceptance of their retirement status and role, insofar as they concede they are no longer part of the labor force, appears to provide them with more psychological composure and a higher degree of social adjustment than the unemployed who say they are not retired. The latter, unwilling to tolerate the economic idleness to which they have been relegated, have the most emphatic minority group reactions of all occupational categories among the chronologically aged. Although they constitute less than one seventh the numerical size of retirants, the reluctantly unemployed in our population deserve far more attention from gerontological researchers than they have been given until now.

Problems of Dynamic Physical and Mental Health

Emphasis in research on the dynamics of health in old age, as we have seen, appears to be misplaced too. Some of our findings definitely suggest that we have been concentrating on problems of physical health when actually we should be studying more intensively the problems of mental health. Physical ailments in the older population are not as severe and widespread as they are generally reputed to be. Although there is more illness and more disability owing to illness in old age than in any other age group, most of the elderly have been found to be in fairly good physical health and the number of invalids among them is relatively small. At the same time the relatively little gerontological research on mental disorders in later life indicates they are more extensive than problems of physical health. The nationwide urban survey conducted at Cornell University revealed that whereas over half of the entire sample (53 per cent) claimed to have no particular problems of physical health, the majority of the urban older people are troubled at least some of the time by psychosomatic symptoms, nervousness, and forgetfulness.

Kaplan, one of the few specialists in mental disorders of the aged, has pointed out that "we are almost wholly ignorant of the factors responsible for the major mental disorders of later life." [2] Much more obviously needs to be known about the social and cultural bases of these mental disorders.

[2] Oscar J. Kaplan, "Psychological Aspects of Aging," *The Annals of the American Academy of Political and Social Science* (Vol. 279, Jan. 1952), p. 41.

Adaptation of Social Science Concepts and Theory to Gerontological Research

Throughout this book we have suggested that the time is long overdue for more utilization of relevant social science concepts and theory in gerontological research on problems of mental health as well as other problems of aging. Several studies have already intimated that the kind of social relations in which older persons participate is a crucial factor in the etiology of their mental disorders. These social relations have been fruitfully characterized by orthodox social science concepts such as Durkheim's "anomie," Jung's "loss of significance," and Faris and Dunham's "isolation."

The theoretical framework basic to much contemporary social psychology, especially that which we associate with the names of George Herbert Mead, Willard Waller, and Harry Stack Sullivan, seems to be especially adaptable to gerontological research on problems of mental health. The attention of gerontological researchers should be drawn to other potentially relevant concepts and theoretical schemes of social science as well. How important is "generational solidarity" in old age? That is, do older people actively seek out company in their own age group? Is "alienation" at work in the separation of age categories from each other, and if so, are the five alternative meanings of alienation: powerlessness, meaninglessness, normlessness, isolation, and self-estrangement, all equally applicable to the aged in American society? [3]

Does the "self-fulfilling prophecy" have any bearing on the dynamics of occupational roles and health in old age? Can we hypothesize that expectations of morbidity and mortality in old age are intensified by the practice of retirement so that they become self-fulfilling prophecies expressed in hypochondria and functional symptoms of illness? Does the Kinsey concept of "psychological fatigue," originally used by sexologists to explain in part the decline in sex activity in old age, help us to understand the attitudes of the aged in other situations, such as occupational activity, in that people simply grow tired of something they have had in abundance all their adult lives? To what extent, if any, does "psychological unemployability" account for the difficulties of the unemployed aged who do not consider themselves retired in returning to

[3] Melvin Seeman, "On the Meaning of Alienation," *American Sociological Review* (Vol. 24, Dec. 1959), pp. 783–91.

gainful employment? Is unplanned, involuntary, and abrupt retirement the kind of experience Goldstein had in mind when he coined the concept "catastrophic reaction?" [4] Hayward's concept, "the need for illness," is another social psychosomatic tool with gerontological possibilities. It refers to a condition which is an outgrowth of repeated frustrations in the individual in attempting to handle complicated problems. The person does not consciously seek illness as an escape, but rather the care that one receives in illness, corresponding to the maternal love given a child who has met difficulties.[5]

Middle-Class Norms in Theory and Research

In this book we have attempted to show that one of the pitfalls to be avoided is the indiscriminate gerontological usurpation of concepts and theoretical frameworks from a social science that has heretofore been youth-biased. Gerontology, in fact, can eventually make a contribution to social science by helping to correct this overdependence on youthful subjects in its concepts and research findings.

Another weakness in gerontology and geriatrics is the heavy reliance on middle-class norms. We need to pause and ask ourselves whether or not "social adjustment," "social satisfaction," and "avocational interest" are truly free of restrictive class connotations. We have seen that there is some basis to the suspicion that educators, scientists, physicians, clergymen, and industrial and business personnel, all of whom are typical middle-class representatives, have played a more important and influential role in defining the problems of aging and introducing these norms to an age-status in urban industrial society that is new and still without a clearly delineated subculture than have the representatives of other social classes. The geriatric as well as gerontologic consequences are self-evident if we ask ourselves why there has been such negligence by older people in preparing and planning for retirement. Many of the norms for such preparation and planning are implicit in such activities as hobbies, travel, education, avocations, and club sociability, for all offer more appeal and meaning to older people of the middle classes than they do to those of lower economic, social, and educational strata. Yet older people in our society, according to re-

[4] R. G. Barker and H. F. Wright, *One Boy's Day: A Specimen Record of Behavior* (New York, Harper & Brothers, 1951), p. 37.

[5] United States Department of Health, Education, and Welfare, *Aging* (Vol. 8, Nov. 1953), p. 4.

search findings, think of themselves socially as belonging to the working classes to a greater extent than they identify with any other social stratum. The working-class aged apparently and logically have not been enthusiastic recipients of middle-class standards.

The Need for New Concepts and Theory in Gerontology

Gerontological research on the dynamics and interrelationships of occupational roles, health, and aging obviously cannot rely completely on concepts and theory already available in the social sciences. There is a need for new, imaginative theoretical formulations, an example being the typology recently put forward by Riesman for analyzing materials gathered in the Kansas City Study of middle age and aging. Riesman pointed out that reaction to aging in American society is largely governed by norms that vary according to social group. Not only do we need to recognize the substrata among older people, but we must also adapt norms to the various substrata. Three suggested types of reaction to aging are the adjusted, the anomic, and the autonomous.[6]

Another fresh idea about aging comes to us in reaction against the rigid and false categorization of all old people, such as those who are sixty-five years of age and over, as being members of a single homogeneous age group. It has been suggested that in planning for employment, housing, pensions, and retirement, it would be more useful to assume a triphasic concept of old age.

According to this concept, old age is realistically divisible into the following three subdivisions:

1. There is an "early-late maturity" between sixty-five and seventy years of age, when there is generally a little psychological fatigue, a marked alteration in skin dryness, no marked deterioration physiologically, no withdrawal from the community, and no marked habit alterations or differences in needs.

2. There is a "middle-late maturity" between seventy and seventy-five years of age, when generally there is a marked slump in energy, recovery rate, reaction time, social participation, participation in the labor force, flexibility, freedom from chronic ailments, and an increase in fatigue and mental disorders.

[6] David Riesman, "Some Clinical and Cultural Aspects of Aging," *American Journal of Sociology* (Vol. 59, 1954), pp. 379–83.

3. There is a "late-late maturity" from seventy-five years of age and up, when there generally is a uniform picture of little energy, fatigue, a high incidence of ailments likely to be terminal, deeply lined skin, a general withdrawal from community life, and little zest.

It should be understood that the concept of triphasic old age runs the risk of building false stereotypes about people seventy years of age and over. At the most it could be useful only in broad planning, for it is superseded by the reality of individual variability in the aging process.[7]

A formidable task that awaits the future gerontologist is to overcome the incongruities between the generally dark picture presented in the theory of aging, and the somewhat less pessimistic portrayal that emerges from gerontological research. Finally, too little of the theory in gerontology makes any attempt to bridge the organic, psychological, and social aspects of aging. This may call for considerably more ingenuity than any of us feel prepared to offer at the present time. But the same basic principle applies here as in any other human endeavor, research or otherwise: "nothing ventured, nothing gained."

Questions and Research Exercises

1. Show how occupational roles and health affect the social psychology of aging.
2. Explain the Mathiasen compromise concerning the interrelationship between occupational roles and health.
3. Discuss the misplaced emphasis in research on the dynamics of occupational roles and of health in old age.
4. What is the difference, if any, between "generational solidarity" in old age and the "alienation" of the aged?
5. If you were testing the validity of the concept that among the aged there is a "need for illness," how would you design your research?
6. Criticize the concept of "triphasic" old age.

Selected Readings

Anderson, John E., ed., *Psychological Aspects of Aging* (Washington, D.C., American Psychological Association, 1956). Theoretical critiques by the outstanding American psychologists of aging.

[7] *Enriching the Years,* New York State Joint Legislative Committee on Problems of the Aging (Legislative Document No. 32, 1953), pp. 7–8.

Donahue, Wilma T., and Tibbitts, Clark, eds., *The New Frontiers of Aging* (Ann Arbor, University of Michigan Press, 1957). Representative researches on aging as presented at the annual Michigan conference on gerontology.

Jones, Harold E., ed., *Research on Aging* (New York, Social Science Research Council, 1950). The proceedings of an early symposium on research, but still important for its suggestions in theory and methodology.

Pollak, Otto, *Social Adjustment in Old Age* (New York: Social Science Research Council, Bulletin No. 59, 1948). A research planning report of the highest order of sophistication; still fruitful in ideas.

Riesman, David, "Some Clinical and Cultural Aspects of Aging," *American Journal of Sociology* (Vol. 59, 1954), pp. 379–83. One of the leading American sociological theorists applies his "Lonely Crowd" concepts to aging.

Appendices

Appendices

BIBLIOGRAPHY

Syllabi and Annotated Bibliographies

Aldridge, Gordon J., and Fauri, Fedele F. *A Syllabus and Annotated Bibliography on Social Welfare and the Aged.* Ann Arbor: Institute for Social Gerontology, University of Michigan, 1959.

Federal Publications on Aging. Washington, D.C.: Federal Council on Aging, 1958.

Franke, Walter H., and Wilcock, Richard C. *A Syllabus and Annotated Bibliography on the Economics of an Aging Population.* Ann Arbor: Institute for Social Gerontology, University of Michigan, 1959.

Kuhlen, Raymond G., and Morris, Woodrow W. *A Syllabus and Annotated Bibliography on the Psychological Aspects of Aging.* Ann Arbor: Institute for Social Gerontology, University of Michigan, 1959.

Neugarten, Bernice L., Havighurst, Robert J., and Ryder, Claire F. *A Syllabus and Annotated Bibliography on an Interdisciplinary Course in Social Gerontology.* Ann Arbor: Institute for Social Gerontology, University of Michigan, 1959.

Shock, Nathan W. *A Classified Bibliography of Gerontology and Geriatrics.* Stanford: Stanford University Press, 1951. *Supplement One—1949–1955.* Stanford: Stanford University Press, 1957.

United States Department of Health, Education, and Welfare. *Selected References on Aging: An Annotated Bibliography.* Washington, D.C.: U.S. Government Printing Office, 1959.

Webber, Irving L. *A Syllabus and Annotated Bibliography on the Sociology of Aging and the Aged.* Ann Arbor: Institute for Social Gerontology, University of Michigan, 1959.

Periodicals

AARP News Bulletin. American Association of Retired Persons, Colonial Building, 15th Street, N.W., Washington 5, D.C. *Quarterly.*

Adding Life to Years. Institute of Gerontology, State University of Iowa, 26 Byington Road, Iowa City, Iowa. *Monthly.*

Aging. U.S. Department of Health, Education, and Welfare. Special Staff on Aging. Superintendent of Documents, U.S. Government Printing Office, Washington 25, D.C. *Monthly.*

Aging in Connecticut. Commission on Services for Elderly Persons in cooperation with The Institute of Gerontology of the University of Connecticut, Storrs, Conn. *Quarterly.*

Geriatrics. Lancet Publications, Inc., 84 South Tenth Street, Minneapolis 3, Minn. *Monthly.*

Journal of the American Geriatrics Society. The Williams & Wilkins Co., Mt. Royal and Guilford Avenue, Baltimore 2, Md. *Monthly.*

Journal of Gerontology. Gerontological Society, Inc., 660 South Kingshighway Boulevard, St. Louis 10, Mo. *Quarterly.*

Journal of Lifetime Living. Lifetime Living Inc., 711 Fifth Avenue, New York 22, N.Y. *Monthly.*

Mature Years. Methodist Publishing House, 810 Broadway, Nashville 2, Tenn. *Quarterly.*

Maturity. California Citizens' Advisory Committee on Aging, 722 Capitol Avenue, Sacramento 14, Calif. *Quarterly.*

Public Health Reports. U.S. Department of Health, Education, and Welfare. Public Health Service. Superintendent of Documents, U.S. Government Printing Office, Washington 25, D.C. *Monthly.*

Retirement Life. National Association of Retired Civil Employees, 1625 Connecticut Avenue, N.W., Washington 9, D.C. *Monthly.*

Senior Citizen. Senior Citizens of America, 1129 Vermont Avenue, N.W., Washington 5, D.C. *Monthly.*

Social Security Bulletin. U.S. Department of Health, Education, and Welfare. Social Security Administration. Superintendent of Documents, U.S. Government Printing Office, Washington 25, D.C. *Monthly.*

Reports of Conferences and Commissions

Council on Social Work Education. *Toward Better Understanding of the Aging.* Seminar on the Aging. Aspen, Colorado, September 1958. New York: The Council, 1959.

Council of State Governments. *Recommended State Action for the Aging and Aged: A Summary of Recommendations on Problems of the Aging as Compiled from Reports of State Agencies.* Chicago: The Council, 1956. *Processed.*

————. *State Action in the Field of Aging, 1956–57.* Chicago: The Council, February 1958. *Processed.*

————. *State Programs for the Aging: A Review of the Problem and of Recent Action in the States.* Chicago: The Council, December 1956. *Processed.*

————. *The States and Their Older Citizens: A Report to the Governors' Conference.* Chicago: The Council, 1955.

Florida, University of. Institute of Gerontology. Southern Conferences on Gerontology. Gainesville: University of Florida Press.

1951. *Problems of America's Aging Population*. T. Lynn Smith (ed.). 1951.

1952. *Living in the Later Years*. T. Lynn Smith (ed.). 1952.

1953. *Health in the Later Years*. John M. Maclachlan (ed.). 1953.

1954. *Economic Problems of Retirement*. George B. Hurff (ed.). 1954.

1955. *Aging and Retirement*. Irving L. Webber (ed.). 1955.

1956. *Aging: A Current Appraisal*. Irving L. Webber (ed.). 1956.

1957. *Services for the Aging*. Irving L. Webber (ed.). 1957.

1958. *Organized Religion and the Older Person*. Delton L. Scudder (ed.). 1958.

Illinois. Public Aid Commission. *Potentials in Aging*. Chicago: The Commission, 1956.

International Association of Gerontology. *Old Age in the Modern World: Report of the Third Congress of the International Association of Gerontology*, London, 1954. Edinburgh: E. and S. Livingstone Ltd., 1955.

————. Social Science Research Committee, European Section. *The Need for Cross-National Surveys of Old Age: Report of a Conference at Copenhagen*, October 19–23, 1956. Ann Arbor: University of Michigan, Division of Gerontology, 1958.

Iowa Conference on Gerontology. *The Middle Years: A Time of Change and Preparation*. Proceedings of the Sixth Annual Iowa Conference on Gerontology. Iowa City: State University of Iowa, Iowa Conference on Gerontology, 1957.

Man and His Years: An Account of the First National Conference on Aging, Sponsored by the Federal Security Agency. Raleigh, N.C.: Health Publications Institute, Inc., 1951.

Michigan, University of. Conferences on Aging. Ann Arbor: University of Michigan Press.

1948. *Living through the Older Years*. Clark Tibbitts (ed.). 1949.

1949. *Planning the Older Years*. Wilma Donahue and Clark Tibbitts (eds.). 1950.

1950. *Growing in the Older Years*. Wilma Donahue and Clark Tibbitts (eds.). 1951.

1951. *Rehabilitation of the Older Worker*. Wilma Donahue, James Rae, Jr., and Roger Berry (eds.). 1953.

1952. *Housing the Aging*. Wilma Donahue (ed.). 1954.

1953. *Earning Opportunities for Older Workers*. Wilma Donahue (ed.). 1954.

1955. *The New Frontiers of Aging*. Wilma Donahue and Clark Tibbitts (eds.). 1957.

1957. *Free Time: Challenge to Later Maturity*. Wilma Donahue, Woodrow W. Hunter, Dorothy H. Coons, and Helen K. Maurice (eds.). 1958.

Minnesota. Commission on Aging. *Minnesota's Aging Citizens: A Report on Their Employment, Recreation, Living Arrangements, Economic Welfare*. St. Paul: The Commission, 1953.

New Jersey. Old Age Study Commission. *A Positive Policy Toward Aging*. Trenton: The Commission, 1957.

New York State. Conference on Financing Health Costs for the Aged. *Financing Health Costs for the Aged*. Albany: Office of the Special Assistant, Problems of Aging, 1957.

————. Governor's Conference on Problems of the Aging. *Charter for the Aging*. Albany: The Conference, 1955.

————. *Salute to the Aging: A Guide to New York State Services for Senior Citizens*. Albany: The Conference, 1958.

New York State Joint Legislative Committee on Problems of the Aging. Newburgh, N.Y.: The Committee.

1948. *Birthdays Don't Count*. Legislative Document No. 61. 1948.

1949. *Never Too Old*. Legislative Document No. 32. 1949.

1950. *Young at Any Age*. Legislative Document No. 12. 1950.

1951. *No Time to Grow Old*. Legislative Document No. 12. 1951.

1952. *Age Is No Barrier*. Legislative Document No. 35. 1952.

1953. *Enriching the Years*. Legislative Document No. 32. 1953.

1954. *Growing with the Years*. Legislative Document No. 32. 1954.

1955. *Making the Years Count*. Legislative Document No. 32. 1955.

1956. *New Channels for the Golden Years*. Legislative Document No. 33. 1956.

1957. *Brightening the Senior Years*. Legislative Document No. 81. 1957.

1958. *Good News for Later Life*. Legislative Document No. 8. 1958.

North Carolina. Governor's Conference on Aging. *Proceedings*. Raleigh: The Conference, 1951.

Pennsylvania. General Assembly, Joint State Government Commission. *Sixty Five: A Report concerning Pennsylvania's Aged*. Harrisburg: The Commission, 1953.

Problems of Aging: Transactions of the Fifteenth Conference, January, 1953, Princeton, New Jersey. Nathan W. Shock (ed.). New York: Josiah Macy, Jr. Foundation, 1954.

Rhode Island. Governor's Commission to Study Problems of the Aged. *Old Age in Rhode Island*. Providence: The Commission, 1953.

General References

The Aged and Aging in the United States: Summary of Expert Views before the Subcommittee on Problems of the Aged and Aging of the Com-

mittee on Labor and Public Welfare, U.S. Senate, June 16–18, 1959. Washington, D.C.: U.S. Government Printing Office, 1959.

The Aged and Society: A Symposium on the Problems of an Aging Population. Milton Derber (ed.). Champaign, Ill.: Industrial Relations Research Association, 1950.

Amulree, Lord. *Adding Life to Years.* London: The National Council of Social Service, 1951.

Birren, James E. (ed.). *Handbook of Aging and the Individual.* Chicago: University of Chicago Press, 1959.

Burgess, Ernest W. (ed.). *Aging in Western Societies.* Chicago: University of Chicago Press, 1960.

Cavan, Ruth S., *et al. Personal Adjustment in Old Age.* Chicago: Science Research Associates, 1949.

Drake, Joseph T. *The Aged in American Society.* New York: The Ronald Press Co., 1958.

Eisenstadt, S. N. *From Generation to Generation: Age Groups and Social Structure.* Glencoe: The Free Press, 1956.

Gilbert, Jeanne G. *Understanding Old Age.* New York: The Ronald Press Co., 1952.

Havighurst, Robert J., and Albrecht, Ruth. *Older People.* New York: Longmans, Green and Co., 1953.

Pinner, Frank A., Jacobs, Paul, and Selznick, Philip. *Old Age and Political Behavior: A Case Study.* Berkeley: University of California Press, 1960.

Pollak, Otto. *Social Adjustment in Old Age: A Research Planning Report.* New York: Social Science Research Council, 1948.

Shenfield, B. E. *Social Policies for Old Age: A Review of Social Provision for Old Age in Great Britain.* London: Routledge and Kegan Paul, Ltd., 1957.

Shock, Nathan W. *Trends in Gerontology* (2d ed.). Stanford: Stanford University Press, 1957.

"Social Contribution by the Aging." Clark Tibbitts (ed.). *The Annals of the American Academy of Political and Social Science,* Vol. 279, January 1952, entire issue.

Soule, George. *Longer Life.* New York: The Viking Press, 1958.

Stieglitz, Edward J. *The Second Forty Years.* Philadelphia: J. B. Lippincott Co., 1952.

Tibbitts, Clark (ed.). *A Handbook of Social Gerontology.* Chicago: University of Chicago Press, 1960.

———, and Donahue, Wilma (eds.). *Aging in Today's Society.* Englewood Cliffs: Prentice-Hall, 1960.

U.S. Congress. Senate Committee on Labor and Public Welfare. *Studies of the Aged and Aging: Selected Documents.* Washington, D.C.: U.S. Government Printing Office, 1956 and 1957. 11 volumes.

U.S. Department of Health, Education, and Welfare. Social Security Administration. *Basic Readings in Social Security: Social Welfare—Social Insurance.* Washington, D.C.: U.S. Government Printing Office, 1957.

Wolff, Kurt. *The Biological, Sociological, and Psychological Aspects of Aging.* Springfield, Ill.: Charles C Thomas, 1959.

Topic References

Biology of Aging

Bourliere, F. "The Comparative Biology of Aging," *Journal of Gerontology,* Vol. 13, April 1958, supplement no. 1, pp. 16–24.

Carlson, Anton J., and Stieglitz, Edward J. "Physiological Changes in Aging," *The Annals of the American Academy of Political and Social Science,* Vol. 279, January 1952, pp. 18–31.

Cowdry's Problems of Ageing: Biological and Medical Aspects (3d ed.). A. I. Lansing (ed.). Baltimore: The Williams & Wilkins Co., 1952.

Lansing, Albert I. "Experiments in Aging," *Scientific American,* Vol. 188, April 1953, pp. 38–42.

Shock, Nathan W. "Age Changes in Some Physiologic Processes," *Geriatrics,* Vol. 12, January 1957, pp. 40–48.

Community Organization, Surveys, and Planning

Abrams, Albert J. "Community Programs for the Aging," *New Channels for the Golden Years.* Newburgh: New York State Joint Legislative Committee on Problems of the Aging, 1956, pp. 109–17.

Frazier, Loudell, and Gebhart, Dorothy L. *The Community and Institutions for the Aged.* Chicago: American Public Welfare Association, 1957.

Hunter, Woodrow W., and Maurice, Helen. *Older People Tell Their Story: A Community Survey and Forum.* Ann Arbor: University of Michigan, Division of Gerontology, 1953.

Kutner, Bernard, Fanshel, David, Togo, Alice M., and Langner, Thomas S. *Five Hundred over Sixty: A Community Survey on Aging.* New York: Russell Sage Foundation, 1956.

Levine, Harry A. "Community Programs for the Elderly," *The Annals of the American Academy of Political and Social Science,* Vol. 279, January 1952, pp. 164–70.

Snyder, Ruth M. *Community Activities for the Aging.* Chicago: Research Council for Economic Security, 1955.

Welfare Council of Metropolitan Chicago. *Community Services for Older People: The Chicago Plan.* Chicago: Wilcox & Follett Company, 1952.

Economic Status of Older Persons

Bond, Floyd A., *et al. Our Needy Aged: A California Study of a National Problem.* New York: Henry Holt & Co., 1954.

Burns, Robert K. "Economic Aspects of Aging and Retirement," *American Journal of Sociology,* Vol. 59, January 1954, pp. 384–90.

Corson, John J., and McConnell, John W. *Economic Needs of Older People.* New York: The Twentieth Century Fund, 1956.

McConnell, John W. "The Impact of Aging on the Economy," *Journal of Gerontology,* Vol. 13, July 1958, supplement no. 2, pp. 42–47.

Steiner, Peter O., and Dorfman, Robert. *The Economic Status of the Aged.* Berkeley: University of California Press, 1957.

Education

"Adult Education." *Review of Educational Research,* Vol. 23, June 1953, entire issue.

Brown, Giles T. "Never Too Old to Learn: A Gerontological Experiment in General Education," *School and Society,* Vol. 74, November 1951, pp. 279–81.

Donahue, Wilma (ed.). *Education for Later Maturity: A Handbook.* New York: Whiteside, Inc., and William Morrow & Co., 1955.

Hurwitz, Sidney, and Guthartz, Jacob C. "Family Life Education with the Aged," *Social Casework,* Vol. 33, November 1952, pp. 382–87.

Employment and the Older Worker

Bancroft, Gertrude. "Older Persons in the Labor Force," *The Annals of the American Academy of Political and Social Science,* Vol. 279, January 1952, pp. 52–61.

Bers, Melvin K. *Union Policy and the Older Worker.* Berkeley: University of California, Institute of Industrial Relations, 1957.

Crook, G. Hamilton, and Heinstein, Martin. *The Older Worker in Industry.* Berkeley: University of California, Institute of Industrial Relations, 1958.

Wolfbein, Seymour L. "The Outlook for the Older Worker," *Personnel and Guidance Journal,* Vol. 36, October 1957, pp. 80–86.

Health and Illness

Boas, Ernst P. *Add Life to Your Years.* New York: The McBride Co., 1954.

Bortz, Edward L. "Stress and Aging," *Geriatrics,* Vol. 10, March 1955, pp. 93–99.

Monroe, Robert T. *Diseases in Old Age.* Cambridge: Harvard University Press, 1951.

Sheldon, Joseph H. *The Social Medicine of Old Age.* London: Oxford University Press, 1948.

Thewlis, Malford W. *The Care of the Aged (Geriatrics)* (6th ed.). St. Louis: The C. V. Mosby Co., 1954.

Homes for the Aged

Abrams, Albert J. "Trends in Old Age Homes and Housing for the Aged in Various Parts of the World," *No Time to Grow Old.* Newburgh: New York State Joint Legislative Committee on Problems of the Aging, 1951, pp. 265–82.

Fisher, Jacob. "Trends in Institutional Care of the Aged," *Social Security Bulletin,* Vol. 16, October 1953, pp. 9–13 ff.

Fox, Flora. "Home Care Programs of Homes for the Aged," *Jewish Social Service Quarterly,* Vol. 29, Spring 1953, pp. 302–9.

Kleemeier, Robert W. "Moosehaven: Congregate Living in a Community of the Retired," *American Journal of Sociology,* Vol. 59, January 1954, pp. 347–51.

De Lourdes, Mother M. Bernadette. *Where Somebody Cares: The Mary Manning Walsh Home and Its Program for Complete Care of the Aging.* New York: G. P. Putnam's Sons, 1959.

Mathiasen, Geneva (ed.). *Planning Homes for the Aged.* New York: Dodge Books, 1959.

Taietz, Philip. *Administrative Practices and Personal Adjustment in Homes for the Aged.* Ithaca: Cornell University Agricultural Experiment Station, Bulletin 899, July 1953.

Housing and Living Arrangements

American Public Health Association. *Housing an Aging Population.* New York: The Association, 1953.

Donahue, Wilma (ed.). *Housing the Aging.* Ann Arbor: University of Michigan Press, 1954.

Nicholson, Edna E. "Housing as a Basic Need of Senior Citizens," *Journal of the American Medical Association,* Vol. 165, October 1957, pp. 1058–62.

Silk, Leonard S. "The Housing Circumstances of the Aged in the United States, 1950," *Journal of Gerontology,* Vol. 7, January 1952, pp. 87–91.

"Symposium: Environmental Needs of the Aging." *Geriatrics,* Vol. 12, April 1957, pp. 209–51.

U.S. Congress. Senate Committee on Banking and Currency. Subcommittee on Housing. *Housing for the Aged.* Washington, D.C.: U.S. Government Printing Office, 1956.

Mental Health and Personality Changes

Andrus, Ruth. "Personality Change in an Older Age Group," *Geriatrics,* Vol. 10, September 1955, pp. 432–35.

Felix, Robert H. "Mental Health in an Aging Population," *Growing in the Older Years.* Ann Arbor: University of Michigan Press, 1951, pp. 23–44.

Kaplan, Oscar J. (ed.). *Mental Disorders in Later Life* (2d ed.). Stanford: Stanford University Press, 1956.

Strecker, Edward A. "Mental Hazards of Aging," *Journal of the American Geriatrics Society,* Vol. 6, March 1958, pp. 210–14.

Watson, Robert I. "The Personality of the Aged: A Review," *Journal of Gerontology,* Vol. 9, July 1954, pp. 309–15.

Middle Age

Desmond, Thomas C. "America's Unknown Middle-Agers," *Brightening the Senior Years.* Newburgh: New York State Joint Legislative Committee on Problems of the Aging, 1957, pp. 57–60.

Gross, Irma H. (ed.). *Potentialities of Women in the Middle Years.* East Lansing: Michigan State University Press, 1956.

Howe, Reuel L. *The Creative Years.* Greenwich: Seabury Press, 1959.

Trent, Sarah. *Women over Forty.* New York: The Macauley Co., 1934.

The Years Between: The Role Today of Women in Middle Age. New York: Jewish Vacation Association, 1957.

Personality and Family Relationships

Albrecht, Ruth. "Relationships of Older Parents with Their Children," *Marriage and Family Living,* Vol. 16, February 1954, pp. 32–35.

Blau, Zena Smith. "Changes in Status and Age Identification," *American Sociological Review,* Vol. 21, April 1956, pp. 198–203.

Glick, Paul C. *American Families.* (Census Monograph Series.) New York: John Wiley & Sons, Inc., 1957.

Gravatt, Arthur E. "Family Relations in Middle and Old Age: A Review," *Journal of Gerontology,* Vol. 8, April 1953, pp. 197–201.

Linden, Maurice E. "The Older Person in the Family," *Social Casework,* Vol. 37, February 1956, pp. 75–81.

Phillips, Bernard S. "A Role Theory Approach to Adjustment in Old Age," *American Sociological Review,* Vol. 22, April 1957, pp. 212–17.

Townsend, Peter. *The Family Life of Old People: An Inquiry in London.* London: Routledge and Kegan Paul, 1957.

Population Changes and Forecasts

Dublin, Louis I., Lotka, Alfred J., and Spiegelman, Mortimer. *Length of Life: A Study of the Life Table.* New York: The Ronald Press Co., 1949.

Sheldon, Henry D. *The Older Population of the United States: The Characteristics and Contributions of the Nation's Older People.* (Census Monograph Series.) New York: John Wiley & Sons, 1958.

Spengler, Joseph J., and Duncan, Otis D. (eds.). *Demographic Analysis: Selected Readings.* Glencoe: The Free Press, 1956.

Taeuber, Conrad, and Taeuber, Irene B. *The Changing Population of the United States.* (Census Monograph Series.) New York: John Wiley & Sons, 1958.

Valaoras, Vasilios G. "Young and Aged Populations," *The Annals of the American Academy of Political and Social Science,* Vol. 316, March 1958, pp. 69–83.

Vance, Rupert B. "The Ecology of Our Aging Population," *Social Forces,* Vol. 32, May 1954, pp. 330–35.

Psychology of Aging

Anderson, John E. (ed.). *Psychological Aspects of Aging: Proceedings of a Conference on Planning Research.* Washington, D.C.: American Psychological Association, 1956.

Bayley, Nancy, and Oden, Melita H. "The Maintenance of Intellectual Ability in Gifted Adults," *Journal of Gerontology,* Vol. 10, January 1955, pp. 91–107.

Birren, James E. "Psychological Limitations that Occur with Age," *Public Health Reports,* Vol. 71, December 1956, pp. 1173–78.

Bromley, Dennis B. "Some Effects of Age on the Quality of Intellectual Output," *Journal of Gerontology,* Vol. 12, July 1957, pp. 318–23.

Kamin, Leon J. "Differential Changes in Mental Abilities in Old Age," *Journal of Gerontology,* Vol. 12, January 1957, pp. 66–70.

Lehman, Harvey C. *Age and Achievement.* Princeton: Princeton University Press, 1953.

Pressey, Sidney L., and Kuhlen, Raymond G. *Psychological Development through the Life Span.* New York: Harper & Brothers, 1957.

Welford, A. T. *Ageing and Human Skill.* London: Oxford University Press, 1958.

Recreation and Creative Activity

Abrams, Albert J. "Golden Age Clubs and Centers in New York State," *Brightening the Senior Years.* Newburgh: New York State Joint Legislative Committee on Problems of the Aging, 1957, pp. 122–29.

Burgess, Ernest W. "Social Relations, Activities, and Personal Adjustment," *American Journal of Sociology,* Vol. 59, January 1954, pp. 352–60.

Desmond, Thomas C. "Recreation in the Later Years," *Making the Years Count.* Newburgh: New York State Joint Legislative Committee on Problems of the Aging, 1955, pp. 147–51.

Havighurst, Robert J. "The Leisure Activities of the Middle-Aged," *American Journal of Sociology,* Vol. 63, September 1957, pp. 152–62.

Kaplan, Jerome. *A Social Program for Older People.* Minneapolis: University of Minnesota Press, 1953.

Kubie, Susan H., and Landau, Gertrude. *Group Work with the Aged.* New York: International Universities Press, Inc., 1953.

McCarthy, Henry L. *Day Centers for Older People.* Chicago: American Public Welfare Association, 1954.

Williams, Arthur. *Recreation for the Aging.* New York: Association Press, 1953.

Religious Programs and Services

Biller, Newman M. "The Role of the Synagogue in Work with Old People," *Jewish Social Service Quarterly,* Vol. 28, March 1952, pp. 284–89.

Mathiasen, Geneva. "Role of Religion in the Lives of Older People," *Charter for the Aging.* Albany: Governor's Conference on Problems of the Aging, 1955, pp. 423–37.

Maves, Paul B., and Cedarleaf, J. Lennart. *Older People and the Church.* Nashville: Abingdon-Cokesbury Press, 1949.

Moberg, David O. "The Christian Religion and Personal Adjustment in Old Age," *American Sociological Review,* Vol. 18, February 1953, pp. 87–90.

O'Reilly, Charles T. "Religious Practice and Personal Adjustment of Older People," *Sociology and Social Research,* Vol. 42, November–December 1957, pp. 119–21.

Retirement

"Aging and Retirement," *American Journal of Sociology,* Vol. 59, January 1954, entire issue.

Buckley, Joseph C. *The Retirement Handbook: A Complete Planning Guide to Your Future* (rev. ed.). New York: Harper & Brothers, 1956.

Friedmann, Eugene, and Havighurst, Robert J. *The Meaning of Work and Retirement*. Chicago: University of Chicago Press, 1954.

Hall, Harold R. *Some Observations on Executive Retirement*. Boston: Harvard University Graduate School of Business Administration, Division of Research, 1953.

Kaplan, Max. "Pressures of Leisure on the Older Individual," *Journal of Gerontology*, Vol. 13, July 1958, supplement no. 2, pp. 36–41.

Mathiasen, Geneva (ed.). *Criteria for Retirement: A Report of a National Conference on Retirement of Older Workers*. New York: G. P. Putnam's Sons, 1953.

Myers, Robert J. "Mortality after Retirement," *Social Security Bulletin*, Vol. 17, June 1954, pp. 3–7.

Pollak, Otto. *Positive Experience in Retirement: A Field Study*. (Pension Research Council Monograph Series.) Homewood, Ill.: Richard D. Irwin, Inc., 1957.

Pollak, Otto. *The Social Aspects of Retirement*. (Pension Research Council Monograph Series.) Homewood, Ill.: Richard D. Irwin, Inc., 1957.

Pressey, Sidney L. "Certain Findings and Proposals Regarding Professional Retirement," *AAUP Bulletin*, Vol. 41, Autumn, 1955, pp. 503–9.

"Retirement." *Journal of Business*, School of Business of the University of Chicago, Vol. 27, April 1954, Part I, entire issue.

Tuckman, Jacob, and Lorge, Irving D. *Retirement and the Industrial Worker: Prospect and Reality*. New York: Columbia University, Teachers College, Bureau of Publications, 1953.

Social Welfare

Affleck, Jane F. "Family Agency Services to Older People," *Social Casework*, Vol. 38, April 1957, pp. 171–76.

Carpenter, Niles. *Programs for Older People in Great Britain*. Buffalo: University of Buffalo Series, 1959.

Cohen, Ruth G. "Casework with Older Persons," *Social Work*, Vol. 2, January 1957, pp. 30–35.

Gordon, Ruth G. "The Place of the Family Agency in a Program for the Aging," *Jewish Social Service Quarterly*, Vol. 28, June 1952, pp. 396–401.

Hale, Mark P. "Foster Home Care for the Aged," *Geriatrics*, Vol. 13, February 1958, pp. 116–19.

Levine, David L. "Casework and Counseling Services for the Aged," *Public Welfare*, Vol. 15, January 1957, pp. 17–20.

Posner, William. "Adapting and Sharpening Social Work Knowledge and

Skills in Serving the Aging," *Social Work,* Vol. 2, October 1957, pp. 37–42.

Shore, Herbert. "The Application of Social Work Disciplines to Group-Work Services in Homes for the Aged," *Social Service Review,* Vol. 26, December 1952, pp. 418–22.

Understanding the Older Client. (Reprinted from *Social Casework.*) New York: Family Service Association of America, 1955.

STUDY AIDS

Films

Adventure in Maturity. STORY: Depicts the emotional problems of an older woman after retirement from active work. PRODUCER: Oklahoma State Department of Health and the University of Oklahoma, 1954. DATA: 16 mm, color, sound, 22 minutes. AVAILABILITY: Rental from Mental Hygiene Division, Oklahoma State Department of Health, 3400 N. Eastern Street, Oklahoma City 5, Oklahoma.

America's Untapped Asset. STORY: Shows how well those who have physical handicaps owing to disability or age fit into the work of a busy business office. Illustrates training techniques as well as results. PRODUCER: President's Committee on Employment of the Physically Handicapped, 1954. DATA: 16 mm, B & W, sound, 13½ minutes. AVAILABILITY: On loan from State Chairman of Governor's Committee on Employment of the Physically Handicapped, Washington 25, D.C., or Bankers Life and Casualty Company of Chicago, 4444 Lawrence Ave., Chicago 30, Ill.

Bunker Hill. STORY: Presents an arresting view of the rather inactive lives of the older residents of a Los Angeles area about to be cleared for urban redevelopment. DATA: 16 mm, B & W, sound, 18 minutes. (1956.) AVAILABILITY: Rental or sale from Audio-Visual Services, Department of Cinema, University of Southern California, Los Angeles 7, California.

Cold Spring Idea. STORY: Documentary showing how retired persons explore and develop potentials for making the most of their later years during a nine-month course at the Cold Spring Institute (New York). PRODUCER: Julius Tannenbaum, 1956. DATA: 16 mm, B & W, sound, 12½ minutes. AVAILABILITY: Rental or sale from Harvey Associates, 424 Madison Ave., New York 17, N.Y.

Confidential File: Old Age. STORY: Compares daily life of a demoralized, aimless, elderly man with lives of three active, creative, productive, older persons. PRODUCER: Guild Films Company, Inc. 1956. DATA: 16 mm, B & W, sound, 26½ minutes. AVAILABILITY: Rental from Public Service Department, Guild Films Co., Inc., 460 Park Avenue, New York 22, N.Y.

Gift of Life. STORY: An examination of four major problem areas in aging (employment, health, housing, leisure time); presented as 15 half-hour

TV shows, using guest authorities, panels, and documentaries. PRODUCER: University of Michigan Television, 1957. DATA: 16 mm (kinescopes), B & W, sound, 29½ minutes each. AVAILABILITY: Rental from University of Michigan TV, 310 Maynard Street, Ann Arbor, Michigan.

Make Way for Tomorrow. STORY: Shows problems created when an elderly widow goes to live with her son's family. PRODUCER: Paramount Pictures Corporation. DATA: 16 mm, B & W, sound, 18 minutes. AVAILABILITY: Rental from Association Films, 206 S. Michigan Avenue, Chicago, Illinois.

Our Senior Citizens. STORY: Documentary illustrating range of activities in an urban day center for the aging, with emphasis on positive mental health values. PRODUCER: New York City Department of Welfare, 1955. DATA: 16 mm, B & W, sound, 30 minutes with introduction, 28 without. AVAILABILITY: Loan from Department of Welfare, 250 Church Street, New York 13, N.Y.

Seventh Age. STORY: Shows living arrangements provided for older people in Denmark. PRODUCER: Danish Government Film Committee, 1947. DATA: 16 mm, B & W, sound (English commentary), 17 minutes. AVAILABILITY: Loan from Danish Information Office, 588 Fifth Avenue, New York 36, N.Y.

Such A Busy Day Tomorrow. STORY: An elderly widower, retired from work and more or less out of contact with his family, is rescued from loneliness and frustration by joining a community senior citizens center. Filmed against the background of the Hodson Center in New York City. PRODUCER: Neptune Productions, 1954. DATA: 16 mm, B & W, sound, 50 minutes. AVAILABILITY: Loan from U.S. Social Security Administration District Offices, or Regional Offices of the Department of Health, Education, and Welfare.

Recordings

Aging in Europe. SUMMARY: A series of interviews, recorded in Europe by Dr. Wilma Donahue, with typical older people in housing experiments or hospitals, leaders in the fields of gerontology and geriatrics, and famous old people. PRODUCER: Station WUOM, University of Michigan, 1956. DATA: Tapes, 14½ minutes each. AVAILABILITY: Loan from Station WUOM, or sale from Audio-Visual Aids, University of Michigan, Ann Arbor, Michigan.

Autumn Harvest. SUMMARY: Adjustment Problems of older people, narrated by a social worker. PRODUCER: National Broadcasting Company in coöperation with the National Institute of Mental Health, 1953. DATA: 16-inch discs, standard cut, 33⅓ rpm, 30 minutes. AVAILABILITY: Sale from Allied Record Manufacturing Company, 1041 N. Las Palmas Ave., Hollywood 38, California.

Humanizing the Aged. SUMMARY: Interviews in which two older citizens talk over their problems, one with an employment counselor, the other with a social worker. Originally produced for public hearings, the unrehearsed interviews sharply point up the problems and potentials of the older worker. PRODUCER: Conference Group on Welfare of the Aged of the Welfare and Health Council of New York City, and the New York State Joint Legislative Committee on Problems of the Aging. DATA: Tapes, 8 minutes each. AVAILABILITY: Loan from Senator Thomas C. Desmond, Chairman, New York State Joint Legislative Committee on Problems of the Aging, 94 Broadway, Newburgh, N.Y.

Transition. SUMMARY: Problems of the late middle years. PRODUCER: National Broadcasting Company in cooperation with the National Institute of Mental Health, 1953. DATA: 16-inch discs, standard cut, 33⅓ rpm, 30 minutes. AVAILABILITY: Sale from Allied Record Manufacturing Company, 1041 N. Las Palmas Avenue, Hollywood 38, California.

Index

The page references given throughout this index indicate only the page on which the discussion begins.

Abrams, Albert J., 56, 67, 162, 250, 252, 255
"adaptation energy," 29
adjustment and religion in old age; *see* religion
Affleck, Jane F., 256
aged
  apartments for, 195
  chronological definition of, 28, 30
  clubs for, 9
  cross-cultural survey of, 25
  discrimination against, 38, 60
  drug service for, 199
  education and recreation for, 200, 201
  educational distribution of, 105
  group therapy for, 9
  health of, 47, 109
  housing of, 41, 192
  inadequate income of, 40, 122, 197
  institutions for, 9, 190, 212
  mental and emotional disorders of, 50
  migration of, 34
  minority characteristics of, 38, 108, 221
  norms for, 69, 72
  occupational status of, 102, 106
  pressure groups of, 9, 57
  problems of, 8, 23, 40
  professional study of, 6
  religiosity of, 171
  religious programs and services for, 169
  rural survey of, 113
  services for, 202
  sex ratio of, 33
  size and distribution of, 30
  sources of income of, 42, 121
  spatial distribution of, 34
  urban survey of, 99

aged (*cont.*)
  urbanization of, 32
  See also aging
aging
  advisory council, committees and commissions on, 16
  beginning point of, 13
  committees and divisions on, 6
  demography of, 7, 30
  mental disorders in, 82
  middle-class norms of, 72
  multidisciplinary interest in, 6, 10
  in nonliterate societies, 25
  preparing and planning for, 70
  problems of, linked with youth problems, 4
  psychological, 29
  religion and, 164
  research on, 3, 10, 12
  in rural societies, 27
  Senate hearings on, 17
  specific causes of problems of, 35
  in urban industrial societies, 28
  variations in, 28
  White House Conference on Aging, 18
  See also gerontology and geriatrics
Albrecht, Ruth, 52, 171, 172, 177, 178, 249, 253
Aldridge, Gordon J., 245
almshouses 9, 188
  See also institutional care
American Association of Retired Persons, 199, 245
American Geriatrics Society, 6
American Medical Association, 6
American Psychological Association, 6
Amulree, Lord Basil, 51, 249
Anderson, John E., 51, 240, 254
Andrus, Ruth, 192, 253

263